MAT
MILLER ANALOGIES TEST

Eve P. Steinberg
William Bader
Daniel S. Burt

Prentice Hall
New York • London • Toronto • Sydney • Tokyo • Singapore

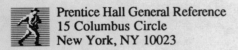

Prentice Hall General Reference
15 Columbus Circle
New York, NY 10023

An Arco Book

Library of Congress Cataloging-in-Publication Data

Steinberg, Eve P.
    MAT, Miller analogies test.

    Rev. ed. of: Mat, Miller analogies test / William
Bader, Daniel S. Burt. 2nd ed. ©1985.
    1. Miller analogies test—Study guides. I. Bader,
William. II. Burt, Daniel S. III. Bader, William. Mat,
Miller analogies test. IV. Title. V. Title: Miller
 analogies test.
LB2367.6.B3   1988   371.2'62   88-24925
ISBN 0-13-563917-4

Manufactured in the United States of America

3   4   5   6   7   8   9   10

Fourth Edition

CONTENTS

PART III: VERBAL ANALOGIES FOR
OTHER GRADUATE-LEVEL EXAMINATIONS

APPENDIX: USEFUL MISCELLANEOUS INFORMATION
FOR THE MILLER ANALOGIES TEST-TAKER

THE MILLER ANALOGIES TEST

WHAT IS THE MAT?

The Miller Analogies Test, commonly referred to as the MAT, is a high-level test of mental ability required by many graduate schools for admission to a master's or doctoral program or as a basis for granting financial aid for graduate study. The test is also required by some business firms and some scientific, social, and educational agencies for employment in jobs calling for a high degree of intellectual ability.

The MAT is not administered on a uniform date throughout the country. Rather, each official Controlled Testing Center determines its own testing schedule and establishes its own fees. Controlled Testing Centers are located throughout the United States, Canada, Australia, Great Britain, and the Philippines. In addition, The Psychological Corporation, administrator of the MAT, can arrange for special testing for applicants who live at great distances from established testing centers and in countries in which the MAT is not regularly offered.

You may obtain a list of Controlled Testing Centers and an Information Bulletin that includes specific information about applying for and taking the MAT by writing to:

The Psychological Corporation
555 Academic Court
San Antonio, TX 78204-2498

THE NATURE OF THE TEST

The MAT consists of 100 analogies—mostly verbal—which are to be answered in only 50 minutes. The questions cover a broad range of subjects with only a smattering of items in any one field of study. Although considered an aptitude test, the MAT presupposes not only an extensive vocabulary but also a firm grounding in literature, social studies, mathematics, and science.

The MAT questions are meant to be arranged in order of difficulty, with the

1

easiest questions at the beginning of the test. "Easiest" is, however, a relative term. Unfamiliarity with the subject matter may make some early questions difficult for you even though the analogy entails an obvious relationship. However, all questions are of equal weight, and no penalty is imposed for incorrect responses. Therefore, it is to your advantage to proceed through the test as quickly as possible, answering every question you can. When you have done this, go back and answer the questions you skipped, even if you have to guess. When fifty minutes have elapsed, you should have no blank spaces on your answer sheet.

HOW SCORES ARE REPORTED

Within a few days after taking the MAT, you will receive a report of your score on a card which you addressed to yourself at the time of the test. This card is for your personal records only.

At about the same time, official reports of your test score will be sent to those institutions, agencies, or companies you designated at examination time. You are entitled to as many as three official score reports provided that you specify complete, correct addresses for each one on the day you take the test. After the test date, you will have to pay an additional fee for any further reports of your test score that you may wish to have sent out.

Only raw scores (that is, number right) are reported by The Psychological Corporation. It is left to the receiving institution to interpret these scores according to its own standards or norms as established through past experience with MAT scores.

WHAT ABOUT RETESTING?

It is *recommended* that you retake the MAT if you are required to submit your score more than two years after taking the test. It is *necessary* to retake the test if scores are required more than five years after the initial test. The Psychological Corporation will not report scores that are more than five years old. If you choose to retake the test in a period of less than twenty-four months, both current and previous scores will be reported. If you retake the exam within a twelve-month period, you must request an alternate form of the examination. The alternate form will be equal in difficulty to the initial examination but will contain different questions.

Part I

Preparing for the MAT

ALL ABOUT ANALOGIES

WHAT IS AN ANALOGY?

An analogy is a verbal proportion presented in the following form:

$$A : B :: C : D$$

In this proportion the sign : stands for *is to* and the sign :: stands for *as*. Therefore, the problem is read A is to B as C is to D.

   On the MAT one of the four terms in each analogy is missing. The missing term may be in the first, second, third, or fourth position in the proportion. In place of the missing term are four options enclosed in parentheses and lettered a, b, c, and d. The task is to choose the one option which best completes the analogy: that is, the option which establishes the same relationship between the terms of the incomplete word pair as you have determined exists between the terms of the given word pair.

SEEKING A RELATIONSHIP BETWEEN THE GIVEN TERMS

The first step in solving an analogy problem is to find a relationship between two of the three given terms. In MAT analogies the relationship may be between the two terms on the left side of the proportion and the two terms on the right side of the proportion such that A is related to B as C is related to D. Or the relationship may cross the proportion sign so that A is related to C as B is related to D. Never give up on an analogy problem until you have considered both of these possibilities. A look at the following sample questions will illustrate this point.

> 1. DOCTOR : SYMPTOM :: DETECTIVE : (a. mystery, b. crime, c. police, d. clue)
> 2. DOCTOR : DETECTIVE :: SYMPTOM : (a. illness, b. mystery, c. crime, d. clue)

In the first sample question, it is fairly obvious that a relationship exists between the first two terms (A and B): to the DOCTOR a SYMPTOM provides the key to the nature of an illness. The same relationship may be established between the third and fourth terms (C and D): to the DETECTIVE a CLUE provides the key to the nature of the crime.

In the second sample question, no relationship is immediately apparent between the first two terms. However, when you consider the first and third terms (A and C) and the second and fourth terms (B and D), the relationship of an investigator to a piece of evidence should come to light.

Bear in mind that it is never acceptable to relate the first and fourth terms (A and D) to the second and third terms (B and C).

Graphically, acceptable analogy forms for the MAT are:

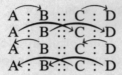

Unacceptable are:

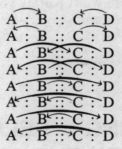

Whether an analogy is in the form of A : B :: C : D or A : C :: B : D, the direction of the relationship must be the same on both sides of the analogy. In other words, if the relationship between the terms of the given word pair is that the first term is part of the second term, then the relationship of the incomplete word pair must also be that the first term is part of the second. Sample question 3 illustrates this point.

3. MINUTE : HOUR :: MONTH : (a. week, b. year, c. time, d. calendar)

The relationship established by terms A and B is one of part to whole; a MINUTE is a part of an HOUR. In order to maintain the same relationship, the second word pair must also be part to whole; a MONTH is a part of a YEAR. If you select WEEK, you are reversing the direction of the relationship required and thus making an unacceptable analogy.

HOW TO SOLVE ANALOGY PROBLEMS

The first step in approaching an analogy problem is to define the given terms. In an MAT problem, this means that you must know the meaning of three terms well enough that you will be able to understand the relationship of two of those terms to each other and of the third term to one of the answer choices. Occasionally the answer choices will give you a clue to the meaning of one mystery term, but generally familiarity with the three given terms is absolutely requisite to completing the analogy. Remember that unlike analogy questions on most aptitude tests, MAT questions are designed to probe the depth of your vocabulary, your competence in the humanities and sciences, and your general knowledge as well. Obviously, you are not equally competent in all of these areas. You will find some analogy questions insoluble because you cannot define or understand the given terms. Don't worry. Guess.

The time pressure of the MAT is very real. Thirty seconds per question is not much. If you do not know the meanings of the words in the related pair, you cannot determine their relationship. If you cannot define the given third term, you cannot determine its relationship to a fourth term. Do not waste your time trying to answer an analogy problem in which you cannot define the terms. You will need that time for puzzling out the problems in which relationships rather than definitions give you trouble. Since MAT scoring carries no penalty for a wrong answer, guess and move on as quickly as possible.

The second step in solving an analogy problem is to determine how two of the given terms are related to each other. There are two techniques that may be employed to determine the nature of the relationship between the terms in a verbal analogy—one using sentences and one using categories. With the Sentence Technique, you begin by making up a short, simple sentence using the two terms you are considering. Then you substitute the other given term, together with each of the answer choices, in the sentence you have created. You should find one combination that exactly parallels the relationship expressed by the original word pair. An analysis of the following sample question illustrates the Sentence Technique for solving analogy problems.

PLAY : AUDIENCE :: BOOK : (a. writer, b. publisher, c. plot, d. reader)

Step 1. Make a short sentence using the first two terms:
　　　　A *play* is meant to entertain an *audience*.
Step 2. Substitute the third term and each of the answer choices in the same sentence.
　(a)　A *book* is meant to entertain a *writer*.
　　　　(It certainly may, but this is hardly the purpose of a book.)
　(b)　A *book* is meant to entertain a *publisher*.
　　　　(Again, a book that entertains publishers only has a very limited appeal.)

(c) A *book* is meant to entertain a *plot*.
(This statement can be eliminated immediately since it makes no sense.)
(d) A *book* is meant to entertain a *reader*.
(This statement is both parallel to the original statement and true; therefore, it is correct.)

With the Sentence Technique, often you can solve an analogy without formally categorizing the relationship between the terms. This is perfectly acceptable; after all, only the correct answer is important. However, if you cannot make sense of an analogy question and so cannot compose a useful sentence, you should try the Category Technique. First define a general relationship, then narrow it to a more specific relationship, if possible. Do not search for unusual relationships in this second step. Search beyond the readily visible relationship only when the more obvious relationship does not yield an answer. Suppose you are confronted with an analogy problem which begins: BRIM : HAT. BRIM and HAT are immediately associated in your mind; therefore, the first relationship which you can describe is that of association. Nearly all words in analogy pairs are associated, so try to narrow the association to more specific relationship. A BRIM is a part of a HAT, so you may refine your relationship as that of a part to a whole. This part to whole relationship will probably be sufficiently narrow to allow you to solve the analogy problem. If you should find two possible answers which offer a part to whole relationship, you might have to return to the original pair and further refine the relationship to "external part to whole" or to "not absolutely necessary part to whole." You should not move to this very narrow definition of the relationship until you have attempted to solve the problem. If your relationship is too specific, you may miss an answer that is based on a broader sense of the relationship.

Once you have isolated a reasonable relationship between the words of the given pair, look at the third given word and then at the choices. You must find among the choices the word that bears the same relationship to the third word that the second word bears to the first. (If the missing term is other than the fourth, this instruction must be rephrased to fit the problem. The basis of an analogy problem is that on both sides of the proportion the second term must bear the same relationship to the first.) Choosing the word which best completes the analogy is done through a process of elimination. Let us further analyze the analogy problem we previously discussed.

BRIM : HAT :: HAND : (a. glove, b. finger, c. foot, d. arm)

Consider each answer choice in turn. HAND is certainly associated with GLOVE, but in no way is it part of a glove. You cannot discount (a) as the answer until you find a part to whole relationship, but chances are that (a) will not be the best answer.

Now look at (b). HAND and FINGER are certainly associated, and, indeed, a finger is part of a hand, But **BEWARE**. BRIM is a part of HAT, or, in other words, HAT is the whole of which BRIM is a part. The relationship in choice (b) is the reverse of the relationship of the original pair. HAND is the whole and FINGER is the part. Your answer must maintain the same relationship *in the same sequence* as the original pair.

The relationship of HAND and FOOT in (c) is only one of association, not of part to whole. This answer is no more likely to be correct than (a). In fact, since you have found two answers which have equal chances of being correct, you can eliminate them both. There must be a single *best* answer.

When you get to (d), you find that *best* answer. A HAND is part of an ARM in the same way that a BRIM is part of a HAT, or, to restate, ARM is the whole of which HAND is a part in the same way that HAT is the whole of which BRIM is the part.

And so the process is:

1. Define the initial terms.
2. Describe the initial relationship.
3. Eliminate incorrect answers.
4. Refine the initial relationship, if necessary.
5. Choose the *best* answer.

Usually your problem will be narrowing to the *best* answer. Sometimes, however, your difficulty will lie in finding even one correct answer. If this happens, you may have to redefine your initial relationship. Consider an analogy that begins: LETTER : WORD. Initially you will probably think, "A LETTER is part of a WORD, therefore the relationship is that of part to whole." If the relationship of the third word to any of the choices is also part to whole, then all is well. However, suppose the question looks like this:

> LETTER : WORD :: SONG : (a. story, b. music, c. note, d. orchestra)

All of the choices offer an association relationship, so clearly you must define the relationship more narrowly than simple association. However, your original definition of the relationship was that of part to whole, and none of the choices offers a whole of which a song must be a part (such as operetta or musical comedy). Therefore, you must return to the original pair and consider other relationships between LETTER and WORD. Rethinking the relationship between two words is not easy. This mental flexibility is one of the factors measured by analogy problems. If LETTER is not "letter of the alphabet" but rather "written communication," then a WORD is part of a LETTER and the relationship of the first word to the second is that of the whole to one of its parts. Now you can find the answer. A SONG is the whole of which a NOTE, (c), is a part. The relationship on both sides of the analogy is the same and in the same sequence.

If you are having a great deal of trouble determining the relationship between the words of the initial pair, you might find it useful to read the analogy backwards. If the relationship becomes clear when you mentally reverse the order of the terms, you must remember to mentally reverse the order of the third and fourth words as well. You must maintain parallel relationships on both sides of the proportion.

Up to this point, we have stressed the importance of the relationship between the terms of an initial pair and the need to maintain this same relationship between the terms of the pair on the other side of the proportion. Sometimes the relationship between the first two words cannot be determined without interaction with the words on the other side of the proportion. In other words, the first word may be related to the third word and the second word may be related to the fourth. There is still a relationship between the first and second words and between the third and fourth words, but that relationship can be defined only after the relationship between the first and third words and the second and fourth words have been determined.

> HAIL : HALE :: (a. farewell, b. greet, c. hearty, d. taxi) : STRONG

HAIL and HALE are homonyms; that is, they sound alike but are spelled differently and have different meanings. Since this is a Miller Analogy, your first thought must be that the fact that these words are homonyms is the basis of their relationship. However, there is no homonym for STRONG, so you must seek another relationship. There is absolutely no meaningful relationship between HAIL, which means "greet," and HALE, which means "healthy and strong." The meaningful relationship among given terms is that between term B and term D; that is, HALE and STRONG are synonyms. Now the task is simplified to finding among the choices a synonym for HAIL. The well-known phrase "hail and farewell" comes immediately to mind but should be quickly discarded. The conjunction *and* is a dead giveaway that the two words are not synonyms. One may hail a taxi. In such an instance the taxi is an object, not a synonym. Choice (b) meets the test of synonym to HAIL and is the correct answer. On each side of the proportion there is no logical connection between the two words, but since the words on both sides of the proportion have the same meanings, the relationship is identical. The standard A : B :: C : D analogy is more common, but you must be alert to the possibility of A : C :: B : D whenever you cannot readily identify the relationship between two words on the same side of the proportion. In order to score high on analogy tests, you must be able to see all the possibilities.

CLASSIFYING ANALOGIES

The Category Technique for classifying analogies involves devising a list of common relationships between words. This list must be comprehensive enough to describe almost every way in which words can be related and yet concise enough to be committed to memory. Through careful analysis of thousands of analogy questions, we were able to distinguish eighteen categories into which the vast majority of analogies fall. These categories are intended to serve as *guidelines* for analogical thinking. They are by no means the only relationships that can exist among terms, nor are they mutually exclusive. A single analogy problem may fit into two—or even three—different categories, as for example, PAINTING : WALL :: RUG : FLOOR. Whether you consider this an analogy of association or place or even purpose, you can still select the correct term to complete the relationship.

The following list of common relationships represents our exhaustive analysis of the analogy question. Study it well, for it will prove invaluable to you as you work your way through the practice tests in this book and, more importantly, as you take the actual MAT.

1. **SYNONYMS OR SIMILAR CONCEPTS**
   DELIVERANCE : (a. rescue, b. oration, c. liberate, d. demise) :: EXERCISE : PRACTICE

   The given terms in this analogy consist of a noun and two verbs. The verbs, EXERCISE and PRACTICE, are synonyms. Therefore, the missing term must be a noun, which means the same as DELIVERANCE, in this case, RESCUE.

2. **ANTONYMS OR CONTRASTING CONCEPTS**
   (a. hostel, b. hostile, c. amenable, d. amoral) : AMICABLE :: CHASTE : LEWD

   The relationship existing between CHASTE (meaning pure or decent) and LEWD (meaning obscene or salacious) is that they are opposites. The opposite of AMICABLE is HOSTILE.

3. **CAUSE AND EFFECT**
   HEREDITY : ENVIRONMENT :: (a. influenza, b. pneumonia, c. hemophilia, d. roseola) : RUBELLA

   In this analogy, the cause-and-effect relationship is easier to see when you consider the second and fourth terms as the given word pair. A virus present in the ENVIRONMENT is the cause of RUBELLA (German measles). Similarly, a sex-linked gene which is part of one's HEREDITY is the cause of HEMOPHILIA (a blood defect characterized by delayed clotting of the blood).

4. **PART TO WHOLE**
   LEAF : TREE :: KEY : (a. lock, b. door, c. typewriter, d. car)

   The relationship between the first two terms is that a LEAF is one small part of the whole TREE. A KEY is used to open a lock or a door or a car, but the only term to which key can be related as one small part of a whole is TYPEWRITER.

5. **PART TO PART**
   FATHER : DAUGHTER :: GILL : (a. fish, b. fin, c. lung, d. wattle)

   FATHER and DAUGHTER are each part of a family. GILL and FIN are each part of a fish. If you pair gill with fish, you are changing the part-to-part relationship required by the first pair of terms to a part-to-whole relationship, thus making an unacceptable analogy.

6. **PURPOSE OR USE**
   GLOVE : BALL :: HOOK : (a. coat, b. line, c. fish, d. curve)

A GLOVE is used to catch a BALL just as a HOOK is used to catch a FISH. A hook may also be used to hold a coat, but this relationship is not as close to the relationship expressed by the given word pair as is hook and fish.

7. **ACTION TO OBJECT**
   PITCH : FIRE :: (a. coal, b. ball, c. sound, d. slope) : GUN

You might be tempted to look for a synonym relationship in this analogy since pitch and fire both mean to hurl with force. However, since none of the answer choices is a synonym for gun, this relationship must be ruled out. On re-examination, look for a relationship between the second and fourth terms. This should lead to the realization that to FIRE is an action taken on a GUN just as to PITCH is an action taken on a BALL.

8. **OBJECT TO ACTION**
   SPRAIN : (a. ankle, b. tape, c. twist, d. swell) :: BITE : ITCH

The problem in this analogy is to determine whether the given terms are being used as nouns or verbs. Once you realize that sprain and bite are used as nouns and itch is used as a verb, you can see the relationship of an object to the action taken upon it. Recognizing this relationship, you can then pinpoint the verb swell as the correct answer, for just as a BITE is likely to ITCH, a SPRAIN is likely to SWELL.

9. **PLACE**
   PARAGUAY : BOLIVIA :: SWITZERLAND : (a. Afghanistan, b. Poland, c. Czechoslovakia, d. Yugoslavia)

Paraguay, Bolivia, and Switzerland are all landlocked countries. So, too, are Afghanistan and Czechoslovakia. In order to complete this analogy, the relationship among the given terms must be further refined. PARAGUAY and BOLIVIA are landlocked countries in South America. SWITZERLAND and CZECHOSLOVAKIA are landlocked countries in Europe. (Afghanistan is in Asia.)

10. **ASSOCIATION**
    MOZART : MUSIC :: PEI : (a. painting, b. architecture, c. sculpture, d. dance)

MOZART, the eighteenth-century Austrian composer, is associated with the field of MUSIC in the same way that PEI, the twentieth-century Chinese-American architect is associated with the field of ARCHITECTURE.

11. **SEQUENCE OR TIME**
    SAIL : STEAM :: PROPELLER : (a. plane, b. engine, c. jet, d. wing)

Ships were propelled first by SAIL and later by STEAM. Similarly, planes were propelled first by means of a PROPELLER and later by means of a JET engine.

12. *CHARACTERISTIC OR DESCRIPTION*
(a. scream, b. ear, c. shrill, d. vocal) : PIERCING :: CRY : PLAINTIVE

A CRY may be described as PLAINTIVE, meaning woeful, just as a SCREAM may be described as PIERCING, meaning loud and shrill. If you have trouble with an analogy such as this in which the missing term is the first term in the question, try reversing the first and second terms. Remember, though, that if you reverse the first pair of terms, you must also reverse the second pair in order to preserve the original relationship. In this example, you may find it easier to choose the correct answer when the adjectives piercing and plaintive are placed before, rather than after, the nouns they modify.

13. *DEGREE*
WARM : HOT :: BRIGHT : (a. dark, b. dim, c. genius, d. illuminate)

WARM is a lesser degree of temperature than HOT. BRIGHT is a lesser degree of intelligence than GENIUS. Remember that the direction of the relationship must be the same on each side of the analogy. Since the progression from warm to hot is an increase in degree, you must choose an answer that represents an increase in degree over the given term *bright*.

14. *MEASUREMENT*
ODOMETER : (a. speed, b. distance, c. pressure, d. temperature) :: CLOCK : TIME

A CLOCK measures TIME passed just as an ODOMETER measures DISTANCE traveled.

15. *GRAMMATICAL*
BROKE : BROKEN :: (a. fled, b. flight, c. flew, d. flung) : FLOWN

BROKE and BROKEN are respectively the past tense and past participle of the verb *break*. FLEW and FLOWN are the past tense and past participle of the verb *fly*. Grammatical analogies may also be concerned with parts of speech and formation of plurals.

16. *MATHEMATICAL*
12 1/2% : (a. 1/4, b. 1/5, c. 1/8, d. 1/3) :: 16 2/3% : 1/6

This problem illustrates one kind of mathematical analogy—an equality. Since percents are fractions whose denominators are always 100, 12 1/2% equals 12 1/2 divided by 100, which equals 1/8. Similarly, 16 2/3% equals 16 2/3 divided by 100, which equals 1/6. Other common mathematical analogies concern geometrical and numerical relationships.

17. **WORKER TO TOOL**
    PHYSICIAN : (a. hospital, b. patient, c. surgeon, d. X-ray) ::
    ACTUARY : STATISTICS

    An ACTUARY uses STATISTICS as a tool in calculating insurance and
    annuity premiums. A PHYSICIAN uses an X-RAY as a tool in diagnos-
    ing and treating a patient.

18. **NONSEMANTIC** — related by sound, in letters in a word
    HOE : ROE :: THOUGH : (a. rough, b. flood, c. flow, d. how)

    In this sample question the terms are related not by meaning but by
    sound. The only relationship among the three given terms is the fact that
    they rhyme. Of the answer choices given, only FLOW rhymes with
    HOE, ROE, and THOUGH.

    EVIL : LIVE :: STEP : (a. stand, b. stop, c. post, d. pest)

    Another common nonsemantic relationship concerns the arrangement of
    letters in a word. In this sample question, EVIL and LIVE are two
    words made up of the same letters in different arrangements; that is, they
    are anagrams. An alternate arrangement of the letters in STEP results in
    the word PEST.

Analogy problems are a real challenge and can even be fun. They also offer
many opportunities for error if every answer is not given careful consideration. A few of the most common pitfalls to avoid are:

- **Reversal of sequence of the relationship**
  Part to Whole is *not* the same as Whole to Part.
  Cause to Effect is *not* the same as Effect to Cause.
  Smaller to Larger is *not* the same as Larger to Smaller.
  Action to Object is *not* the same as Object to Action.

- **Confusion of relationship**
  Part to Part (geometry : calculus) is *not* the same as Part to Whole
    (algebra : mathematics).
  Cause and Effect (fire : smoke) is *not* the same as Association
    (man : woman).
  Degree (drizzle : downpour) is *not* the same as Antonyms (dry : wet).
  Association (walk : limp) is *not* the same as Synonyms (eat :
    consume).

- **Grammatical inconsistency**
  The grammatical relationship of your first two words must be retained
  throughout the analogy. Consider this analogy: IMPRIS-
  ONED : LION :: CAGE : PARROT. While the meaningful relationship is the same on both sides of the proportion, the analogy is not
  parallel in construction. To be correct, the analogy would have to read
  either: PRISON : LION :: CAGE : PARROT or IMPRIS-
  ONED : LION :: CAGED : PARROT. In analogy problems, you
  have to create a pair which is grammatically consistent with the first
  pair as well as meaningfully correct.

- **Concentration on the meanings of words instead of on their relationships**
    In this type of error, you see FEATHERS : BEAK and you think "bird" instead of "Part-to-Part relationship." Then you choose as your answer WING : BIRD instead of WING : FOOT.

SUBJECT AREAS

In its attempt to provide accurate prediction of success in graduate study, the Miller Analogies Test measures both substantive knowledge and ability to see relationships and to think creatively. The substantive knowledge that the exam measures is based on a lifetime of experience and learning as well as on undergraduate coursework. It is impossible to map out a course of study now for the content of questions on the MAT. Rest assured that weakness in one or two areas will in no way disqualify you from admittance to the graduate program of your choice. Each content area is represented by only a handful of questions, and there is sufficient breadth of subject matter to allow every intelligent, well-educated person to understand a large proportion of the questions. The area from which you as an adult are most likely to be distanced is that of mythology. If you have the time and inclination for any substantive brush-up, we recommend that you renew your acquaintance with the gods of the Greek and Roman pantheons.

The Appendix at the end of this book will give you a quick brush-up in a number of significant subject areas. The mythology section lists and defines some of the major gods and goddesses and a number of lesser deities as well. Other sources will recount the myths involving these gods and their relationships with mortals. MAT questions may refer to these myths, to the superhuman heroes such as Hercules, Perseus, and Theseus, and to the great epics such as the *Aeneid* and the *Odyssey*.

The second section of the Appendix lists some of the nations of the world and names by which they have been known in earlier times. Other sources will cover world geography and world history in greater depth.

The final section of the Appendix, Mathematics, is self-explanatory. Learn what you can. The more information you bring into your exam, the easier it will be to recognize relationships and to complete analogies.

Some substantive areas from which your questions are sure to be drawn include:

General Knowledge—sports terminology; relationships between common words like *up* and *down*; frequently used abbreviations like *et al.*; parts of buildings; universally accepted concepts like the relationship between crime and punishment; common metaphors like the proverbial wisdom of owls; and so on

Vocabulary—analogies based on words that are not often used in ordinary conversation but which may have been learned through education and wide reading

Literature—mythology, Shakespeare, ancient and modern drama, poetry, classics and current novels

Music—musical terms, composers and their works, instruments

Art—artists and their creations, artistic periods

History—ancient history, world history, American history, documents, people, historians

Philosophy

Psychology

Geography—ancient and modern place names

Sciences—biology, chemistry, physics, medicine, terminology and concepts

Mathematics—algebra, geometry, calculus, terminology, equivalencies, simple calculations

Grammar—singulars and plurals, adjective and adverb endings, tenses, participles

Other—spelling; anagrams; homophones; rhymes; configurations

You should be aware, as well, that within any question two different substantive areas may be represented. For instance, a completed analogy involving a creator/creation relationship might be: WERTHEIMER : GESTALT :: GROFE : GRAND CANYON SUITE, drawing on the realms of psychology and music.

Obviously, it is not within the scope of this book to provide a complete knowledge review. Instead, we will concentrate on presenting exercises to familiarize you with relationships and formats. The classified analogies tests will give you practice with many kinds of relationships. Along with the correct answers, we have provided a simple sentence by which you might also have chosen the correct answer and, where appropriate, explanation of the thinking process involved in choosing the answer. Study **EVERY** answer explanation in this book in order to expand your own arsenal of approaches to analogy questions.

The full-length Sample Exams in Part II offer you the best practice available. These exams are not actual MATs, of course; the Miller Analogies Test is a secure exam, and the sample MATs released to the public may not be duplicated. However, the simulated exams in this book are closely patterned on the actual exam in terms of subject matter, variety of relationships, and difficulty. The explanations that follow the correct answers should prove useful to you as you develop and refine your skills in answering MAT questions. Do NOT skip over the explanations, even though you may have chosen the correct answers.

Part III of this book gives practice with another style of analogy question, the paired analogy. If you expect to take the GRE, you should give equal attention to this question style. If the MAT is the only exam you expect to take, try to allow yourself time to answer the paired analogy questions anyway. The more analogy questions you puzzle through, the better prepared you will be for your MAT. And the explanations to the paired analogy questions can give you more information and further insights.

Before you begin the classified analogies tests that follow, read through the following Analogy Test-Taking Tips. Read them again before you begin the Sample Exams. Give them a final reading the day before you take the Miller Analogies Test.

ANALOGY TEST-TAKING TIPS

1. Read each question carefully and try to categorize the relationship expressed by the given word pair. First look for a relationship between the two given words separated by a single colon (A and B or C and D). If you find no relationship between these terms, then look for a relationship between the first and third or the second and fourth terms (A and C or B and D).

2. Read each answer choice. It has been shown that the questions most likely to be answered incorrectly are those in which the correct answer is the last option. The most probable reason for this is that candidates tend to choose the first plausible answer they see, rather than examining all four options to determine which is truly the best answer to the question.

3. Use context clues to solve analogy problems containing one or more unfamiliar terms. While all four terms in an analogy question need not be the same part of speech, there will be no more than two parts of speech represented in any one question (unless the question is a nonsemantic analogy). With this fact in mind, you can immediately eliminate any option which introduces a third part of speech into an analogy problem.

4. Answer every question in order. MAT scores are based solely on the number of questions you answer correctly. Since there is no penalty imposed for incorrect responses, it is to your advantage to mark an answer for every question. Even if you are only guessing, you just might hit the right answer and add valuable points to your score. You lose nothing if you are wrong. You might make a mark in the test booklet next to the number of each question on which you are taking an educated or a wild guess. If you have time, you can easily locate the questions that you would like to rethink. If you work right down to the wire, you will have left no blanks and will not have run the risk of marking answers in the wrong spaces while skipping questions.

5. Work quickly. You have only fifty minutes to answer one hundred analogy problems. That means you should allow fewer than thirty seconds per question. Don't waste time stewing over a difficult analogy. If the answer does not come easily, guess, mark the question, and go on to the next one. Answer every question. Try to save a few minutes at the end of the test so that you can go back and take another look at the questions on which you guessed. The intensive practice in this book should give you ample opportunity to learn to pace yourself so that you can finish the actual MAT with time to spare to look back. If you do find yourself running out of time, however, use the last few seconds to mark all the remaining questions with the same answer, preferably not (a), since (a) is the correct answer least often. By the law of averages, you should get some answers right.

6. Come to the examination supplied with a watch and two or three pencils with erasers. Because it is so important for you to pace yourself on the MAT, it is essential that you be aware of the time. It is faster and easier to glance at your own watch than to look around the room for a clock to track your progress. Obviously, you do not want to waste precious time sharpening pencils or searching for an eraser to change an answer.

7. Become familiar with MAT question types by working through each of the practice tests and sample exams in this book. While the test you take may not have any of the same questions as the practice tests, it will certainly cover many of the same relationships between terms. As you sharpen your ability to recognize these relationships, you will be increasing your chances of scoring high on the MAT.

ANSWER SHEET FOR ANALOGY TESTS
CLASSIFIED BY CATEGORY

Test I. Synonyms and Definitions

1 Ⓐ Ⓑ Ⓒ Ⓓ	6 Ⓐ Ⓑ Ⓒ Ⓓ	11 Ⓐ Ⓑ Ⓒ Ⓓ	16 Ⓐ Ⓑ Ⓒ Ⓓ	21 Ⓐ Ⓑ Ⓒ Ⓓ	26 Ⓐ Ⓑ Ⓒ Ⓓ
2 Ⓐ Ⓑ Ⓒ Ⓓ	7 Ⓐ Ⓑ Ⓒ Ⓓ	12 Ⓐ Ⓑ Ⓒ Ⓓ	17 Ⓐ Ⓑ Ⓒ Ⓓ	22 Ⓐ Ⓑ Ⓒ Ⓓ	
3 Ⓐ Ⓑ Ⓒ Ⓓ	8 Ⓐ Ⓑ Ⓒ Ⓓ	13 Ⓐ Ⓑ Ⓒ Ⓓ	18 Ⓐ Ⓑ Ⓒ Ⓓ	23 Ⓐ Ⓑ Ⓒ Ⓓ	
4 Ⓐ Ⓑ Ⓒ Ⓓ	9 Ⓐ Ⓑ Ⓒ Ⓓ	14 Ⓐ Ⓑ Ⓒ Ⓓ	19 Ⓐ Ⓑ Ⓒ Ⓓ	24 Ⓐ Ⓑ Ⓒ Ⓓ	
5 Ⓐ Ⓑ Ⓒ Ⓓ	10 Ⓐ Ⓑ Ⓒ Ⓓ	15 Ⓐ Ⓑ Ⓒ Ⓓ	20 Ⓐ Ⓑ Ⓒ Ⓓ	25 Ⓐ Ⓑ Ⓒ Ⓓ	

Test II. Antonyms

1 Ⓐ Ⓑ Ⓒ Ⓓ	6 Ⓐ Ⓑ Ⓒ Ⓓ	11 Ⓐ Ⓑ Ⓒ Ⓓ	16 Ⓐ Ⓑ Ⓒ Ⓓ	21 Ⓐ Ⓑ Ⓒ Ⓓ	26 Ⓐ Ⓑ Ⓒ Ⓓ
2 Ⓐ Ⓑ Ⓒ Ⓓ	7 Ⓐ Ⓑ Ⓒ Ⓓ	12 Ⓐ Ⓑ Ⓒ Ⓓ	17 Ⓐ Ⓑ Ⓒ Ⓓ	22 Ⓐ Ⓑ Ⓒ Ⓓ	
3 Ⓐ Ⓑ Ⓒ Ⓓ	8 Ⓐ Ⓑ Ⓒ Ⓓ	13 Ⓐ Ⓑ Ⓒ Ⓓ	18 Ⓐ Ⓑ Ⓒ Ⓓ	23 Ⓐ Ⓑ Ⓒ Ⓓ	
4 Ⓐ Ⓑ Ⓒ Ⓓ	9 Ⓐ Ⓑ Ⓒ Ⓓ	14 Ⓐ Ⓑ Ⓒ Ⓓ	19 Ⓐ Ⓑ Ⓒ Ⓓ	24 Ⓐ Ⓑ Ⓒ Ⓓ	
5 Ⓐ Ⓑ Ⓒ Ⓓ	10 Ⓐ Ⓑ Ⓒ Ⓓ	15 Ⓐ Ⓑ Ⓒ Ⓓ	20 Ⓐ Ⓑ Ⓒ Ⓓ	25 Ⓐ Ⓑ Ⓒ Ⓓ	

Tear Here

Test III. Cause and Effect/Effect and Cause

1 Ⓐ Ⓑ Ⓒ Ⓓ	6 Ⓐ Ⓑ Ⓒ Ⓓ	11 Ⓐ Ⓑ Ⓒ Ⓓ	16 Ⓐ Ⓑ Ⓒ Ⓓ	21 Ⓐ Ⓑ Ⓒ Ⓓ	26 Ⓐ Ⓑ Ⓒ Ⓓ
2 Ⓐ Ⓑ Ⓒ Ⓓ	7 Ⓐ Ⓑ Ⓒ Ⓓ	12 Ⓐ Ⓑ Ⓒ Ⓓ	17 Ⓐ Ⓑ Ⓒ Ⓓ	22 Ⓐ Ⓑ Ⓒ Ⓓ	
3 Ⓐ Ⓑ Ⓒ Ⓓ	8 Ⓐ Ⓑ Ⓒ Ⓓ	13 Ⓐ Ⓑ Ⓒ Ⓓ	18 Ⓐ Ⓑ Ⓒ Ⓓ	23 Ⓐ Ⓑ Ⓒ Ⓓ	
4 Ⓐ Ⓑ Ⓒ Ⓓ	9 Ⓐ Ⓑ Ⓒ Ⓓ	14 Ⓐ Ⓑ Ⓒ Ⓓ	19 Ⓐ Ⓑ Ⓒ Ⓓ	24 Ⓐ Ⓑ Ⓒ Ⓓ	
5 Ⓐ Ⓑ Ⓒ Ⓓ	10 Ⓐ Ⓑ Ⓒ Ⓓ	15 Ⓐ Ⓑ Ⓒ Ⓓ	20 Ⓐ Ⓑ Ⓒ Ⓓ	25 Ⓐ Ⓑ Ⓒ Ⓓ	

Test IV. Part to Whole/Whole to Part

1 Ⓐ Ⓑ Ⓒ Ⓓ	6 Ⓐ Ⓑ Ⓒ Ⓓ	11 Ⓐ Ⓑ Ⓒ Ⓓ	16 Ⓐ Ⓑ Ⓒ Ⓓ	21 Ⓐ Ⓑ Ⓒ Ⓓ	26 Ⓐ Ⓑ Ⓒ Ⓓ
2 Ⓐ Ⓑ Ⓒ Ⓓ	7 Ⓐ Ⓑ Ⓒ Ⓓ	12 Ⓐ Ⓑ Ⓒ Ⓓ	17 Ⓐ Ⓑ Ⓒ Ⓓ	22 Ⓐ Ⓑ Ⓒ Ⓓ	
3 Ⓐ Ⓑ Ⓒ Ⓓ	8 Ⓐ Ⓑ Ⓒ Ⓓ	13 Ⓐ Ⓑ Ⓒ Ⓓ	18 Ⓐ Ⓑ Ⓒ Ⓓ	23 Ⓐ Ⓑ Ⓒ Ⓓ	
4 Ⓐ Ⓑ Ⓒ Ⓓ	9 Ⓐ Ⓑ Ⓒ Ⓓ	14 Ⓐ Ⓑ Ⓒ Ⓓ	19 Ⓐ Ⓑ Ⓒ Ⓓ	24 Ⓐ Ⓑ Ⓒ Ⓓ	
5 Ⓐ Ⓑ Ⓒ Ⓓ	10 Ⓐ Ⓑ Ⓒ Ⓓ	15 Ⓐ Ⓑ Ⓒ Ⓓ	20 Ⓐ Ⓑ Ⓒ Ⓓ	25 Ⓐ Ⓑ Ⓒ Ⓓ	

Test V. Part to Part

1 Ⓐ Ⓑ Ⓒ Ⓓ	6 Ⓐ Ⓑ Ⓒ Ⓓ	11 Ⓐ Ⓑ Ⓒ Ⓓ	16 Ⓐ Ⓑ Ⓒ Ⓓ	21 Ⓐ Ⓑ Ⓒ Ⓓ	26 Ⓐ Ⓑ Ⓒ Ⓓ
2 Ⓐ Ⓑ Ⓒ Ⓓ	7 Ⓐ Ⓑ Ⓒ Ⓓ	12 Ⓐ Ⓑ Ⓒ Ⓓ	17 Ⓐ Ⓑ Ⓒ Ⓓ	22 Ⓐ Ⓑ Ⓒ Ⓓ	
3 Ⓐ Ⓑ Ⓒ Ⓓ	8 Ⓐ Ⓑ Ⓒ Ⓓ	13 Ⓐ Ⓑ Ⓒ Ⓓ	18 Ⓐ Ⓑ Ⓒ Ⓓ	23 Ⓐ Ⓑ Ⓒ Ⓓ	
4 Ⓐ Ⓑ Ⓒ Ⓓ	9 Ⓐ Ⓑ Ⓒ Ⓓ	14 Ⓐ Ⓑ Ⓒ Ⓓ	19 Ⓐ Ⓑ Ⓒ Ⓓ	24 Ⓐ Ⓑ Ⓒ Ⓓ	
5 Ⓐ Ⓑ Ⓒ Ⓓ	10 Ⓐ Ⓑ Ⓒ Ⓓ	15 Ⓐ Ⓑ Ⓒ Ⓓ	20 Ⓐ Ⓑ Ⓒ Ⓓ	25 Ⓐ Ⓑ Ⓒ Ⓓ	

Test VI. Purpose, Use or Function

1 Ⓐ Ⓑ Ⓒ Ⓓ	6 Ⓐ Ⓑ Ⓒ Ⓓ	11 Ⓐ Ⓑ Ⓒ Ⓓ	16 Ⓐ Ⓑ Ⓒ Ⓓ	21 Ⓐ Ⓑ Ⓒ Ⓓ	26 Ⓐ Ⓑ Ⓒ Ⓓ
2 Ⓐ Ⓑ Ⓒ Ⓓ	7 Ⓐ Ⓑ Ⓒ Ⓓ	12 Ⓐ Ⓑ Ⓒ Ⓓ	17 Ⓐ Ⓑ Ⓒ Ⓓ	22 Ⓐ Ⓑ Ⓒ Ⓓ	
3 Ⓐ Ⓑ Ⓒ Ⓓ	8 Ⓐ Ⓑ Ⓒ Ⓓ	13 Ⓐ Ⓑ Ⓒ Ⓓ	18 Ⓐ Ⓑ Ⓒ Ⓓ	23 Ⓐ Ⓑ Ⓒ Ⓓ	
4 Ⓐ Ⓑ Ⓒ Ⓓ	9 Ⓐ Ⓑ Ⓒ Ⓓ	14 Ⓐ Ⓑ Ⓒ Ⓓ	19 Ⓐ Ⓑ Ⓒ Ⓓ	24 Ⓐ Ⓑ Ⓒ Ⓓ	
5 Ⓐ Ⓑ Ⓒ Ⓓ	10 Ⓐ Ⓑ Ⓒ Ⓓ	15 Ⓐ Ⓑ Ⓒ Ⓓ	20 Ⓐ Ⓑ Ⓒ Ⓓ	25 Ⓐ Ⓑ Ⓒ Ⓓ	

Test VII. Action to Object/Object to Action

1 Ⓐ Ⓑ Ⓒ Ⓓ	6 Ⓐ Ⓑ Ⓒ Ⓓ	11 Ⓐ Ⓑ Ⓒ Ⓓ	16 Ⓐ Ⓑ Ⓒ Ⓓ	21 Ⓐ Ⓑ Ⓒ Ⓓ	26 Ⓐ Ⓑ Ⓒ Ⓓ
2 Ⓐ Ⓑ Ⓒ Ⓓ	7 Ⓐ Ⓑ Ⓒ Ⓓ	12 Ⓐ Ⓑ Ⓒ Ⓓ	17 Ⓐ Ⓑ Ⓒ Ⓓ	22 Ⓐ Ⓑ Ⓒ Ⓓ	
3 Ⓐ Ⓑ Ⓒ Ⓓ	8 Ⓐ Ⓑ Ⓒ Ⓓ	13 Ⓐ Ⓑ Ⓒ Ⓓ	18 Ⓐ Ⓑ Ⓒ Ⓓ	23 Ⓐ Ⓑ Ⓒ Ⓓ	
4 Ⓐ Ⓑ Ⓒ Ⓓ	9 Ⓐ Ⓑ Ⓒ Ⓓ	14 Ⓐ Ⓑ Ⓒ Ⓓ	19 Ⓐ Ⓑ Ⓒ Ⓓ	24 Ⓐ Ⓑ Ⓒ Ⓓ	
5 Ⓐ Ⓑ Ⓒ Ⓓ	10 Ⓐ Ⓑ Ⓒ Ⓓ	15 Ⓐ Ⓑ Ⓒ Ⓓ	20 Ⓐ Ⓑ Ⓒ Ⓓ	25 Ⓐ Ⓑ Ⓒ Ⓓ	

Test VIII. Actor to Object/Object to Actor and Actor to Action/Action to Actor

1 Ⓐ Ⓑ Ⓒ Ⓓ	6 Ⓐ Ⓑ Ⓒ Ⓓ	11 Ⓐ Ⓑ Ⓒ Ⓓ	16 Ⓐ Ⓑ Ⓒ Ⓓ	21 Ⓐ Ⓑ Ⓒ Ⓓ	26 Ⓐ Ⓑ Ⓒ Ⓓ
2 Ⓐ Ⓑ Ⓒ Ⓓ	7 Ⓐ Ⓑ Ⓒ Ⓓ	12 Ⓐ Ⓑ Ⓒ Ⓓ	17 Ⓐ Ⓑ Ⓒ Ⓓ	22 Ⓐ Ⓑ Ⓒ Ⓓ	
3 Ⓐ Ⓑ Ⓒ Ⓓ	8 Ⓐ Ⓑ Ⓒ Ⓓ	13 Ⓐ Ⓑ Ⓒ Ⓓ	18 Ⓐ Ⓑ Ⓒ Ⓓ	23 Ⓐ Ⓑ Ⓒ Ⓓ	
4 Ⓐ Ⓑ Ⓒ Ⓓ	9 Ⓐ Ⓑ Ⓒ Ⓓ	14 Ⓐ Ⓑ Ⓒ Ⓓ	19 Ⓐ Ⓑ Ⓒ Ⓓ	24 Ⓐ Ⓑ Ⓒ Ⓓ	
5 Ⓐ Ⓑ Ⓒ Ⓓ	10 Ⓐ Ⓑ Ⓒ Ⓓ	15 Ⓐ Ⓑ Ⓒ Ⓓ	20 Ⓐ Ⓑ Ⓒ Ⓓ	25 Ⓐ Ⓑ Ⓒ Ⓓ	

Tear Here

Test IX. Place or Location

1 Ⓐ Ⓑ Ⓒ Ⓓ 6 Ⓐ Ⓑ Ⓒ Ⓓ 11 Ⓐ Ⓑ Ⓒ Ⓓ 16 Ⓐ Ⓑ Ⓒ Ⓓ 21 Ⓐ Ⓑ Ⓒ Ⓓ 26 Ⓐ Ⓑ Ⓒ Ⓓ
2 Ⓐ Ⓑ Ⓒ Ⓓ 7 Ⓐ Ⓑ Ⓒ Ⓓ 12 Ⓐ Ⓑ Ⓒ Ⓓ 17 Ⓐ Ⓑ Ⓒ Ⓓ 22 Ⓐ Ⓑ Ⓒ Ⓓ
3 Ⓐ Ⓑ Ⓒ Ⓓ 8 Ⓐ Ⓑ Ⓒ Ⓓ 13 Ⓐ Ⓑ Ⓒ Ⓓ 18 Ⓐ Ⓑ Ⓒ Ⓓ 23 Ⓐ Ⓑ Ⓒ Ⓓ
4 Ⓐ Ⓑ Ⓒ Ⓓ 9 Ⓐ Ⓑ Ⓒ Ⓓ 14 Ⓐ Ⓑ Ⓒ Ⓓ 19 Ⓐ Ⓑ Ⓒ Ⓓ 24 Ⓐ Ⓑ Ⓒ Ⓓ
5 Ⓐ Ⓑ Ⓒ Ⓓ 10 Ⓐ Ⓑ Ⓒ Ⓓ 15 Ⓐ Ⓑ Ⓒ Ⓓ 20 Ⓐ Ⓑ Ⓒ Ⓓ 25 Ⓐ Ⓑ Ⓒ Ⓓ

Test X. Association

1 Ⓐ Ⓑ Ⓒ Ⓓ 6 Ⓐ Ⓑ Ⓒ Ⓓ 11 Ⓐ Ⓑ Ⓒ Ⓓ 16 Ⓐ Ⓑ Ⓒ Ⓓ 21 Ⓐ Ⓑ Ⓒ Ⓓ 26 Ⓐ Ⓑ Ⓒ Ⓓ
2 Ⓐ Ⓑ Ⓒ Ⓓ 7 Ⓐ Ⓑ Ⓒ Ⓓ 12 Ⓐ Ⓑ Ⓒ Ⓓ 17 Ⓐ Ⓑ Ⓒ Ⓓ 22 Ⓐ Ⓑ Ⓒ Ⓓ
3 Ⓐ Ⓑ Ⓒ Ⓓ 8 Ⓐ Ⓑ Ⓒ Ⓓ 13 Ⓐ Ⓑ Ⓒ Ⓓ 18 Ⓐ Ⓑ Ⓒ Ⓓ 23 Ⓐ Ⓑ Ⓒ Ⓓ
4 Ⓐ Ⓑ Ⓒ Ⓓ 9 Ⓐ Ⓑ Ⓒ Ⓓ 14 Ⓐ Ⓑ Ⓒ Ⓓ 19 Ⓐ Ⓑ Ⓒ Ⓓ 24 Ⓐ Ⓑ Ⓒ Ⓓ
5 Ⓐ Ⓑ Ⓒ Ⓓ 10 Ⓐ Ⓑ Ⓒ Ⓓ 15 Ⓐ Ⓑ Ⓒ Ⓓ 20 Ⓐ Ⓑ Ⓒ Ⓓ 25 Ⓐ Ⓑ Ⓒ Ⓓ

Test XI. Sequence

1 Ⓐ Ⓑ Ⓒ Ⓓ 6 Ⓐ Ⓑ Ⓒ Ⓓ 11 Ⓐ Ⓑ Ⓒ Ⓓ 16 Ⓐ Ⓑ Ⓒ Ⓓ 21 Ⓐ Ⓑ Ⓒ Ⓓ 26 Ⓐ Ⓑ Ⓒ Ⓓ
2 Ⓐ Ⓑ Ⓒ Ⓓ 7 Ⓐ Ⓑ Ⓒ Ⓓ 12 Ⓐ Ⓑ Ⓒ Ⓓ 17 Ⓐ Ⓑ Ⓒ Ⓓ 22 Ⓐ Ⓑ Ⓒ Ⓓ
3 Ⓐ Ⓑ Ⓒ Ⓓ 8 Ⓐ Ⓑ Ⓒ Ⓓ 13 Ⓐ Ⓑ Ⓒ Ⓓ 18 Ⓐ Ⓑ Ⓒ Ⓓ 23 Ⓐ Ⓑ Ⓒ Ⓓ
4 Ⓐ Ⓑ Ⓒ Ⓓ 9 Ⓐ Ⓑ Ⓒ Ⓓ 14 Ⓐ Ⓑ Ⓒ Ⓓ 19 Ⓐ Ⓑ Ⓒ Ⓓ 24 Ⓐ Ⓑ Ⓒ Ⓓ
5 Ⓐ Ⓑ Ⓒ Ⓓ 10 Ⓐ Ⓑ Ⓒ Ⓓ 15 Ⓐ Ⓑ Ⓒ Ⓓ 20 Ⓐ Ⓑ Ⓒ Ⓓ 25 Ⓐ Ⓑ Ⓒ Ⓓ

Test XII. Characteristic

1 Ⓐ Ⓑ Ⓒ Ⓓ 6 Ⓐ Ⓑ Ⓒ Ⓓ 11 Ⓐ Ⓑ Ⓒ Ⓓ 16 Ⓐ Ⓑ Ⓒ Ⓓ 21 Ⓐ Ⓑ Ⓒ Ⓓ 26 Ⓐ Ⓑ Ⓒ Ⓓ
2 Ⓐ Ⓑ Ⓒ Ⓓ 7 Ⓐ Ⓑ Ⓒ Ⓓ 12 Ⓐ Ⓑ Ⓒ Ⓓ 17 Ⓐ Ⓑ Ⓒ Ⓓ 22 Ⓐ Ⓑ Ⓒ Ⓓ
3 Ⓐ Ⓑ Ⓒ Ⓓ 8 Ⓐ Ⓑ Ⓒ Ⓓ 13 Ⓐ Ⓑ Ⓒ Ⓓ 18 Ⓐ Ⓑ Ⓒ Ⓓ 23 Ⓐ Ⓑ Ⓒ Ⓓ
4 Ⓐ Ⓑ Ⓒ Ⓓ 9 Ⓐ Ⓑ Ⓒ Ⓓ 14 Ⓐ Ⓑ Ⓒ Ⓓ 19 Ⓐ Ⓑ Ⓒ Ⓓ 24 Ⓐ Ⓑ Ⓒ Ⓓ
5 Ⓐ Ⓑ Ⓒ Ⓓ 10 Ⓐ Ⓑ Ⓒ Ⓓ 15 Ⓐ Ⓑ Ⓒ Ⓓ 20 Ⓐ Ⓑ Ⓒ Ⓓ 25 Ⓐ Ⓑ Ⓒ Ⓓ

Tear Here

Test XIII. Degree

1 Ⓐ Ⓑ Ⓒ Ⓓ 6 Ⓐ Ⓑ Ⓒ Ⓓ 11 Ⓐ Ⓑ Ⓒ Ⓓ 16 Ⓐ Ⓑ Ⓒ Ⓓ 21 Ⓐ Ⓑ Ⓒ Ⓓ 26 Ⓐ Ⓑ Ⓒ Ⓓ
2 Ⓐ Ⓑ Ⓒ Ⓓ 7 Ⓐ Ⓑ Ⓒ Ⓓ 12 Ⓐ Ⓑ Ⓒ Ⓓ 17 Ⓐ Ⓑ Ⓒ Ⓓ 22 Ⓐ Ⓑ Ⓒ Ⓓ
3 Ⓐ Ⓑ Ⓒ Ⓓ 8 Ⓐ Ⓑ Ⓒ Ⓓ 13 Ⓐ Ⓑ Ⓒ Ⓓ 18 Ⓐ Ⓑ Ⓒ Ⓓ 23 Ⓐ Ⓑ Ⓒ Ⓓ
4 Ⓐ Ⓑ Ⓒ Ⓓ 9 Ⓐ Ⓑ Ⓒ Ⓓ 14 Ⓐ Ⓑ Ⓒ Ⓓ 19 Ⓐ Ⓑ Ⓒ Ⓓ 24 Ⓐ Ⓑ Ⓒ Ⓓ
5 Ⓐ Ⓑ Ⓒ Ⓓ 10 Ⓐ Ⓑ Ⓒ Ⓓ 15 Ⓐ Ⓑ Ⓒ Ⓓ 20 Ⓐ Ⓑ Ⓒ Ⓓ 25 Ⓐ Ⓑ Ⓒ Ⓓ

Test XIV. Grammatical

1 Ⓐ Ⓑ Ⓒ Ⓓ 6 Ⓐ Ⓑ Ⓒ Ⓓ 11 Ⓐ Ⓑ Ⓒ Ⓓ 16 Ⓐ Ⓑ Ⓒ Ⓓ 21 Ⓐ Ⓑ Ⓒ Ⓓ 26 Ⓐ Ⓑ Ⓒ Ⓓ
2 Ⓐ Ⓑ Ⓒ Ⓓ 7 Ⓐ Ⓑ Ⓒ Ⓓ 12 Ⓐ Ⓑ Ⓒ Ⓓ 17 Ⓐ Ⓑ Ⓒ Ⓓ 22 Ⓐ Ⓑ Ⓒ Ⓓ
3 Ⓐ Ⓑ Ⓒ Ⓓ 8 Ⓐ Ⓑ Ⓒ Ⓓ 13 Ⓐ Ⓑ Ⓒ Ⓓ 18 Ⓐ Ⓑ Ⓒ Ⓓ 23 Ⓐ Ⓑ Ⓒ Ⓓ
4 Ⓐ Ⓑ Ⓒ Ⓓ 9 Ⓐ Ⓑ Ⓒ Ⓓ 14 Ⓐ Ⓑ Ⓒ Ⓓ 19 Ⓐ Ⓑ Ⓒ Ⓓ 24 Ⓐ Ⓑ Ⓒ Ⓓ
5 Ⓐ Ⓑ Ⓒ Ⓓ 10 Ⓐ Ⓑ Ⓒ Ⓓ 15 Ⓐ Ⓑ Ⓒ Ⓓ 20 Ⓐ Ⓑ Ⓒ Ⓓ 25 Ⓐ Ⓑ Ⓒ Ⓓ

Test XV. Miscellaneous

1 Ⓐ Ⓑ Ⓒ Ⓓ 6 Ⓐ Ⓑ Ⓒ Ⓓ 11 Ⓐ Ⓑ Ⓒ Ⓓ 16 Ⓐ Ⓑ Ⓒ Ⓓ 21 Ⓐ Ⓑ Ⓒ Ⓓ 26 Ⓐ Ⓑ Ⓒ Ⓓ
2 Ⓐ Ⓑ Ⓒ Ⓓ 7 Ⓐ Ⓑ Ⓒ Ⓓ 12 Ⓐ Ⓑ Ⓒ Ⓓ 17 Ⓐ Ⓑ Ⓒ Ⓓ 22 Ⓐ Ⓑ Ⓒ Ⓓ
3 Ⓐ Ⓑ Ⓒ Ⓓ 8 Ⓐ Ⓑ Ⓒ Ⓓ 13 Ⓐ Ⓑ Ⓒ Ⓓ 18 Ⓐ Ⓑ Ⓒ Ⓓ 23 Ⓐ Ⓑ Ⓒ Ⓓ
4 Ⓐ Ⓑ Ⓒ Ⓓ 9 Ⓐ Ⓑ Ⓒ Ⓓ 14 Ⓐ Ⓑ Ⓒ Ⓓ 19 Ⓐ Ⓑ Ⓒ Ⓓ 24 Ⓐ Ⓑ Ⓒ Ⓓ
5 Ⓐ Ⓑ Ⓒ Ⓓ 10 Ⓐ Ⓑ Ⓒ Ⓓ 15 Ⓐ Ⓑ Ⓒ Ⓓ 20 Ⓐ Ⓑ Ⓒ Ⓓ 25 Ⓐ Ⓑ Ⓒ Ⓓ

Tear Here

ANALOGY TESTS
CLASSIFIED BY CATEGORY

Start your preparation for the MAT by taking each of the tests that follow. These tests provide intensive practice with the Category Technique for solving analogy problems. Each test consists of twenty-six questions which are indicative of the range of possibilities within a given category. The thirteen-minute time limit for each test simulates the pace of the MAT, a pace that requires quick decisions and allows for no dawdling over elusive relationships.

When you have completed these tests, check your answers with the correct answers at the end of the chapter. Read through all of the explanations. If you are not satisfied with your performance on the practice tests, try them again. When your scores show that you have a good grasp of the analogy question, move on to tackle the seven full-length sample exams that follow.

The sample exams contain a mixture of analogy problems very much like the mixture on the actual MAT. In addition to correct answers, explanations are provided after each exam to show you where and how you may have gone astray in answering each question. Take time to read these explanations since they may help to keep you from making some of the more common errors on your exam.

VERBAL ANALOGIES TEST I.
SYNONYMS AND DEFINITIONS

Time: 13 Minutes. 26 Questions.

Directions: Each of these test questions consists of three CAPITALIZED words and four lettered words enclosed in parentheses. Two of the capitalized words are related in some way. Find the two related words and establish the nature of the relationship. Then study the four words lettered a, b, c, and d. Select the one lettered word which is related to the remaining capitalized word in the same way that the first two capitalized words are related. Mark the answer sheet for the letter preceding the word you select.

1. DILIGENT : UNREMITTING :: DIAMETRIC : (a. pretentious, b. geographical, c. adamant, d. antithetical)

23

2. FRAUDULENT : (a. deceit, b. slander, c. fallacious, d. plausible) :: REMUNERATIVE : PROFITABLE

3. EXTORT : WREST :: CONSPIRE : (a. entice, b. plot, c. deduce, d. respire)

4. DOWAGER : WIDOW :: (a. enemy, b. constable, c. companion, distaff) : CONSORT

5. GAUDY : OSTENTATIOUS :: DEJECTED : (a. oppressed, b. inform, c. rejected, d. depressed)

6. (a. intermediate, b. feminine, c. alto, d. high) : SOPRANO :: LOW : BASS

7. LUXURY : ELEGANCE :: (a. penury, b. misery, c. poorhouse, d. hunger) : POVERTY

8. ARTFULNESS : FINESSE :: INEPT : (a. inefficient, b. artistic, c. tricky, d. insatiable)

9. REGALE : (a. endure, b. remain, c. entertain, d. cohere) :: REGISTER : ENROLL

10. BEGIN : (a. evening, b. seasonal, c. equinoctial, d. nightly) :: ESTABLISH : NOCTURNAL

11. STREW : STRAY :: DISPERSE : (a. deviate, b. utter, c. dredge, d. relegate)

12. VERTICAL : (a. circular, b. plumb, c. horizontal, d. inclined) :: PROSTRATE : FLAT

13. (a. indigenous, b. Indian, c. foreign, d. godly) : NATIVE :: REMOTE : DISTANT

14. BLAST : GUST :: BLARE : (a. uncover, b. roar, c. blaze, d. icicle)

15. (a. slavery, b. wrong, c. abolition, d. end) : DAILY :: ABOLISH : DIURNAL

16. BEGINNING : INCIPIENT :: (a. irrelevant, b. corresponding, c. reflexive, d. congregated) : CONGRUENT

17. SUFFICIENT : INTRODUCTION :: ENOUGH : (a. salutation, b. lecturer, c. conclusion, d. prologue)

18. DIN : NOISE :: CONTORTION : (a. disease, b. writhing, c. exploitation, d. contingency)

19. RESTRAINT : CONTINENCE :: (a. rift, b. glacier, c. depth, d. mountain) : CREVASSE

20. REFINED : URBANE :: EQUITABLE : (a. equine, b. just, c. recurrent, d. ambiguous)

21. FINIAL : PEDIMENT :: PINNACLE : (a. basement, b. lineage, c. gable, d. obstruction)

22. HISTORY : (a. reality, b. war, c. peace, d. geography) :: TALE : SUPPOSITION

23. JABBER : GIBBERISH :: QUIDNUNC : (a. quisling, b. gossip, c. theorist, d. testator)

24. DIAPASON : (a. diaphragm, b. clef, c. chord, d. organ) :: KEY-NOTE : TONIC

25. PALLID : BLANCHED :: (a. form, b. sum, c. purpose, d. begin) : INSTITUTE

26. CREPUSCULAR : CURSORY :: INDISTINCT : (a. profane, b. egregious, c. superficial, d. unique)

VERBAL ANALOGIES TEST II.
ANTONYMS

Time: 13 Minutes. 26 Questions.

Directions: Each of these test questions consists of three CAPITALIZED words and four lettered words enclosed in parentheses. Two of the capitalized words are related in some way. Find the two related words and establish the nature of the relationship. Then study the four words lettered a, b, c, and d. Select the one lettered word which is related to the remaining capitalized word in the same way that the first two capitalized words are related. Mark the answer sheet for the letter preceding the word you select.

1. SUNDER : CONSOLIDATE :: TANGIBLE : (a. abstract, b. tasty, c. possible, d. tangled)

2. ACCORD : BREACH :: CONNECTION : (a. tie, b. dissociation, c. association, d. distrust)

3. BIRTH : CATCALL :: DEATH : (a. oblivion, b. meow, c. acceptance, d. backyard)

4. MAGNANIMITY : TOLERANCE :: PARSIMONY : (a. advocacy, b. totality, c. urgency, d. bigotry)

5. (a. elongated, b. useless, c. everlasting, d. heavenly) : DERISION :: EPHEMERAL : ENCORE

6. (a. clumsy, b. clandestine, c. graceful, d. lugubrious) : GAUCHE :: WEALTHY : INDIGENT

7. MATURE : COUNTERFEIT :: (a. spotted, b. rotten, c. unripe, d. grown) : REAL

8. MANIFEST : (a. latent, b. many-sided, c. obvious, d. manipulated) :: INQUISITIVE : INCURIOUS

9. IDIOT : GENIUS :: VALLEY : (a. plateau, b. moron, c. mountain, d. field)

10. MISCELLANEOUS : PERMANENT :: (a. collective, b. undetermined, c. righteous, d. single) : TEMPORARY

11. IMPROMPTU : (a. ad lib, b. memorized, c. verbose, d. prolific) :: SPONTANEOUS : CALCULATED

12. MEDLEY : (a. victory, b. enjoyment, c. criticize, d. succeed) :: ONE : PRAISE

13. WHITE : VALOR :: (a. color, b. dim, c. pigment, d. black) : COWARDICE

14. HYPOCRISY : HONESTY :: HOSTILITY : (a. war, b. amity, c. hospitality, d. hostage)

15. PLETHORA : CUNNING :: DEARTH : (a. dull, b. earthy, c. foxy, d. cute)

16. PERTINENT : (a. pert, b. cloudy, c. irrelevant, d. perceptive) :: INCLEMENT : CLEAR

17. BOMBASTIC : (a. stringent, b. medicinal, c. fishy, d. filthy) :: PLAINSPOKEN : LAX

18. (a. pursue, b. abstain, c. hunt, d. find) : INDULGE :: AVOID : SEEK

19. DISHONESTY : OBVIOUS :: INTEGRITY : (a. oblong, b. invidious, c. surreptitious, d. honest)

20. REVERE : (a. composed, b. reprehensible, c. completed, d. inscrutable) :: BLASPHEME : COMPREHENSIBLE

21. IMMATURITY : (a. anger, b. childhood, c. adulthood, d. incompatibility) :: COMPETITION : MONOPOLY

22. REPUGN : COMPROMISE :: RESCIND : (a. refuse, b. rest, c. decipher, d. validate)

23. DEGRADE : MARTIAL :: LAUD : (a. military, b. noisy, c. worried, d. halcyon)

24. SCARCE : WARLIKE :: (a. fear, b. hardly, c. few, d. abundant) : PEACEFUL

25. INTIMIDATE : ENCOURAGE :: (a. interdict, b. comply, c. expect, d. continue) : ALLOW

26. COSTLY : SCARCE :: CHEAP : (a. abundant, b. tinny, c. difficult, d. puny)

VERBAL ANALOGIES TEST III.
CAUSE AND EFFECT/
EFFECT AND CAUSE

Time: 13 Minutes. 26 Questions.

Directions: Each of these test questions consists of three CAPITALIZED words and four lettered words enclosed in parentheses. Two of the capitalized words are related in some way. Find the two related words and establish the nature of the relationship. Then study the four words lettered a, b, c, and d. Select the one lettered word which is related to the remaining capitalized word in the same way that the first two capitalized words are related. Mark the answer sheet for the letter preceding the word you select.

1. CURIOSITY : ENLIGHTENMENT :: VERACITY : (a. credulousness, b. credibility, c. validity, d. cognizance)

2. TENACITY : (a. adversity, b. antagonism, c. attainment, d. lassitude) :: MONOTONY : BOREDOM

3. SATISFACTION : GOOD DEED :: IMPROVEMENT : (a. sin, b. criticism, c. diligence, d. kindness)

4. (a. yolk, b. crack, c. bird, d. shell) : EGG :: PLANT : SEED

5. CARE : (a. avoidance, b. accident, c. fruition, d. safety) :: ASSI-
   DUITY : SUCCESS

6. GRAPE : (a. vintage, b. vine, c. wine, d. fruit) :: WHEAT : FLOUR

7. WAR : GRIEF :: (a. joy, b. peace, c. soldier, d. finish) : HAPPINESS

8. MOON : LIGHT :: ECLIPSE : (a. violence, b. darkness, c. cruelty,
   d. whistling)

9. WATER : (a. sky, b. rain, c. lake, d. H₂O) :: HEAT : FIRE

10. SCAR : WOUND :: (a. damage, b. case, c. car, d. murder) : AC-
    CIDENT

11. HEALTH : DISEASE :: SANITATION : (a. filth, b. measles, c. care-
    lessness, d. illness)

12. COLD : (a. water, b. ice, c. gas, d. crystals) :: HEAT : STEAM

13. LAZINESS : STRATEGY :: FAILURE : (a. mentality, b. brutality,
    c. company, d. victory)

14. (a. starvation, b. indigestion, c. energy, d. life) : FOOD :: SUFFO-
    CATION : AIR

15. RESPONSE : (a. answer, b. stimulus, c. correct, d. effect) ::
    PREDICAMENT : CARELESSNESS

16. PAIN : (a. punishment, b. crime, c. defiance, d. distress) :: FALL :
    DISOBEDIENCE

17. FAITH : DESPERATION :: PRAYER : (a. blasphemy, b. crime,
    c. salvation, d. despair)

18. FANATICISM : (a. infirmity, b. criticism, c. intolerance, d. enthusi-
    asm) :: BIGOTRY : HATRED

19. CONVICTION : (a. revenge, b. contrition, c. justice, d. vindica-
    tion) :: GUILT : INNOCENCE

20. LIQUOR : ALCOHOLISM :: CANDY : (a. confectionery, b. blem-
    ish, c. obesity, d. overindulgence)

21. TAXATION : (a. rebellion, b. slavery, c. prohibition, d. cotton)
    :: REVOLUTION : CIVIL WAR

22. FIRE : SMOKE :: PROFLIGACY : (a. debt, b. prodigality, c. disper-
    sal, d. deceit)

23. WORK : (a. employment, b. entertainment, c. office, d. income) :: FOOD : GROWTH

24. ERROR : (a. recklessness, b. caution, c. indifference, d. accident) :: INEXPERIENCE : CARELESSNESS

25. AIR : WATER :: (a. fluorine, b. charcoal, c. smoke, d. fog) : CHLORINE

26. FLAME : BURN :: INSULT : (a. disdain, b. anger, c. reparation, d. approbation)

VERBAL ANALOGIES TEST IV.
PART TO WHOLE/WHOLE TO PART

Time: 13 Minutes. 26 Questions.

Directions: Each of these test questions consists of three CAPITALIZED words and four lettered words enclosed in parentheses. Two of the capitalized words are related in some way. Find the two related words and establish the nature of the relationship. Then study the four words lettered a, b, c, and d. Select the one lettered word which is related to the remaining capitalized word in the same way that the first two capitalized words are related. Mark the answer sheet for the letter preceding the word you select.

1. VERSAILLES : PALACE :: BASTILLE : (a. parkway, b. Paris, c. prison, d. France)

2. PLAY : PROLOGUE :: CONSTITUTION : (a. preamble, b. laws, c. article, d. amendment)

3. SENTENCE : (a. structure, b. word, c. composition, d. correctness) :: PARAGRAPH : SENTENCE

4. BEAD : (a. ball, b. iron, c. link, d. strength) :: NECKLACE : CHAIN

5. PEACH : PIT :: (a. planet, b. moon, c. orbit, d. solar system) : SUN

6. SLICE : LOAF :: ISLAND : (a. land, b. archipelago, c. peninsula, d. ocean)

7. PEAK : (a. water, b. storm, c. crest, d. ocean) :: MOUNTAIN : WAVE

8. (a. carpenter, b. market, c. roast, d. cowboy) : MEAT :: RANCH : STEER

9. INGREDIENT : YELLOW :: RECIPE : (a. yolk, b. green, c. liver, d. age)

10. (a. crystallization, b. mine, c. foliage, d. forest) : QUARRY :: LUMBER : STONE

11. GRANITE : MARBLE :: (a. hardness, b. polish, c. quartz, d. fragility) : LIMESTONE

12. STEEL : ALLOY :: IRON : (a. compound, b. element, c. alloy, d. mixture)

13. MAN : (a. wound, b. woman, c. fist, d. shield) :: BEE : STINGER

14. PART : (a. United States, b. Lake Erie, c. Ontario, d. North America) :: WHOLE : CANADA

15. CADET : WEST POINT :: (a. seabee, b. plebe, c. ensign, d. Navy) : ANNAPOLIS

16. BOOK : HOTEL :: PREFACE : (a. room, b. guest, c. manager, d. lobby)

17. BANQUET : TOASTMASTER :: (a. speaker, b. orator, c. assembly, d. speech) : CHAIRMAN

18. POETRY : SONNET :: (a. symphony, b. song, c. music, d. etude) : CONCERTO

19. (a. coat, b. rabbit, c. warm, d. women) : FLOWER :: FUR : PETAL

20. CHEMISTRY : ELEMENTS :: GRAMMAR : (a. teacher, b. English, c. subject, d. parts of speech)

21. PINE : (a. Christmas, b. tree, c. fir, d. loss) :: POINSETTIA : FLOWER

22. CARROT : COW :: PLANT : (a. meat, b. herd, c. animal, d. stockyard)

23. CORPORATION : (a. mayor, b. state, c. nation, d. government) :: PRESIDENT : GOVERNOR

24. (a. face, b. eye, c. head, d. brain) : TEAM :: EAR : PLAYER

25. CHINESE : MONGOLIAN :: ENGLISH : (a. clever, b. race, c. Caucasian, d. language)

26. WHEAT : (a. bushel, b. chaff, c. stalk, d. bread) :: WINE : DREGS

VERBAL ANALOGIES TEST V.
PART TO PART

Time: 13 Minutes. 26 Questions.

Directions: Each of these test questions consists of three CAPITAL-IZED words and four lettered words enclosed in parentheses. Two of the capitalized words are related in some way. Find the two related words and establish the nature of the relationship. Then study the four words lettered a, b, c, and d. Select the one lettered word which is related to the remaining capitalized word in the same way that the first two capitalized words are related. Mark the answer sheet for the letter preceding the word you select.

1. NEPHEW : NIECE :: UNCLE : (a. man, b. relative, c. father, d. aunt)

2. HAND : ELBOW :: FOOT : (a. muscle, b. knee, c. leg, d. toe)

3. SNEAKER : SHOE :: (a. hand, b. foot, c. mitten, d. boot) : GLOVE

4. CONTRALTO : (a. opera, b. soprano, c. woman, d. song) :: BAR-ITONE : TENOR

5. ROBIN : (a. St. Bernard, b. calico, c. redbreast, d. duck) :: BLUEJAY :: SPANIEL

6. HEART : LUNGS :: BRAIN : (a. appendix, b. intelligence, c. liver, d. breathing)

7. LAWNMOWER : MOP :: (a. fertilizer, b. rake, c. gardener, d. grass) : BUCKET

8. HIGH JUMP : BROAD JUMP :: HOCKEY : (a. bowling, b. surfing, c. soccer, d. tennis)

9. PEN : (a. ink, b. paper, c. point, d. pencil) :: PAPER : SLATE

10. NICOTINE : MILK :: (a. alcohol, b. cigarettes, c. cancer, d. to-bacco) : ORANGE JUICE

11. PERCH : TROUT :: PUPPY : (a. Great Dane, b. wolf, c. dog, d. kitten)

12. CARROT : LETTUCE :: POTATO : (a. grape, b. cabbage, c. radish, d. onion)

13. FORWARD : (a. batter, b. referee, c. goaltender, d. fullback) :: GUARD : POINT KICKER

14. (a. box, b. Egypt, c. pentagon, d. triangle) : SQUARE :: PYRAMID : CUBE

15. GOOSE : GANDER :: (a. cow, b. hog, c. pig, d. lamb) : BULL

16. SENEGAL : TUNISIA :: (a. Brazil, b. Bolivia, c. Surinam, d. Guyana) : COLOMBIA

17. FOOT : (a. pound, b. degree, c. mile, d. ampere) :: INCH : CENTIMETER

18. OPHELIA : HAMLET :: PORTIA : (a. Shylock, b. Macbeth, c. Iago, d. Henry VIII)

19. (a. cob, b. corn, c. swan, d. bitch) : DOE :: COCK : EWE

20. CLAM : OYSTER :: COW : (a. pig, b. sheep, c. dog, d. squirrel)

21. AIRPLANE : (a. kite, b. ship, c. bird, d. helicopter) :: BUS : TRAIN

22. GELDING : CAPON :: (a. stallion, b. waterfowl, c. steer, d. mongrel) : EUNUCH

23. EYE : SHIRT :: EAR : (a. button, b. pants, c. cotton, d. clothing)

24. FINGER : PALM :: (a. shoe, b. foot, c. sole, d. limb) : HEEL

25. (a. car, b. bicycle, c. bumper, d. night) : SEAM :: HEADLIGHT : BUTTON

26. WING : BEAK :: PAW : (a. tail, b. foot, c. cat, d. dog)

VERBAL ANALOGIES TEST VI.
PURPOSE, USE, OR FUNCTION

Time: 13 Minutes. 26 Questions.

Directions: Each of these test questions consists of three CAPITALIZED words and four lettered words enclosed in parentheses. Two of the capitalized words are related in some way. Find the two related words and establish the nature of the relationship. Then study the four words lettered a, b, c, and d. Select the one lettered word which is related to the remaining capitalized word in the same way that the first two capitalized words are related. Mark the answer sheet for the letter preceding the word you select.

1. HORSE : HITCHING POST :: CRAFT : (a. parapet, b. moorage, c. running, d. vessel)

2. BALL : BAT :: SHUTTLECOCK : (a. battledore, b. badminton, c. plumage, d. game)

3. WIRELESS : (a. message, b. speed, c. transoceanic, d. communication) :: AIRPLANE : TRANSPORTATION

4. CALF : GOOSE :: SHOE : (a. gander, b. pillow, c. roast, d. feathers)

5. (a. wood, b. chair, c. house, d. cloth) : CURTAIN :: TABLE : WINDOW

6. EXERCISE : (a. action, b. drama, c. stage, d. performance) :: GYMNASIUM : THEATER

7. CRATER : VOLCANO :: CHIMNEY : (a. fire, b. house, c. flue, d. smoke)

8. SIPHON : (a. shovel, b. pipette, c. sponge, d. spoon) :: GASOLINE : COAL

9. ARCHAEOLOGIST : ANTIQUITY :: ICHTHYLOGIST : (a. theology, b. marine life, c. horticulture, d. mysticism)

10. SCOPE : (a. tele, b. enlarge, c. see, d. range) :: METER : MEASURE

11. (a. wool, b. sheep, c. animal, d. farm) : MUTTON :: PIG : PORK

12. PRINT : PRESS :: (a. efface, b. board, c. chalk, d. rubber) : ERASER

13. AGAR : (a. jelly, b. skin, c. culture, d. medium) :: BREAD : MOLD

14. MENU : MEAL :: MAP : (a. road, b. distance, c. trip, d. scale)

15. HEW : AX :: (a. punch, b. tack, c. clear, d. auger) : AWL

16. CONE : PINE :: ACORN : (a. nut, b. squirrel, c. tree, d. oak)

17. GUN : HOLSTER :: SWORD : (a. pistol, b. scabbard, c. warrior, d. slay)

18. MESSENGER : LETTER CARRIER :: (a. value, b. dispatches, c. easy, d. complicated) : MAIL

19. BANDAGE : STRING :: WOUND : (a. package, b. cling, c. rope, d. twine)

20. (a. tobacco, b. fire, c. flame, d. flue) : SIPHON :: SMOKE : LIQUID

21. MAN : BREAD :: HORSE : (a. stable, b. duck, c. barn, d. hay)

22. HANG : (a. gallows, b. nail, c. murderer, d. picture) :: BEHEAD : GUILLOTINE

23. BARREL : SILO :: WINE : (a. horses, b. floss, c. grain, d. refuse)

24. HAIR : (a. grass, b. fish, c. scales, d. orangutan) :: FEATHER : OSTRICH

25. (a. steel, b. head, c. combat, d. football) : FACE :: HELMET : MASK

26. WING : BIRD :: (a. gill, b. tail, c. fin, d. scales) : FISH

VERBAL ANALOGIES TEST VII.
ACTION TO OBJECT/OBJECT TO ACTION

Time: 13 Minutes. 26 Questions.

Directions: Each of these test questions consists of three CAPITALIZED words and four lettered words enclosed in parentheses. Two of the capitalized words are related in some way. Find the two related words and establish the nature of the relationship. Then study the four words lettered a, b, c, and d. Select the one lettered word which is related to the remaining capitalized word in the same way that the first two capitalized words are related. Mark the answer sheet for the letter preceding the word you select.

1. HEAR : SOUND :: SEE : (a. move, b. taste, c. picture, d. visible)

2. SCRUB : SCOUR :: FLOOR : (a. sweep, b. pan, c. kitchen, d. cleanse)

3. BANANA : (a. sea, b. fish, c. sand, d. oyster) :: PEEL : SHUCK

4. (a. book, b. remodeling, c. correction, d. content) : REVISION :: GARMENT : ALTERATION

5. SCENE : VIEW :: (a. taste, b. concert, c. odor, d. color) : HEAR

6. STUDY : TRY :: LEARN : (a. begin, b. attempt, c. tail, d. succeed)

7. DREDGE : SCOOP :: SILT : (a. ladle, b. ice cream, c. shovel, d. newspaper)

8. (a. store, b. coat, c. wool, d. sheep) : BREAD :: WEAR : EAT

9. HONE : WHET :: (a. hunger, b. knife, c. meat, d. fork) : APPETITE

10. PRESIDE : (a. court, b. jury, c. judge, d. subject) :: REIGN : KING

11. OVERLOOK : MISTAKE :: ADVOCATE : (a. recommend, b. cause, c. consideration, d. error)

12. ASSUAGE : (a. appease, b. reassure, c. fear, d. joy) :: ARTIC-ULATE : DESIRE

13. KNOWLEDGE : (a. culture, b. erudition, c. deception, d. debt) :: ASSIMILATE : ASSUME

14. THWART : ASPIRATIONS :: STIFLE : (a. heat, b. air, c. anger, d. sense)

15. (a. reject, b. contend, c. love, d. reply) : HATE :: FRIEND : ENEMY

16. CHECK : FORGERY :: COPYRIGHT : (a. bank, b. infringement, c. book, d. author)

17. DECAY : (a. dampness, b. rust, c. steel, d. ore) :: WOOD : IRON

18. (a. college, b. research, c. library, d. paper) : THESIS :: ANAL-YSIS : DIAGNOSIS

19. SHIP : ARMY :: MUTINY : (a. court-martial, b. desertion, c. offi-cer, d. navy)

20. IRRIGATION : (a. oxygen, b. respiration, c. ventilation, d. atmos-phere) :: WATER : AIR

21. (a. wardrobes, b. tears, c. silverware, d. fall) : CLOTHING :: BREAK : DISHES

22. TONE : HEARING :: COLOR : (a. pigment, b. sight, c. melody, d. picture)

23. GRIND : (a. wear, b. tear, c. see, d. darn) :: KNIFE : STOCKING

24. PLAY : REHEARSE :: GAME : (a. football, b. practice, c. coach, d. players)

25. (a. buying, b. cheating, c. bravery, d. praying) : SELLING :: FAME : PROFIT

26. MARBLE : (a. palace, b. engraving, c. agate, d. quarry) :: SALT : MINE

VERBAL ANALOGIES TEST VIII.
ACTOR TO OBJECT/OBJECT TO ACTOR
AND ACTOR TO ACTION/
ACTION TO ACTOR

Time: 13 Minutes. 26 Questions.

Directions: Each of these test questions consist of three CAPITAL-IZED words and four lettered words enclosed in parentheses. Two of the capitalized words are related in some way. Find the two related words and establish the nature of the relationship. Then study the four words lettered a, b, c, and d. Select the one lettered word which is related to the remaining capitalized word in the same way that the first two capitalized words are related. Mark the answer sheet for the letter preceding the word you select.

1. SALESMAN : PRODUCT :: TEACHER : (a. principal, b. English, c. pupils, d. subject)

2. EARTH : (a. Mars, b. moon, c. sky, d. sun) :: MOON : EARTH

3. TEACHER : (a. parent, b. dolly, c. youngster, d. obey) :: PUPIL : CHILD

4. BARK : ROAR :: DOG : (a. lion, snake, c. lamb, d. train)

5. (a. vocalist, b. singing, c. chorus, d. music) : ACTRESS :: SING : ACT

6. COACH : PLAYER :: COUNSELOR : (a. tutor, b. supervisor, c. leader, d. camper)

7. MUSIC : (a. typewriter, b. book, c. piano, d. character) :: COMPOSER : AUTHOR

8. WITHER : BLOOM :: PASS : (a. time, b. study, c. fail, d. excuse)

9. CONSTITUTION : MISTAKE :: (a. preamble, b. amendment, c. law, d. unconstitutional) : ERASER

10. DOCTOR : (a. operation, b. disease, c. poverty, d. therapy) :: PSYCHIATRIST : MALADJUSTMENT

11. POLISH : MANICURIST :: POLISH : (a. bootblack, b. shoe, c. buff, d. nail)

12. COMMAND : OBEY :: (a. performance, b. parents, c. army, d. result) : CHILDREN

13. WOODSMAN : (a. cut, b. hew, c. plumber, d. cobbler) :: AX : AWL

14. (a. fish, b. pool, c. pier, d. boat) : MAN :: SWIMS : WALKS

15. SCALPEL : SURGEON :: (a. mallet, b. cleaver, c. chisel, d. wrench) : BUTCHER

16. HEAL : LEND :: PHYSICIAN : (a. money, b. banker, c. give, d. bank)

17. MAN : (a. ditty, b. bird, c. communication, d. tune) :: SPEECH : SONG

18. (a. house, b. wall, c. lodge, d. trowel) : MASON :: SAW : CARPENTER

19. TAILOR : PATTERN :: ARCHITECT : (a. house, b. drawing board, c. plan, d. artist)

20. SEED : EGG :: (a. sow, b. pollinate, c. germinate, d. plant) : HATCH

21. VIBRATION : TONE :: REFRACTION : (a. light, b. noise, c. rays, d. color)

22. REFEREE : RULES :: CONSCIENCE : (a. thought, b. regulations, c. morals, d. Freud)

23. UREA FORMALDEHYDE FOAM : FREON :: (a. preservation, b. insulation, c. levitation, d. aggravation) : REFRIGERATION

24. SLUICE : (a. juice, b. garbage, c. mine, d. water) :: DAM : WATER

25. MUTE : CUSHION :: HORN : (a. chair, b. padding, c. soften, d. pillow)

26. WATER : (a. wet, b. ink, c. water, d. fuel) :: CORK : OIL

VERBAL ANALOGIES TEST IX.
PLACE OR LOCATION

Time: 13 Minutes. 26 Questions.

Directions: Each of the test questions consists of three CAPITAL-IZED words and four lettered words enclosed in parentheses. Two of the capitalized words are related in some way. Find the two related words and establish the nature of the relationship. Then study the four words lettered a, b, c, and d. Select the one lettered word which is related to the remaining capitalized word in the same way that the first two capitalized words are related. Mark the answer sheet for the letter preceding the word you select.

1. THIMBLE : FINGER :: SOCK : (a. band, b. felt, c. hat rack, d. foot)

2. KING : PEASANT :: (a. queen, b. royalty, c. serf, d. palace) : HOVEL

3. BODY : (a. arteries, b. hands, c. brain, d. muscles) :: COUNTRY : RAILROADS

4. BANK : (a. intelligence, b. blackboard, c. books, d. riches) :: MONEY : KNOWLEDGE

5. RACE : TRACK :: SWIM : (a. stroke, b. breathe, c. meet, d. pool)

6. LAND : (a. captain, b. ravage, c. bounty, d. sea) :: GENERAL : ADMIRAL

7. TREE : VINE :: (a. limb, b. leaf, c. pear, d. earth) : MELON

8. SUBMARINE : FISH :: AIRPLANE : (a. aquarium, b. bird, c. wing, d. hanger)

9. BLOOD : (a. corpuscle, b. body, c. vein, d. plasma) :: WATER : AQUEDUCT

10. (a. pizza, b. Mexico, c. pestle, d. England) : PESO :: FRANCE : FRANC

11. FJORD : PENINSULA :: MAINLAND : (a. boats, b. sea, c. cape, d. Massachusetts)

12. ILLINOIS : CHICAGO :: MASSACHUSETTS : (a. Boston, b. Kentucky, c. Kennedy, d. Europe)

13. SHANGRI-LA : (a. Tibet, b. heaven, c. *Lost Horizon*, d. paradise) :: EDEN : BIBLE

14. (a. sail, b. sea, c. yacht, d. plane) : BOAT :: AIR : WATER

15. CARRIAGE : BABY :: (a. woman, b. automobile, c. child, d. adult) : MAN

16. FRANCE : (a. Norway, b. Hungary, c. Spain, d. Portugal) :: THAILAND : CAMBODIA

17. HOSPITAL : NURSE :: SCHOOL : (a. student, b. apple, c. test, d. teacher)

18. (a. engineer, b. driver, c. butler, d. servant) : CHAUFFEUR :: TRAIN : AUTOMOBILE

19. BAGPIPE : (a. harp, b. guitar, c. piano, d. trumpet) :: SCOTLAND : SPAIN

20. CAPE : CONTINENT :: GULF : (a. ocean, b. lake, c. reservoir, d. water)

21. LONDON : (a. Florence, b. Madrid, c. Milan, d. Rome) :: GLOBE THEATER : LA SCALA

22. RUSSIA : STEPPES :: ARGENTINA : (a. mountains, b. pampas, c. tundra, d. valleys)

23. (a. mechanic, b. machinery, c. smoke, d. production) : FACTORY :: TYPIST : OFFICE

24. FACULTY : STAFF :: UNIVERSITY : (a. intern, b. patient, c. workers, d. hospital)

25. EAGLE : (a. eaglet, b. aerie, c. hawk, d. rabbit) :: RABBIT : BURROW

26. TRAIN : (a. steamer, b. pier, c. water, d. track) :: STATION : WHARF

VERBAL ANALOGIES TEST X.
ASSOCIATION

Time: 13 Minutes. 26 Questions.

Directions: Each of these test questions consist of three CAPITAL-IZED words and four lettered words enclosed in parentheses. Two of the capitalized words are related in some way. Find the two related words and establish the nature of the relationship. Then study the four words lettered a, b, c, and d. Select the one lettered word which is related to the remaining capitalized word in the same way that the first two capitalized words are related. Mark the answer sheet for the letter preceding the word you select.

1. SILK : RAYON :: BUTTER : (a. margarine, b. oil, c. cream, d. bread)

2. BOAT : (a. rescue, b. sink, c. life preserver, d. safety) :: AIR-PLANE : PARACHUTE

3. NUTRITION : (a. vision, b. bulb, c. electricity, d. watt) :: FOOD : LIGHT

4. (a. deed, b. request, c. person, d. thanks) : FAVOR :: FEE : SERVICE

5. ELECTRICITY : RUBBER :: FIRE : (a. ashes, b. heat, c. asbestos, d. melting)

6. (a. horse, b. hoof, c. neigh, d. army) : FOOT :: CAVALRY : INFANTRY

7. REWARD : PRESENT :: (a. accomplishment, b. punishment, c. medal, d. money) : BIRTHDAY

8. BALLET : TERPSICHORE :: POETRY : (a. Zeus, b. music, c. Mt. Olympus, d. Erato)

9. HOSTAGE : (a. criminal, b. ransom, c. murder, d. threat) :: LAW-BREAKER : BAIL

10. LIBRARY : GYMNASIUM :: (a. sick, b. school, c. books, d. knowledge) : HEALTH

11. PEAS : CARROTS :: MEAT : (a. dinner, b. fish, c. potatoes, d. beef)

12. (a. vote, b. freedom, c. people, d. republic) : DEMOCRACY :: KING : MONARCHY

13. APARTHEID : SOUTH AFRICA :: (a. miscegenation, b. equality, c. segregation, d. libertarianism) : SWEDEN

14. SORROW : (a. joy, b. smile, c. girls, d. sadness) :: TEARS : LAUGHTER

15. ROBIN : SPRING :: (a. seagull, b. mud, c. corn, d. goldfish) : SUMMER

16. BIBLIOPHILE : PHILATELIST :: BOOKS : (a. pharmacy, b. coins, c. stamps, d. jewelry)

17. NAIAD : WATER :: DRYAD : (a. land, b. tree, c. elm, d. wringer)

18. (a. river, b. irrigation, c. dam, d. water) : FOOD :: DROUGHT : FAMINE

19. ROYAL : SAD :: PURPLE : (a. white, b. chartreuse, c. pauper, d. blue)

20. THIRTEEN : THREE-ON-A-MATCH :: (a. broken mirror, b. rabbit's foot, c. will-o'-the-wisp, d. cat-o'-nine-tails) : IDES OF MARCH

21. HALF-MAST : ELEGY :: UPSIDE DOWN : (a. excitement, b. error, c. confusion, d. distress)

22. (a. October, b. autumn, c. season, d. sadness) : SPRING :: LEAVES : FEVER

23. WET SUIT : SCUBA :: TUTU : (a. church, b. Africa, c. snorkel, d. ballet)

24. CULINARY : (a. bedroom, b. closet, c. knife, d. kitchen) :: ECUMENICAL : CHURCH

25. (a. teacher, b. player, c. actor, d. surgeon) : TEAM :: OSCAR : PENNANT

26. MIDAS : BRYAN :: GOLD : (a. silver, b. politician, c. miser, d. tail)

VERBAL ANALOGIES TEST XI.
SEQUENCE

Time: 13 Minutes. 26 Questions.

Directions: Each of these test questions consists of three CAPITALIZED words and four lettered words enclosed in parentheses. Two of the capitalized words are related in some way. Find the two related words and establish the nature of the relationship. Then study the four words lettered a, b, c, and d. Select the one lettered word which is related to the remaining capitalized word in the same way that the first two capitalized words are related. Mark the answer sheet for the letter preceding the word you select.

1. MAY : FEBRUARY :: NOVEMBER : (a. August, b. January, c. October, d. July)

2. THIRD : FIRST :: JEFFERSON : (a. Washington, b. White House, c. president, d. Jackson)

3. G : (a. K, b. C, c. D, d. F) :: Q : M

4. EFH : ABD :: (a. MNO, b. NOP, c. NOO, d. MNP) : IJL

5. (a. Sunday, b. Monday, c. Wednesday, d. Friday) : SATURDAY :: THURSDAY : TUESDAY

6. MIDDLE AGES : RENAISSANCE :: 1700 : (a. Dark Ages, b. 1500, c. ancient Greece, d. 20th century)

7. TALKIES : (a. tube, b. broadcast, c. television, d. space travel) : SILENTS : RADIO

8. (a. bone, b. bark, c. pup, d. kennel) : LAMB :: DOG : SHEEP

9. TODAY : YESTERDAY :: PRESENT : (a. yesterday, b. tomorrow, c. past, d. now)

10. STALLION : (a. water, b. river, c. brook, d. puddle) :: COLT : STREAM

11. (a. child, b. grandfather, c. boy, d. father) : SON :: MOTHER : DAUGHTER

12. DUSK : (a. twilight, b. dawn, c. night, d. rain) :: SENILITY : CHILDHOOD

13. SPRING : WINTER :: (a. end, b. continuation, c. birth, d. sorrow) : DEATH

14. APRIL : JUNE :: JANUARY : (a. November, b. March, c. February, d. August)

15. MATURITY : ADOLESCENCE :: CHILDHOOD : (a. manhood, b. infancy, c. school, d. immaturity)

16. INTERN : APPRENTICE :: PHYSICIAN : (a. doctor, b. lawyer, c. trade, d. craftsman)

17. (a. individual, b. baby, c. adult, d. male) : OAK :: INFANT : ACORN

18. HANDPLOW : (a. building, b. skyscraper, c. stairs, d. feet) :: TRACTOR : ELEVATOR

19. TOMORROW : YESTERDAY :: FUTURE : (a. present, b. unknown, c. year, d. past)

20. HORSE : (a. telephone, b. letter, c. communication, d. transportation) :: AUTOMOBILE : TELEGRAM

21. (a. eat, b. money, c. dough, d. yeast) : COAL :: BREAD : COKE

22. INFANT : TODDLER :: BOY : (a. man, b. youth, c. adult, d. masculine)

23. CLUB : (a. prehistoric, b. cave, c. cannon, d. rampage) :: GUN : HOUSE

24. (a. throne, b. prince, c. kingdom, d. majesty) : FILLY :: KING : MARE

25. TWIG : (a. thorn, b. branch, c. leaf, d. rose) :: BUD : FLOWER

26. MOTORCYCLE : BICYCLE :: AUTOMOBILE : (a. bus, b. airplane, c. transportation, d. wagon)

VERBAL ANALOGIES TEST XII. CHARACTERISTIC

Time: 13 Minutes. 26 Questions.

Directions: Each of these test questions consists of three CAPITALIZED words and four lettered words enclosed in parentheses. Two of the capitalized words are related in some way. Find the two related words and establish the nature of the relationship. Then study the four words lettered a, b, c, and d. Select the one lettered word which is related to the remaining capitalized word in the same way that the first two capitalized words are related. Mark the answer sheet for the letter preceding the word you select.

1. RICH : OWN :: WISE : (a. know, b. teach, c. divulge, d. save)

2. LION : (a. kingly, b. animal, c. carnivorous, d. omnipotent) :: MAN : OMNIVOROUS

3. SWALLOW : MIGRATION :: (a. chicken, b. lobster, c. bear, d. hummingbird) : HIBERNATION

4. IRON : (a. steak, b. crowd, c. humor, d. diamond) :: COMMON : RARE

5. (a. complaining, b. weakness, c. insistence, d. solitude) : STING-INESS :: HERMIT : MISER

6. NOISE : AUDIBLE :: (a. picture, b. honesty, c. distance, d. heaven) : VISIBLE

7. ALERT : (a. strong, b. cruel, c. kind, d. steady) :: PILOT : MARKS-MAN

8. LOUD : THUNDER :: LARGE : (a. monkey, b. midget, c. whale, d. blatancy)

9. (a. coat, b. industry, c. fur, d. mammal) : BEAVER :: WIS-DOM : OWL

10. SUGAR : (a. malaria, b. quinine, c. saccharine, d. acidity) :: SWEET : BITTER

11. CLOUD : FEVER :: (a. sky, b. cold, c. storm, d. weather) : SICKNESS

12. (a. harmful, b. loud, c. orchestrated, d. pleasing) : HARMONY :: DISTRACTING : NOISE

13. GOURMET : DISCRIMINATION :: GLUTTON : (a. excess, b. food, c. charity, d. obesity)

14. (a. traffic, b. direct, c. speed, d. distance) : MEANDERING :: HIGHWAY : STREAM

15. RAIN : SNOW :: (a. wet, b. summer, c. cold, d. flood) : WINTER

16. NOVICE : EXPERT :: INSECURITY : (a. tools, b. confidence, c. difficulty, d. money)

17. IRON : (a. bread, b. penicillin, c. virus, d. disease) :: RUST : MOLD

18. SINKS : ROCK :: FLOATS :: (a. feather, b. light, c. flies, d. drowns)

19. SAGE : FOX :: (a. brains, b. student, c. school, d. wisdom) : CUNNING

20. BUOYANT : CORK :: (a. jewel, b. watch, c. brilliant, d. extravagant) : DIAMOND

21. SHIVER : COLD :: TREMBLE : (a. hot, b. happiness, c. fear, d. intelligence)

22. TUNDRA : DESERT :: (a. exotic, b. dry, c. salty, d. frozen) : DRY

23. INGENUE : KNAVE :: NAIVETY : (a. chivalry, b. chicanery, c. morality, d. subtlety)

24. SEER : (a. Hispanic, b. Black, c. minority, d. bigot) :: PRE-
SCIENCE : PREJUDICE

25. HERO : VALOR :: HERETIC : (a. dissent, b. bravado, c. reverence,
d. discretion)

26. (a. loud, b. resounding, c. response, d. echo) : BALL :: RESONANT
: RESILIENT

VERBAL ANALOGIES TEST XIII.
DEGREE

Time: 13 Minutes. 26 Questions.

Directions: Each of these test questions consists of three CAPITAL-
IZED words and four lettered words enclosed in parentheses. Two
of the capitalized words are related in some way. Find the two related words and establish the nature of the relationship. Then study
the four words lettered a, b, c, and d. Select the one lettered word
which is related to the remaining capitalized word in the same way
that the first two capitalized words are related. Mark the answer sheet
for the letter preceding the word you select.

1. POSSIBLE : PROBABLE :: HOPE : (a. expect, b. deceive, c. resent,
d. prove)

2. GRAY : BLACK :: DISCOMFORT : (a. green, b. pain, c. hospital,
d. mutilation)

3. BANQUET : (a. festival, b. party, c. ball, d. snack) :: ORA-
TION : CHAT

4. HUT : INCH :: (a. foundation, b. skyscraper, c. building, d. abode)
: MILE

5. (a. rain, b. sunshine, c. climate, d. cyclone) : CLOUDBURST ::
BREEZE : SHOWER

6. MONTH : WEEK :: WEEK : (a. day, b. month, c. year, d. hour)

7. EAGLE : (a. forest, b. mountain, c. grass, d. tree) :: HUM-
MINGBIRD : SHRUB

8. (a. eagle, b. whale, c. giant, d. elephant) : HORSEFLY :: MIN-
NOW : FLEA

9. CENTURY : DECADE :: DIME : (a. lucre, b. cent, c. age, d. nickel)

10. SQUARE INCH : (a. inch, b. cubic inch, c. foot, d. yard) :: INCH : SQUARE INCH

11. SLEET : MIST :: (a. breathe, b. gulp, c. chew, d. devour) : SIP

12. PLEAD : (a. beggar, b. selfishness, c. charity, d. philanthropist) :: BEG : ALMS

13. (a. pronunciation, b. stammer, c. crutch, d. speech) : LIMP :: TALK : WALK

14. NONE : LITTLE :: NEVER : (a. maybe, b. frequently, c. negative, d. seldom)

15. WORSE : (a. bad, b. good, c. best, d. better) :: WORST : WORSE

16. (a. heat, b. molecules, c. ice, d. matter) : WATER :: WATER : STEAM

17. RAGE : (a. irk, b. annoy, c. anger, d. mischief) :: DEMONIC : NAUGHTY

18. HOUR : MINUTE :: MINUTE : (a. time, b. day, c. second, d. moment)

19. LAUGH : (a. bathe, b. lather, c. water, d. dry) :: SMILE : WASH

20. RUN : WALK :: (a. number, b. total, c. multiply, d. subtract) : ADD

21. GUSH : (a. torpid, b. torrid, c. frigid, d. comfortable) :: TRICKLE : TEPID

22. WEEK : DAY :: DAY : (a. month, b. second, c. hour, d. night)

23. (a. guess, b. value, c. calculate, d. worth) : RECOMMEND :: ESTIMATE : SUGGEST

24. PRAISE : (a. exhort, b. exclaim, c. extort, d. extol) :: DRONE : DECLAIM

25. QUART : PINT :: GALLON : (a. inch, b. gram, c. liter, d. quart)

26. COVET : (a. acquire, b. want, c. possess, d. pretext) :: GRIEF : DISTRESS

VERBAL ANALOGIES TEST XIV.
GRAMMATICAL

Time: 13 Minutes. 26 Questions.

Directions: Each of these test questions consists of three CAPITAL-IZED words and four lettered words enclosed in parentheses. Two of the capitalized words are related in some way. Find the two related words and establish the nature of the relationship. Then study the four words lettered a, b, c, and d. Select the one lettered word which is related to the remaining capitalized word in the same way that the first two capitalized words are related. Mark the answer sheet for the letter preceding the word you select.

1. SPRING : SPRUNG :: LIE : (a. lie, b. lain, c. lies, d. lay)

2. ROSE : RISE :: WENT : (a. going, b. gone, c. go, d. return)

3. SHABBILY : (a. harp, b. harmonica, c. harmoniously, d. harmony) : SHABBY : HARMONIOUS

4. INFAMY : (a. infamous, b. inflammatory, c. infernal, d. infantile) :: PLAUSIBILITY : PLAUSIBLE

5. (a. you, b. your, c. ladies, d. we) : THEIR :: BABIES' : ITS

6. SHEEP : ALUMNUS :: EWE : (a. alumna, b. alumni, c. alumnae, d. alumnas)

7. RAT : RATS :: MOUSE : (a. mouses, b. mice, c. cats, d. trap)

8. I : (a. mine, b. they, c. us, d. we) :: MOOSE : MOOSE

9. LIES : DRINKS :: LAIN : (a. drunk, b. drink, c. drinked, d. drank)

10. HIM : (a. me, b. us, c. them, d. you) :: HE : WE

11. (a. fourth, b. third, c. second, d. first) : ONE :: THIRD : THREE

12. SPOKE : SPEAK :: (a. sang, b. talk, c. told, d. tale) : TELL

13. REVERT : REVERSION :: SYMPATHIZE : (a. sympathetic, b. symposium, c. sympathy, d. sympathizer)

14. LB. : CAPT. :: (a. building, b. lawyer, c. pound, d. ton) : CAPTAIN

15. DOWN : DOWNY :: AGE : (a. aging, b. old, c. ageless, d. historic)

16. REGRESS : (a. sterilization, b. sterilize, c. sterility, d. sterilizer) :: REGRESSIVE : STERILE

17. (a. men, b. his, c. man's, d. mine) : MINE :: MAN : I

18. LAY : LIES :: ATE : (a. eater, b. eats, c. eating, d. eat)

19. (a. their, b. your, c. we're, d. one's) : THEY'RE :: NE'ER : E'ER

20. HIS : (a. its, b. it's, c. her's, d. their's) :: MINE : YOURS

21. RELIEF : BELIEVE :: RECEIVE : (a. friend, b. deceit, c. belief, d. brief)

22. LEAF : (a. leafs, b. leave, c. left, d. leaves) :: MEDIUM : MEDIA

23. LIVES : LIFE :: (a. brother-in-laws, b. brothers-in-law, c. brother-in-law's, d. brother's-in-law) : BROTHER-IN-LAW

24. BRING : BROUGHT :: WRITE : (a. wrought, b. writer, c. writing, d. wrote)

25. (a. radii, b. radial, c. radices, d. radiums) : ANALYSES :: RADIUS : ANALYSIS

26. SIMPLEST : (a. fewest, b. myriad, c. more, d. most) :: SIMPLE : MANY

VERBAL ANALOGIES TEST XV.
MISCELLANEOUS

Time: 13 Minutes. 26 Questions.

Directions: Each of these test questions consists of three CAPITALIZED words and four lettered words enclosed in parentheses. Two of the capitalized words are related in some way. Find the two related words and establish the nature of the relationship. Then study the four words lettered a, b, c, and d. Select the one lettered word which is related to the remaining capitalized word in the same way that the first two capitalized words are related. Mark the answer sheet for the letter preceding the word you select.

1. ALVA : (a. Benjamin, b. stove, c. lightning, d. Delano) :: THOMAS : FRANKLIN

2. DISABLED : FREEDOM FIGHTER :: (a. retarded, b. entitled, c. privileged, d. underprivileged) : REBEL

3. (a. 11, b. 13, c. 14, d. 17) : 3 :: SONNET : HAIKU

4. JENNY LIND : TOM THUMB :: *THE GREATEST SHOW ON EARTH* : (a. circus, b. *The Ten Commandments,* c. *Gone with the Wind,* d. P.T. Barnum)

5. ELLERY QUEEN, JR. : (a. Ellery Queen, b. Upton Sinclair, c. Samuel Clemens, d. Agatha Christie) :: FRANKLIN W. DIXON : CAROLYN KEENE

6. (a. COD, b. RFD, c. CIA, d. SOS) : LAX :: FBI : JFK

7. *THE SILENT SPRING* : (a. *Nigger of the Narcissus,* b. *Of Human Bondage,* c. *The Way of All Flesh,* d. *Uncle Tom's Cabin*) :: ENVIRONMENTAL EXPLOITATION : BLACK EXPLOITATION

8. (a. fry, b. bake, c. braise, d. stew) : SAUTE :: BOIL : STEAM

9. MUHAMMAD ALI : CASSIUS CLAY :: (a. Matthew Henson, b. Malcom X, c. Kareem Abdul Jabbar, d. Adam Clayton Powell) : LEW ALCINDOR

10. πr^2 : $\frac{bh}{2}$ :: CIRCLE : (a. trapezoid, b. rhombus, c. pyramid, d. triangle)

11. SAMSON : ACHILLES :: (a. lion, b. hair, c. Delilah, d. pillars) : HEEL

12. BRACES : (a. suspenders, b. belt, c. band, d. tram) :: LORRY : TRUCK

13. ENGLAND : DENMARK :: (a. Sweden, b. China, c. France, d. Namibia) : ISRAEL

14. JELLO® : GELATIN :: XEROX® : (a. IBM®, b. carbon paper, c. toner, d. photocopier)

15. AK : MN:: (a. AS, b. AZ, c. NB, d. IO) : PA

16. ETYMOLOGY : WORDS :: HAGIOLOGY : (a. saints, b. senility, c. selling, d. writing)

17. (a. Apollo, b. Janus, c. Eros, d. Jupiter) : JUNO :: ZEUS : HERA

18. GESUNDHEIT : AL DENTE :: CAVEAT EMPTOR : (a. buyer beware, b. *amicus curiae,* c. *savoir faire,* d. thank goodness)

19. HEW : (a. hue, b. mow, c. toe, d. hew) :: SANCTION : SANCTION

20. "PASTORALE" : "EMPEROR :: "EROICA" : (a. "Brandenburg," b. "Egmont," c. "Nutcracker," d. Beethoven)

21. (a. proboscis, b. smell, c. olfactory, d. redolent) : TACTILE :: NOSE : FINGER

22. KOESTLER : (a. Kreisler, b. Hemingway, c. Rhineland, d. Beethoven) :: DARKNESS : MOONLIGHT

23. (a. Jacob, b. Benjamin, c. Isaac, d. David) : JOSEPH :: MISS LILLIAN : AMY

24. MILK : BROCCOLI :: (a. potato chips, b. liver, c. caviar, d. cake) : TWINKIES®

25. TANZANIA : UNITED ARAB EMIRATES :: KOREA : (a. England, b. Laos, c. Brazil, d. Germany)

26. CARTON : DARNAY :: DAMON : (a. Runyan, b. Heloise, c. Romeo, d. Pythias)

CORRECT ANSWERS FOR ANALOGY TESTS CLASSIFIED BY CATEGORY

Test I. Synonyms and Definitions

1. d	5. d	9. c	13. a	17. a	21. c	25. d
2. c	6. d	10. d	14. b	18. b	22. a	26. c
3. b	7. a	11. a	15. d	19. a	23. b	
4. c	8. a	12. b	16. b	20. b	24. c	

Explanatory Answers

1. **(d)** DILIGENT means UNREMITTING; ANTITHETICAL means OPPOSITE.

2. **(c)** FRAUDULENT means FALLACIOUS; REMUNERATIVE means PROFITABLE. Deceit and slander are varieties of fraud, but you must choose precise synonyms as in the analogous pair.

3. **(b)** To EXTORT is to WREST; to CONSPIRE is to PLOT.

4. **(c)** A DOWAGER (by one definition) is a WIDOW; a COMPANION is a CONSORT.

5. **(d)** That which is GAUDY is OSTENTATIOUS; one who is DEJECTED is DEPRESSED.

6. **(d)** This analogy is more easily read and solved in a B : A :: D : C sequence. A SOPRANO voice is HIGH : a BASS voice is LOW.

7. **(a)** LUXURY is ELEGANCE; PENURY is POVERTY.

8. **(a)** ARTFULNESS means FINESSE and both mean the ability to handle difficulties skillfully; an INEPT person is INEFFICIENT.

9. **(c)** To REGALE is to ENTERTAIN; to REGISTER is to ENROLL.

10. **(d)** This is an A : C :: B : D relationship. To BEGIN is to ESTABLISH. NOCTURNAL means NIGHTLY or at night. While there is absolutely no relationship between the two pairs of words, each pair represents a pair of true synonyms.

11. **(a)** With this analogy you have no choice but A : C :: B : D. To STREW is to DISPERSE; to STRAY is to DEVIATE.

12. **(b)** VERTICAL means PLUMB or straight up and down; PROSTRATE means FLAT.

13. **(a)** Read B : A :: D : C. NATIVE means INDIGENOUS; DISTANT means REMOTE. While native Americans are called Indians, *Indian* is in no way a synonym for *native*.

14. **(b)** A BLAST is a GUST (as in wind); a BLARE is a ROAR (as in noise).

15. **(d)** DIURNAL means DAILY; to ABOLISH is to END. Do not get involved in the significance of words; concentrate on relationships.

16. **(b)** BEGINNING means INCIPIENT; CORRESPONDING means CONGRUENT.

17. **(a)** SUFFICIENT means ENOUGH. The SALUTATION is the INTRODUCTION to a letter.

18. **(b)** DIN means NOISE; CONTORTION means WRITHING or twisting.

19. **(a)** RESTRAINT means CONTINENCE or holding back; a RIFT (in rock) is a CREVASSE.

20. **(b)** A REFINED person is URBANE or extremely polished: an EQUITABLE person is JUST.

21. **(c)** Actually all four terms in this analogy are synonyms or near synonyms. A FINIAL is a top ornament, as the top of a lampshade. A PEDIMENT is the triangular space which forms a gable. A PINNACLE is a lofty peak or a church spire. A GABLE is the triangular end at the top of a building. The other three choices do not refer to peaks.

22. **(a)** HISTORY is REALITY and is factual; a TALE is SUPPOSITION or fiction.

23. **(b)** JABBER and GIBBERISH are both nonsense; QUIDNUNC is a GOSSIP.

24. **(c)** DIAPASON is the full range of harmonic sound, hence a CHORD played on an organ. The TONIC, also known as KEYNOTE, is the first note of a diatonic scale.

25. **(d)** PALLID means BLANCHED or pale; to BEGIN is to INSTITUTE.

26. **(c)** CREPUSCULAR means INDISTINCT or dim; CURSORY means SUPERFICIAL. The analogy reads A : C :: B : D

Test II. Antonyms

1. a	5. c	9. c	13. d	17. a	21. c	25. a
2. b	6. c	10. d	14. b	18. b	22. d	26. a
3. c	7. c	11. b	15. a	19. c	23. d	
4. d	8. a	12. c	16. c	20. d	24. d	

Explanatory Answers

1. **(a)** To SUNDER is the opposite of to CONSOLIDATE; TANGIBLE is the opposite of ABSTRACT.

2. **(b)** The opposite of ACCORD is BREACH; the opposite of CONNECTION is DISSOCIATION.

3. **(c)** BIRTH is clearly the opposite of DEATH. A CATCALL is a noisy expression of disapproval at a sporting event or at a performance of any sort. Clearly, where there are CATCALLs there is no ACCEPTANCE. Since the events are mutually exclusive, they may be considered to be opposites.

4. **(d)** The only relationship here is A : C :: B : D. MAGNANIMITY is the opposite of PARSIMONY; TOLERANCE is the opposite of BIGOTRY.

5. **(c)** Where there is DERISION there will be no ENCORE. The rationale is the same as in question 3. That which is EPHEMERAL is temporary and therefore is not EVERLASTING.

6. **(c)** GRACEFUL is the opposite of GAUCHE, which means crude; WEALTHY is the opposite of INDIGENT, which means poor.

7. **(c)** MATURE is the opposite of UNRIPE; COUNTERFEIT is the opposite of REAL.

8. **(a)** Ordinarily, the prefix *in* means *not,* but in the word *inquisitive* the prefix *in* means *into,* hence the meaning of *inquisitive* is *questioning.* In the word *incurious,* the prefix *in* does indeed mean *not,* hence the meaning *not curious.* MANIFEST, meaning obvious, is the opposite of LATENT, meaning dormant or hidden; INQUISITIVE is the opposite of INCURIOUS.

9. **(c)** An IDIOT is the opposite of a GENIUS; a VALLEY, in its depth, is the opposite of a MOUNTAIN, in its height.

10. **(d)** That which is PERMANENT is not TEMPORARY. MISCELLANEOUS has to do with many different things while SINGLE has to do with only one. When you know that the analogy will be based upon an-

tonyms, it is easy to answer. When your analogies are unclassified, you must look harder to determine whether your answer depends on an A : B :: C : D relationship or A : C :: B : D.

11. **(b)** That which is IMPROMPTU has not been MEMORIZED; that which is SPONTANEOUS has not been CALCULATED.

12. **(c)** That which is a MEDLEY is a mixture of many things, the opposite of ONE. To PRAISE is the opposite of to CRITICIZE.

13. **(d)** WHITE is the opposite of BLACK; VALOR is the opposite of COW-ARDICE.

14. **(b)** HYPOCRISY is the opposite of HONESTY; HOSTILITY is the opposite of AMITY, which means *friendship*. The choice "hospitality" is a clever distractor. At first thought, one who is hostile is not hospitable, but one may grudgingly offer hospitality. It is important to choose the BEST completion for each analogy.

15. **(a)** PLETHORA means excess; its opposite, DEARTH, means lack. CUNNING means clever, clearly the opposite of DULL.

16. **(c)** PERTINENT is the opposite of IRRELEVANT; INCLEMENT weather is not CLEAR.

17. **(a)** A BOMBASTIC speech is inflated and pretentious and is not PLAIN-SPOKEN; one who is STRINGENT and strict in observance is not LAX.

18. **(b)** To ABSTAIN is precisely the opposite of to INDULGE; to AVOID is the exact opposite of to SEEK.

19. **(c)** DISHONESTY is clearly the opposite of INTEGRITY; that which is OBVIOUS is the opposite of that which is SURREPTITIOUS or secret.

20. **(d)** To REVERE is to be respectful while to BLASPHEME is to revile; to be INSCRUTABLE is the opposite of being COMPREHENSIBLE.

21. **(c)** IMMATURITY is a trait associated with childhood, therefore a near opposite of ADULTHOOD; COMPETITION is a trait associated with open trade and hence is a near opposite of MONOPOLY. If the terms of the initial pair are not exact opposites, the second pair need not be exact opposites either, but their relationship must parallel the relationship of the first pair.

22. **(d)** REPUGN, oppose, is the opposite of COMPROMISE; RESCIND, take back, is the opposite of VALIDATE, confirm.

23. **(d)** To DEGRADE is the opposite of to LAUD; MARTIAL, military, is the opposite of HALCYON, peaceful.

24. **(d)** WARLIKE is the opposite of PEACEFUL; SCARCE is the opposite of ABUNDANT.

25. **(a)** To INTIMIDATE is to discourage which is the opposite of ENCOURAGE; to INTERDICT is to prohibit which is the opposite of to ALLOW.

26. **(a)** That which is COSTLY is not CHEAP; that which is SCARCE is not ABUNDANT.

Test III. Cause and Effect/Effect and Cause

1.	b	5.	d	9.	b	13.	d	17.	b	21.	b	25.	b
2.	c	6.	c	10.	a	14.	a	18.	c	22.	a	26.	b
3.	c	7.	b	11.	a	15.	b	19.	d	23.	d		
4.	c	8.	b	12.	b	16.	a	20.	c	24.	d		

Explanatory Answers

1. **(b)** One's CURIOSITY (when acted upon) leads to one's ENLIGHTENMENT; one's VERACITY (when recognized by others) leads to one's CREDIBILITY.

2. **(c)** TENACITY leads to ATTAINMENT; MONOTONY leads to BOREDOM.

3. **(c)** One's own GOOD DEED gives one a feeling of SATISFACTION; one's own DILIGENCE leads to one's IMPROVEMENT. Criticism may also lead one to improve, but criticism comes from someone else. In creating analogies, look for the greatest number of parallelisms.

4. **(c)** A BIRD comes from an EGG; a PLANT comes from a SEED.

5. **(d)** Taking CARE leads to SAFETY; ASSIDUITY or diligence leads to SUCCESS. Taking care may also lead to avoidance of misfortune, but care's leading to safety is a more positive statement in line with assiduity's leading to success.

6. **(c)** WINE is made from the GRAPE; FLOUR is made from WHEAT.

7. **(b)** WAR causes GRIEF; PEACE causes HAPPINESS.

8. **(b)** When the MOON is shining, we have LIGHT; during an ECLIPSE, there is DARKNESS.

9. **(b)** HEAT comes from FIRE; WATER comes from RAIN.

10. **(a)** A SCAR is caused by a WOUND; DAMAGE is caused by an ACCIDENT

11. **(a)** This is an C : A :: D : B analogy. SANITATION leads to HEALTH; FILTH leads to DISEASE. You might refuse to accept this an a cause/effect relationship and simply call it association. How you personally categorize a relationship does not matter. The only requirement is that you choose the right answer.

12. **(b)** COLD creates ICE; HEAT creates STEAM. When speaking of the action of temperature upon water, you might correctly state that cold creates crystals. But ice is a collection of crystals as steam is a collection of droplets.

13. **(d)** A : C :: B : D. LAZINESS leads to FAILURE as having a STRATEGY leads to VICTORY.

14. **(a)** Lack of FOOD leads to STARVATION; lack of AIR leads to SUFFOCATION.

15. **(b)** A STIMULUS leads to a RESPONSE; CARELESSNESS may well land one in a PREDICAMENT. The terms on one side of the equation are in no way related to the terms on the other side, but the relationship within each pair is the same—cause and effect.

16. **(a)** C : A :: D : B. A FALL leads to PAIN; DISOBEDIENCE leads to PUNISHMENT.

17. **(b)** FAITH leads one to PRAYER; DESPERATION may well lead one to CRIME. Desperation does not lead one to despair because the words are basically synonyms, both used to describe a state of hopelessness.

18. **(c)** FANATICISM is excessive enthusiasm, and it leads to INTOLERANCE; BIGOTRY is excessive belief in the superiority of one's own group, and it leads to HATRED.

19. **(d)** If the justice system is working correctly, GUILT leads to CONVICTION and INNOCENCE leads to VINDICATION.

20. **(c)** Overindulgence in LIQUOR may lead to ALCOHOLISM; overindulgence in CANDY may lead to OBESITY.

21. **(b)** TAXATION without representation was one of the causes of the American REVOLUTION; disagreement over SLAVERY was one of the causes of the CIVIL WAR.

22. **(a)** A FIRE very often causes SMOKE; PROFLIGACY, extravagant spending, very often leads one into DEBT. Prodigality is a synonym for profligacy.

23. **(d)** WORK creates INCOME; FOOD promotes GROWTH.

24. **(d)** In this case, either cause may have either effect, but maintaining the analogy: INEXPERIENCE may lead to an ERROR while CARELESS-NESS may lead to an ACCIDENT.

25. **(b)** C : A :: B : D. CHARCOAL serves to purify AIR just as CHLO-RINE is used to purify WATER.

26. **(b)** A FLAME may BURN you; an INSULT may ANGER you.

Test IV. Part to Whole/Whole to Part

1. c	5. d	9. b	13. c	17. c	21. b	25. c
2. a	6. b	10. d	14. c	18. c	22. c	26. b
3. b	7. c	11. c	15. b	19. b	23. b	
4. c	8. b	12. b	16. d	20. d	24. c	

Explanatory Answers

1. **(c)** VERSAILLES is part of the class of buildings called PALACE: the BASTILLE is a part of the class of buildings called PRISON.

2. **(a)** The PROLOGUE is the first part of a PLAY; the PREAMBLE is the first part of our CONSTITUTION. Article and amendment are also parts of our constitution, but the fact that the prologue is the *first* part governs the analogy and the answer.

3. **(b)** Read this analogy D : C :: B : A. A SENTENCE is part of a PAR-AGRAPH; a WORD is part of a SENTENCE.

4. **(c)** A : C :: B : D. A BEAD is a component part of a NECKLACE; a LINK is a component part of a CHAIN.

5. **(d)** A PIT is at the center of a PEACH; the SUN is at the center of our SOLAR SYSTEM. While this is definitely a part to the whole analogy, you would be equally correct classifying it as a relationship based on location.

6. **(b)** A SLICE is a member of a group of slices that form a LOAF; an IS-LAND is a member of a group of islands that form an ARCHIPELAGO.

7. **(c)** The PEAK is the high point of a MOUNTAIN; the CREST is the high point of a WAVE.

8. **(b)** MEAT is one of the items that makes up the wares of a MARKET; a STEER is one of the animals that makes up the livestock on a RANCH. Again, you could legitimately classify this as a relationship based upon location or place.

9. **(b)** An INGREDIENT is an integral part of a RECIPE; YELLOW is an integral part of the color GREEN. Be careful to think beyond simple association before choosing your answer.

10. **(d)** A STONE is part of the QUARRY; LUMBER is part of the FOREST. Once more, place serves well as a rationale. This analogy reads D : B :: C : A.

11. **(c)** GRANITE is a rock of the QUARTZ family; MARBLE is a rock of the LIMESTONE family. You could equally say that GRANITE is composed of QUARTZ, and MARBLE is composed of LIMESTONE.

12. **(b)** STEEL is one of many ALLOYs; IRON is one of many ELEMENTs.

13. **(c)** His FIST is part of a MAN; its STINGER is part of a BEE. You could easily interpret this as a purposeful relationship. The purpose of the STINGER is for the BEE's self-defense. The purpose of the FIST is for the MAN's self-defense. A shield is also used for defense, but its not part of a man.

14. **(c)** Be careful. PART is to WHOLE; ONTARIO is part of CANADA. You were probably tempted to choose North America, but that would be a reversal of the relationship which can also be stated: the WHOLE is CANADA; its PART is ONTARIO.

15. **(b)** CADET and PLEBE are generally interchangeable terms, both referring to a student at a military academy. Thus, the position of a CADET as part of the student body at WEST POINT is analogous to the position of a PLEBE as a member of the student body at ANNAPOLIS.

16. **(d)** The PREFACE is the entry to a BOOK; the LOBBY is the entry to a HOTEL. Of course, a room is also part of a hotel, but your analogy must be as specific as possible.

17. **(c)** The TOASTMASTER is the chairman of a BANQUET; a CHAIRMAN chairs an ASSEMBLY.

18. **(c)** POETRY is the larger class of which a SONNET is a kind or a part; MUSIC is the larger class of which a CONCERTO is a variety or part. Symphony, song, and etude are all other examples of the larger class called music.

19. **(b)** A PETAL is part of a FLOWER; FUR is part of a RABBIT.

20. **(d)** ELEMENTS are part of the subject of CHEMISTRY; PARTS OF SPEECH are part of the subject of GRAMMAR. Grammar also concerns itself with subjects and predicates, but since *subject* may have more than one definition you must choose the most certainly correct completion.

21. **(b)** PINE is a kind of TREE; POINSETTIA is a kind of FLOWER. Beware of associations that do not constitute true analogies.

22. **(c)** A CARROT is a PLANT; a COW is an ANIMAL. In order for *meat* to be the correct answer, the analogy would have to read "carrot : cow :: vegetable : meat."

23. **(b)** A PRESIDENT is part of a CORPORATION, in fact its head. The GOVERNOR is part of the STATE government; in fact he is its head.

24. **(c)** A PLAYER is part of a TEAM; and EAR is part of a HEAD. Be careful. The ear usually is behind the face.

25. **(c)** The CHINESE are part of the MONGOLIAN race; the ENGLISH are part of the CAUCASIAN race.

26. **(b)** The worthless part of the WINE is the DREGS; the worthless part of the WHEAT is the CHAFF.

Test V. Part to Part

1. d	5. a	9. d	13. d	17. c	21. d	25. c
2. b	6. c	10. a	14. d	18. a	22. c	26. a
3. c	7. b	11. d	15. a	19. a	23. b	
4. b	8. c	12. b	16. b	20. b	24. c	

Explanatory Answers

1. **(d)** This is a difficult analogy to verbalize, though it is an easy one to answer. Basically NEPHEW and NIECE are related to any one individual in the same way as UNCLE and AUNT are related to any one individual. In addition, NEPHEW and NIECE are of the opposite sex, so UNCLE and AUNT parallel that aspect of the relationship as well.

2. **(b)** HAND and ELBOW are both parts of the arm; FOOT and KNEE are both parts of the leg. In addition, the relationship of end of the appendage to middle joint is the same. While toe is also part of leg, it is more immediately part of foot, and the initial pair does not constitute a part to whole relationship.

3. **(c)** SNEAKER and SHOE are both footwear; MITTEN and GLOVE are both handwear.

4. **(b)** CONTRALTO and SOPRANO are both female voices; BARITONE and TENOR are both male voices.

5. **(a)** ROBIN and BLUEJAY are both birds; ST. BERNARD and SPANIEL are both dogs.

6. **(c)** HEART and LUNGS are both vital organs; BRAIN and LIVER are also vital organs. In this case, the relationship is not only parallel but identical. The appendix is an internal organ, but it is not a vital organ.

7. **(b)** LAWNMOWER and RAKE are both garden tools; MOP and BUCKET are both floor-cleaning tools.

8. **(c)** HIGH JUMP and BROAD JUMP are both track and field events; HOCKEY and SOCCER are both team sports which involve a goal net.

9. **(d)** PEN and PENCIL are both writing implements; PAPER and SLATE are both surfaces upon which one can write. If pen were paired with chalk, one could create a purposeful relationship as well.

10. **(a)** NICOTINE and ALCOHOL are both harmful, addictive substances; MILK and ORANGE JUICE are both healthful, nonaddictive substances.

11. **(d)** PERCH and TROUT are both kinds of fish; PUPPY and KITTEN are both young animals. There is absolutely no relationship between the terms on the two sides of the proportion, but on each side the relationship of the terms is part to part, and that is sufficient to create an analogy.

12. **(b)** CARROT and POTATO are both root vegetables; LETTUCE and CABBAGE are both leaf vegetables that grow above ground. Beware of choosing a fourth term that is related to two related terms instead of a fourth term bearing the same relationship to the third term as the two related terms bear to each other. Both radish and onion are distractors of this type.

13. **(d)** The FORWARD and GUARD both play basketball; the FULLBACK and POINT KICKER both play football.

14. **(d)** A TRIANGLE and a SQUARE are both plane figures; a PYRAMID and a CUBE are both solid figures. In addition, the pyramid is the solid figure based upon a triangle and the cube is the solid figure based upon a square.

15. **(a)** A GOOSE and GANDER are female and male but they are both geese. A COW and BULL are female and male but they are both cows or cattle.

16. **(b)** SENEGAL and TUNISIA are both part of Africa and both are former French colonies. BOLIVIA and COLOMBIA are both part of South America and both are former Spanish colonies. All four choices are in South America, therefore the analogy must be based upon the fact that the related countries are both part of a group called "former Spanish colonies."

17. **(c)** FOOT, MILE, INCH, and CENTIMETER are all measures of length or distance. This is the only relationship that matters in this analogy question.

18. **(a)** OPHELIA and HAMLET are both characters in Shakespeare's play *Hamlet*. PORTIA and SHYLOCK are both characters in Shakespeare's play *The Merchant of Venice*.

19. **(a)** EWE and DOE are females; COCK and COB are males.

20. **(b)** CLAM and OYSTER are mollusks; COW and SHEEP are ruminants.

21. **(d)** BUS and TRAIN are both forms of ground transportation; AIRPLANE and HELICOPTER are both forms of air transportation.

22. **(c)** All four terms of this analogy represent parts of the same class. A GELDING is a castrated horse; a CAPON is a castrated chicken; a STEER is a castrated bull; a EUNUCH is a castrated human male.

23. **(b)** EYE and EAR are both sensory organs; SHIRT and PANTS are both articles of clothing.

24. **(c)** FINGER and PALM are both parts of the hand; SOLE and HEEL are both parts of the foot. The relationship of the parts from one side of the equation to the other is not analogous, but, since no other part to part choices are offered, a more precise relationship is not required.

25. **(c)** BUTTON and SEAM are both parts of an article of clothing; HEADLIGHT and BUMPER are both parts of a car.

26. **(a)** WING and BEAK are both parts of a bird; PAW and TAIL are both parts of an animal. *Foot* is not the correct answer because *paw* and *foot* are two names for the same part.

Test VI. Purpose, Use, or Function

1. b	5. d	9. b	13. c	17. b	21. d	25. b
2. a	6. d	10. c	14. c	18. b	22. a	26. c
3. d	7. b	11. b	15. a	19. a	23. c	
4. b	8. a	12. a	16. d	20. d	24. d	

Explanatory Answers

1. **(b)** A HITCHING POST serves as a place to tie up a HORSE; a MOOR-AGE serves as a place to tie up a CRAFT. The distractor, vessel, which is a synonym of craft, is very tempting.

2. **(a)** The purpose of the BAT is to hit the BALL; the purpose of the BAT-TLEDORE is to hit the SHUTTLECOCK. Even if the word *battledore* is unfamiliar to you, you should be able to choose the correct answer because no other choice could possibly bear the same relationship to *shuttlecock* as *bat* does to *ball*.

3. **(d)** The function of the AIRPLANE is to provide TRANSPORTATION; the function of the WIRELESS is to provide COMMUNICATION. A wireless transmits a message, a functional relationship to be sure, but the relationship is not the same as that of airplane to transportation.

4. **(b)** The skin of the CALF is tanned to make leather from which is made a SHOE; the feather of a GOOSE is plucked to stuff a PILLOW.

5. **(d)** A CLOTH serves as a TABLE-dressing in the same way as a CUR-TAIN serves as a WINDOW-dressing.

6. **(d)** A GYMNASIUM serves as a place in which one can enjoy EXER-CISE; a THEATER serves as a place in which one can enjoy a PER-FORMANCE. If you wanted to classify this analogy as one of place, you would not be wrong. Classification is personal and the category you assign is irrelevant; you just need to create a correct analogy.

7. **(b)** A CRATER serves as the opening through which smoke and gases escape from a VOLCANO; a CHIMNEY serves as the conduit through which smoke and gasses escape from a HOUSE. The flue is the effective portion of the chimney, but the chimney to flue relationship is the reverse of the crater to volcano relationship.

8. **(a)** A SIPHON serves to transfer GASOLINE; a SHOVEL serves to transfer COAL.

9. **(b)** The purpose of an ARCHAEOLOGIST is to study ANTIQUITY; the purpose of an ICHTHYOLOGIST is to study MARINE LIFE.

10. **(c)** The function of a METER is to MEASURE; the function of a SCOPE is to SEE—a telescope is to see things that are far away, while a microscope is to see things that are tiny.

11. **(b)** The purpose for raising a PIG is to provide PORK; one purpose for raising SHEEP is to provide MUTTON.

12. **(a)** The role of the PRESS is to PRINT; the role of the ERASER is to EF-FACE.

13. **(c)** AGAR serves as a host medium for the growing of a CULTURE; BREAD serves as a host medium for growing MOLD.

14. **(c)** A MENU serves as a guide to the MEAL; a MAP serves as a guide to a TRIP.

15. **(a)** One's purpose in using an AX is to HEW; one's purpose in using an AWL is to PUNCH holes, usually in leather.

16. **(d)** A CONE serves as the seed pod, as the means of propagation of a PINE tree; an ACORN serves exactly the same role for an OAK tree.

17. **(b)** A HOLSTER serves as protective carrying case for a PISTOL; a SCABBARD serves as protective carrying case for a SWORD.

18. **(b)** A LETTER CARRIER carries the MAIL; a MESSENGER carries DISPATCHES of any sort.

19. **(a)** The function of a BANDAGE is to close up a WOUND; the function of a STRING is to close up a PACKAGE.

20. **(d)** A SIPHON serves as a conduit for FLUID; a FLUE serves as a conduit for SMOKE.

21. **(d)** The purpose of BREAD is to sustain MAN; the purpose of HAY is to sustain a HORSE.

22. **(a)** On both sides of the analogy we have effective manners of execution. The GALLOWS is used to HANG the victim; the GUILLOTINE is used to BEHEAD.

23. **(c)** A BARREL serves to store WINE; a SILO serves to store GRAIN.

24. **(d)** FEATHERS serve as outside covering of an OSTRICH; HAIR serves as the outside covering of an ORANGUTAN.

25. **(b)** A MASK serves as protection for the FACE; a HELMET serves as protection for the HEAD.

26. **(c)** The WING is the BIRD'S means of locomotion; the FIN is the FISH's means of locomotion. The wing and the fin serve analogous purposes for the bird and the fish.

Test VII. Action to Object/Object to Action

1. c	5. b	9. b	13. d	17. b	21. b	25. c
2. b	6. d	10. c	14. c	18. b	22. b	26. d
3. d	7. b	11. b	15. c	19. b	23. d	
4. a	8. b	12. c	16. b	20. c	24. b	

Explanatory Answers

1. **(c)** You can HEAR a SOUND; you can SEE a PICTURE.

2. **(b)** You SCRUB the FLOOR; you SCOUR a PAN.

3. **(d)** To reach the edible portion, you PEEL a BANANA and SHUCK an OYSTER.

4. **(a)** When making changes, you make an ALTERATION to a GARMENT and make a REVISION to a BOOK.

5. **(b)** You VIEW a SCENE; you HEAR a CONCERT.

6. **(d)** When you STUDY, the object is to LEARN; when you TRY, the object is to SUCCEED.

7. **(b)** You DREDGE SILT; you SCOOP ICE CREAM. The action of dragging and lifting is identical.

8. **(b)** You EAT BREAD; you WEAR a COAT.

9. **(b)** WHET and HONE both mean sharpen. In common usage, you WHET an APPETITE and HONE a KNIFE.

10. **(c)** The KING REIGNs; the JUDGE PRESIDEs.

11. **(b)** A charitable person will OVERLOOK a MISTAKE; a dedicated person will ADVOCATE a CAUSE.

12. **(c)** One may ARTICULATE or express a DESIRE; one may ASSUAGE or calm a FEAR. Reassurance is a means for assuaging a fear.

13. **(d)** You ASSIMILATE KNOWLEDGE; you ASSUME a DEBT.

14. **(c)** You THWART the ASPIRATIONS of another; you STIFLE your own ANGER. Both have the effect of stopping a potential action.

15. **(c)** You HATE your ENEMY but LOVE your FRIEND.

16. **(b)** A CHECK is the object of a FORGERY; a COPYRIGHT is the object of INFRINGEMENT. Both are illegal activities.

17. **(b)** WOOD DECAYs; IRON RUSTs.

18. **(b)** ANALYSIS of a misfunction or disease hopefully leads to DIAGNOSIS; RESEARCH on almost any topic often results in a THESIS, a theory or a dissertation.

19. **(b)** MUTINY, rebellion or resistance to authority, on a SHIP is analogous to DESERTION, absenting oneself without authorization, from the ARMY.

20. **(c)** IRRIGATION brings in WATER as VENTILATION brings in AIR.

21. **(b)** DISHES BREAK; CLOTHING TEARS; accidents happen.

22. **(b)** The object of HEARING is a TONE; the object of SIGHT is COLOR.

23. **(d)** By way of repairing, you GRIND a KNIFE and DARN a STOCKING.

24. **(b)** In a quest for perfection, the cast will REHEARSE the PLAY; the team will PRACTICE the GAME.

25. **(c)** If things go well, SELLING leads to a PROFIT; BRAVERY brings one FAME.

26. **(d)** One MINEs SALT; one QUARRYs MARBLE. This might just as well be an analogy of place. SALT comes from a MINE; MARBLE comes from a QUARRY.

Test VIII. Actor to Object/Object to Actor and Actor to Action/Action to Actor

1. d	5. a	9. b	13. d	17. b	21. d	25. a
2. d	6. d	10. b	14. a	18. d	22. c	26. c
3. a	7. b	11. a	15. b	19. c	23. b	
4. a	8. a	12. b	16. b	20. c	24. d	

Explanatory Answers

1. **(d)** A SALESMAN promotes a PRODUCT; a TEACHER promotes a SUBJECT. While the action of a teacher directly impacts pupils, the analogous object of the salesman's activity would have to be customers.

2. **(d)** The MOON travels around the EARTH; the EARTH travels around the SUN.

3. **(a)** The PUPIL is guided by the TEACHER; the CHILD is guided by its PARENT.

4. **(a)** A DOG BARKs; a LION ROARs.

5. **(a)** An ACTRESS ACTs; a VOCALIST SINGs.

6. **(d)** The COACH guides the PLAYER; the COUNSELOR guides the CAMPER.

7. **(b)** A COMPOSER writes MUSIC; an AUTHOR writes a BOOK.

8. **(a)** A BLOOM (blossom) WITHERs; TIME PASSes.

9. **(b)** A MISTAKE is changed by the action of an ERASER; the CONSTITUTION is changed by the action of an AMENDMENT.

10. **(b)** The activity of the DOCTOR is to treat a DISEASE; the activity of the PSYCHIATRIST (a specific type of doctor) is to treat MALADJUSTMENT.

11. **(a)** A MANICURIST POLISHes nails; a BOOTBLACK POLISHes shoes.

12. **(b)** PARENTS COMMAND; CHILDREN OBEY, usually.

13. **(d)** A WOODSMAN uses an AX; a COBBLER uses an AWL.

14. **(a)** FISH SWIMS; MAN WALKS.

15. **(b)** A SURGEON uses a SCALPEL to cut; a BUTCHER uses a CLEAVER to cut. The butcher also uses a mallet in his work, but the implement for cutting is the cleaver.

16. **(b)** The activity of the PHYSICIAN is HEALing; the activity of the BANKER is LENDing. The bank also lends, but the analogy is better stated person to person.

17. **(b)** The MAN makes a SPEECH; the BIRD sings a SONG.

18. **(d)** A CARPENTER uses a SAW in his work; the MASON uses a TROWEL.

19. **(c)** A TAILOR creates a PATTERN before any cloth is cut; an ARCHITECT draws up a PLAN before building begins.

20. **(c)** An EGG HATCHes; a SEED GERMINATEs; there is rebirth.

21. **(d)** VIBRATION of sound waves creates TONE; REFRACTION of light rays creates COLOR.

22. **(c)** The REFEREE enforces the RULES; one's CONSCIENCE enforces one's MORALS.

23. **(b)** FREON gas is used in REFRIGERATION; UREA FORMALDEHYDE FOAM has been used for INSULATION. Urea formaldehyde foam has fallen into disuse even though it has been exonerated as a carcinogen. It is an effective insulator.

24. **(d)** A DAM blocks the free passage of WATER, collects it, then releases the water to flow in a controlled manner. A SLUICE does the same, also to WATER, though the term SLUICE is more often applied to the opening while the term DAM is applied to obstruction.

25. **(a)** A MUTE softens the sound of a HORN; a CUSHION softens the seat of a CHAIR.

26. **(c)** CORK floats on WATER; OIL floats on WATER.

Test IX. Place or Location

1. d	5. d	9. c	13. c	17. d	21. c	25. b
2. d	6. d	10. b	14. d	18. a	22. b	26. a
3. a	7. c	11. b	15. b	19. b	23. a	
4. c	8. b	12. a	16. c	20. a	24. d	

Explanatory Answers

1. **(d)** A THIMBLE belongs on a FINGER; a SOCK belongs on a FOOT.

2. **(d)** The PEASANT lives in a HOVEL; the KING lives in a PALACE.

3. **(a)** RAILROADS carry sustenance from one part of the COUNTRY to another; ARTERIES carry blood from one part of the BODY to another. Place alone is not enough categorization for solving this analogy. Three of the four choices are located in the body. The answer involves a combination of place and function.

4. **(c)** MONEY may be found in a BANK; KNOWLEDGE may be found in BOOKS.

5. **(d)** You RACE at the TRACK; you SWIM at the POOL.

6. **(d)** A GENERAL is a military leader on LAND; an ADMIRAL is a military leader at SEA.

7. **(c)** A MELON is a fruit that grows on a VINE; a PEAR is a fruit that grows on a TREE. Again note the refinement beyond place in order to form the most complete analogy.

8. **(b)** SUBMARINE and FISH are found in the water; AIRPLANE and BIRD are found in the sky. Note that in this analogy, the related terms share a location.

9. **(c)** BLOOD is carried in a VEIN just as WATER is carried by an AQUEDUCT.

10. **(b)** FRANC is the unit of currency used in FRANCE; PESO is the unit of currency used in MEXICO.

11. **(b)** A FJORD is a narrow arm of water that juts into the MAINLAND; A PENINSULA is a narrow arm of land that juts into the SEA.

12. **(a)** CHICAGO is a city in ILLINOIS; BOSTON is a city in MASSACHU-SETTS.

13. **(c)** EDEN is a land in the BIBLE; SHANGRI-LA is a place in James Hilton's novel *Lost Horizon*. In the novel, Shangri-La is located in Tibet, but the location of the analogy is literature.

14. **(d)** A BOAT may be found on WATER; the location of a PLANE is the AIR.

15. **(b)** Look for the BABY in the CARRIAGE; the MAN may be found in an AUTOMOBILE.

16. **(c)** THAILAND and CAMBODIA are adjoining countries in Eastern Asia; FRANCE and SPAIN are adjoining countries in Europe. All the choices are countries in Europe, but only Spain adjoins France as Cambodia adjoins Thailand.

17. **(d)** A NURSE works in a HOSPITAL; a TEACHER works in a SCHOOL. A student also works in school, but the student's work is not nearly as analogous to the nurse's work as is the teacher's.

18. **(a)** The CHAUFFEUR drives the AUTOMOBILE; the ENGINEER drives the TRAIN.

19. **(b)** The BAGPIPE is an instrument associated with SCOTLAND; the GUITAR is the instrument of SPAIN.

20. **(a)** A CAPE is a promontory of a CONTINENT; a GULF is a promontory of an OCEAN. Categories do overlap. You may call this Part/Whole if you wish.

21. **(c)** The GLOBE THEATER is in LONDON; LA SCALA opera house is in MILAN.

22. **(b)** STEPPES are large, level treeless plains of RUSSIA; PAMPAS are large, level grass-covered plains of ARGENTINA.

23. **(a)** A TYPIST works in an OFFICE; a MECHANIC works in a FAC-TORY.

24. **(d)** The FACULTY is a major functional unit of the UNIVERSITY; the STAFF serves the same function in the HOSPITAL. An intern is a member of the staff.

25. **(b)** An EAGLE lives in an AERIE, its nest high in the treetops; a RABBIT lives in a BURROW.

26. **(a)** The TRAIN pulls in to the STATION; the STEAMER pulls in at the WHARF. Resist the temptation to choose *pier*, the synonym of *wharf*.

Test X. Association

1. a	5. c	9. b	13. b	17. b	21. d	25. c
2. c	6. a	10. d	14. a	18. d	22. b	26. a
3. a	7. a	11. c	15. c	19. d	23. d	
4. d	8. d	12. c	16. c	20. a	24. d	

Explanatory Answers

1. **(a)** RAYON is artificial SILK; MARGARINE is artificial BUTTER. This analogy is as much one of definition as it is simple association.

2. **(c)** A PARACHUTE is rescue equipment associated with an AIRPLANE; a LIFE PRESERVER is rescue equipment associated with a BOAT.

3. **(a)** FOOD is associated with NUTRITION; LIGHT is associated with VISION. This is not a cause and effect relationship because light does not cause vision. Light is, of course, associated with all four choices, but its relationship to vision most closely parallels the relationship of food to nutrition.

4. **(d)** A SERVICE deserves a FEE; a FAVOR deserves THANKS.

5. **(c)** RUBBER is associated with ELECTRICITY in that RUBBER impedes the passage of ELECTRICITY; likewise, ASBESTOS impedes the passage of FIRE.

6. **(a)** A FOOT soldier is in the INFANTRY; a HORSE-mounted soldier is in the CAVALRY.

7. **(a)** You can get a PRESENT for your BIRTHDAY; you may get a REWARD for an ACCOMPLISHMENT.

8. **(d)** TERPSICHORE is the muse connected with BALLET; ERATO is the muse of POETRY.

9. **(b)** The LAWBREAKER gets out of jail on BAIL; the release of a HOSTAGE is obtained by paying RANSOM.

10. **(d)** The GYMNASIUM is associated with HEALTH; the LIBRARY is associated with KNOWLEDGE. The library is also commonly associated with books, but books in the library would be analogous to equipment in the gymnasium.

11. **(c)** This analogy is based upon association in common parlance. PEAS and CARROTS go together as do MEAT and POTATOES.

12. **(c)** The KING rules in the MONARCHY; the PEOPLE rule in a DEMOCRACY.

13. **(b)** APARTHEID is the state policy of SOUTH AFRICA; EQUALITY is the state policy of SWEDEN.

14. **(a)** TEARS are associated with SORROW as LAUGHTER is associated with JOY.

15. **(c)** When you think ROBIN you think of SPRING; when you think of CORN you think of SUMMER.

16. **(c)** A BIBLIOPHILE loves BOOKS; a PHILATELIST collects STAMPS.

17. **(b)** A NAIAD is a WATER nymph; a DRYAD is a TREE nymph.

18. **(d)** FAMINE is caused by lack of FOOD; DROUGHT is caused by lack of WATER.

19. **(d)** The color PURPLE is associated with ROYALty; the color BLUE is associated with SADness.

20. **(a)** All four terms of this analogy are associated with bad luck. A rabbit's foot is associated with good luck. The other two choices have nothing to do with luck.

21. **(d)** The flag at HALF-MAST is a symbol of mourning; an ELEGY is a funeral dirge. The flag being flown UPSIDE DOWN is a signal of DISTRESS and a call for help.

22. **(b)** This analogy is based on words that often appear in conjunction. SPRING FEVER and AUTUMN LEAVES simply go together.

23. **(d)** A WET SUIT is the garb associated with SCUBA diving; a TUTU is clothing associated with BALLET.

24. **(d)** ECUMENICAL has to do with the CHURCH; CULINARY has to do with the KITCHEN or with cooking.

25. **(c)** A TEAM wins a PENNANT; an ACTOR wins an OSCAR.

26. **(a)** King MIDAS had a touch of GOLD; William Jennings BRYAN, as an orator had a SILVER tongue. Bryan is further associated with silver in that he advocated replacing the gold standard with a silver standard.

Test XI. Sequence

1.	a	5.	b	9.	c	13.	c	17.	c	21.	c	25.	b
2.	a	6.	d	10.	b	14.	b	18.	c	22.	b	26.	d
3.	b	7.	c	11.	d	15.	b	19.	d	23.	b		
4.	d	8.	c	12.	b	16.	d	20.	b	24.	b		

Explanatory Answers

1. **(a)** MAY follows FEBRUARY with two months intervening (FEBRU-ARY, March, April, MAY); NOVEMBER follows AUGUST with two months intervening (AUGUST, September, October, NOVEMBER).

2. **(a)** JEFFERSON was the THIRD president; WASHINGTON was the FIRST.

3. **(b)** The letter Q follows the letter M with three letters intervening (M nop Q): the letter G follows the letter C with three letters intervening (C def G).

4. **(d)** All the terms of this analogy bear the same internal relationships. EFgH : ABcD :: MNoP : IJkL.

5. **(b)** By now you should have a system for solving letters of the alphabet, days of the week, months of the year sequence questions. TUESDAY (Wednesday) THURSDAY :: SATURDAY (Sunday) MONDAY.

6. **(d)** The RENAISSANCE followed the MIDDLE AGES; the only choice which followed 1700 is the 20TH CENTURY.

7. **(c)** SILENTS preceded TALKIES on the movie screen; RADIO preceded TELEVISION over the airwaves.

8. **(c)** A LAMB develops into a SHEEP; a PUP develops into a DOG.

9. **(c)** YESTERDAY preceded TODAY; the PAST preceded the PRESENT. Yesterday also preceded the present. When offered two choices which maintain the relationship, you must choose the best answer on some other basis. In this case look for parallelisms in the word forms. This particular

question poses especially distracting distractors. The relationship of *present* to *tomorrow* is a reversal of the initial relationship; *now* is a synonym of *present*.

10. **(b)** A COLT is an incipient STALLION; a STREAM may grow into a RIVER. *Stream* and *brook* are synonyms.

11. **(d)** The MOTHER is female parent to the female child, DAUGHTER; the FATHER is the male parent to the male child, SON.

12. **(b)** DAWN is the beginning of the day, DUSK is the end; CHILDHOOD is the beginning of a lifetime, SENILITY is near its end.

13. **(c)** As in the previous analogy, we deal here with beginning and end. SPRING is associated with rebirth, it is the beginning of the growing season; WINTER is associated with the end of the year and the absence of new growth. The analogous relationship of BIRTH to DEATH should be clear.

14. **(b)** APRIL, May, JUNE :: JANUARY, February, MARCH.

15. **(b)** MATURITY follows ADOLESCENCE; CHILDHOOD follows IN-FANCY.

16. **(d)** An INTERN, after a period of supervised experience, becomes a PHYSICIAN; an APPRENTICE, after a period of supervised experience, becomes a CRAFTSMAN.

17. **(c)** Great OAKs from little ACORNs grow; an INFANT grows into an ADULT.

18. **(c)** The HANDPLOW preceded the TRACTOR as the implement for preparing the fields for planting; the STAIRS preceded the ELEVATOR as a means for reaching higher floors of a building. The analogy is based upon sequence of technological development. This is a commonly used analogy form.

19. **(d)** TOMORROW, today, YESTERDAY :: FUTURE, present, PAST.

20. **(b)** Technology again. The HORSE is a less sophisticated means of transportation than the AUTOMOBILE; the LETTER is a less technologically sophisticated means of communication than is the TELEGRAM.

21. **(c)** COKE is a byproduct that follows COAL; BREAD is the product that follows DOUGH. The relationship is strictly sequential. There is no A : B :: C : D relationship. The dough and coal are related only insofar as they precede bread and coke.

22. **(b)** The INFANT proceeds to the very next stage and becomes a TOD-DLER; the BOY proceeds to the very next stage and becomes a YOUTH. Proximity of stages as well as sequence enters into your correct choice.

23. **(b)** A CLUB, as a weapon, long preceded the GUN. In fact, the club is from the same prehistoric era as the CAVE which preceded the HOUSE.

24. **(b)** A FILLY grows up to become a MARE; a PRINCE grows up to become a KING.

25. **(b)** A BUD develops and becomes a FLOWER; a TWIG develops and becomes a BRANCH.

26. **(d)** A MOTORCYCLE is a technologically sophisticated BICYCLE; an AUTOMOBILE is similarly related to a WAGON.

Test XII. Characteristic

1.	a	5.	d	9.	b	13.	a	17.	a	21.	c	25.	a
2.	c	6.	a	10.	b	14.	b	18.	a	22.	d	26.	d
3.	c	7.	d	11.	c	15.	b	19.	d	23.	b		
4.	d	8.	c	12.	d	16.	b	20.	c	24.	d		

Explanatory Answers

1. **(a)** If you are RICH, you OWN; if you are WISE, you KNOW.

2. **(c)** MAN is OMNIVOROUS, he eats both animal and vegetable matter; a LION is CARNIVOROUS, eating only meat.

3. **(c)** The characteristic way in which a SWALLOW deals with cold weather is by MIGRATION to warmer climates; a BEAR characteristically chooses HIBERNATION.

4. **(d)** IRON is COMMONly found; DIAMONDs are RARE.

5. **(d)** The characteristic associated with a MISER is STINGINESS; the characteristic associated with a HERMIT is SOLITUDE.

6. **(a)** NOISE is AUDIBLE; a PICTURE is VISIBLE.

7. **(d)** A PILOT must be ALERT; a MARKSMAN must be STEADY.

8. **(c)** THUNDER is LOUD; a WHALE is LARGE.

9. **(b)** The characteristic associated with an OWL is WISDOM; the characteristic associated with a BEAVER is INDUSTRY—"wise as an owl" and "busy as a beaver."

10. **(b)** SUGAR is SWEET; QUININE is BITTER. Saccharine leaves a bitter aftertaste, but it is basically a sweetener.

11. **(c)** FEVER is characteristic of SICKNESS; CLOUDs are characteristic of a STORM.

12. **(d)** NOISE is DISTRACTING; HARMONY is PLEASING.

13. **(a)** The GOURMET chooses to enjoy only the finest food; his characteristic behavior is DISCRIMINATION. The GLUTTON enjoys food in large quantities; his characteristic behavior is EXCESS. Obesity is likely to be a characteristic of the glutton, but not necessarily. Some gluttons remain slim.

14. **(b)** Characteristically, a STREAM does not travel in a straight line; it tends to be MEANDERING. A HIGHWAY tends to be a DIRECT route from one place to the next.

15. **(b)** As SNOW is to WINTER, so RAIN is to SUMMER. Some analogies are so simple as to be disconcerting.

16. **(b)** INSECURITY is characteristic of the NOVICE as CONFIDENCE is characteristic of the EXPERT.

17. **(a)** IRON RUSTs; BREAD gets MOLDy.

18. **(a)** A ROCK SINKS; a FEATHER FLOATS.

19. **(d)** A FOX is known for its CUNNING; a SAGE is known for his WISDOM.

20. **(c)** A CORK is BUOYANT; a DIAMOND is BRILLIANT.

21. **(c)** You SHIVER with COLD; you TREMBLE with FEAR. With happiness, you quiver.

22. **(d)** The DESERT is DRY; the TUNDRA is FROZEN.

23. **(b)** A characteristic of the INGENUE is her NAIVETY; a characteristic of the KNAVE is CHICANERY, trickery or artful deception.

24. **(d)** The SEER is known for PRESCIENCE; the BIGOT is known for PREJUDICE.

25. **(a)** The HERO's stock in trade is VALOR; the HERETIC makes a mark by DISSENT or nonconformity.

26. **(d)** A BALL is RESILIENT; an ECHO is RESONANT. Both bounce.

Test XIII. Degree

1.	a	5.	d	9.	b	13.	b	17.	c	21.	b	25.	d
2.	b	6.	a	10.	b	14.	d	18.	c	22.	c	26.	b
3.	d	7.	d	11.	b	15.	a	19.	a	23.	c		
4.	b	8.	b	12.	c	16.	c	20.	c	24.	d		

Explanatory Answers

1. **(a)** PROBABLE is more likely than POSSIBLE; EXPECT connotes a greater degree of certainty than HOPE.

2. **(b)** BLACK is more intense than GRAY; PAIN is greater than DISCOMFORT.

3. **(d)** An ORATION is longer and more formal than a CHAT; a BANQUET is longer, larger, and more formal than a SNACK.

4. **(b)** A MILE is very much longer than an INCH; a SKYSCRAPER is very much taller than a HUT.

5. **(d)** A SHOWER represents a gentle rain, whereas a CLOUDBURST is a very heavy rainfall. A BREEZE is a gentle wind, whereas a CYCLONE is a heavy windstorm.

6. **(a)** A MONTH is longer than a WEEK; a WEEK is longer than a DAY. A week is also longer than an hour, but since *week* is the next smallest unit to *month,* your best choice in completing the analogy is to choose the next smallest unit to *week,* which is *day.*

7. **(d)** An EAGLE is larger than a HUMMINGBIRD; a TREE is larger than a SHRUB.

8. **(b)** A HORSEFLY is an insect which is larger than another insect, a FLEA; a WHALE is a sea creature which is larger than another sea creature, a MINNOW.

9. **(b)** A CENTURY is ten times longer than a DECADE; a DIME is ten times more valuable than a CENT.

10. **(b)** An INCH times an inch equals a SQUARE INCH; a SQUARE INCH times an inch equals a cubic inch. Anyway, a square inch is larger than an INCH; a CUBIC INCH is larger than a SQUARE INCH.

11. **(b)** SLEET is a much more intensive form of precipitation than is MIST; a GULP is a much more intensive intake of fluid than is a SIP.

12. **(c)** To BEG is on a smaller scale and less intensive than to PLEAD; ALMS is generally on a small change scale while CHARITY is generally associated with larger scale giving. Philanthropy is the highest degree of giving, but *philanthropist* is the wrong answer because the person does not parallel another term.

13. **(b)** A LIMP is a flawed WALK; a STAMMER is a flawed TALK.

14. **(d)** LITTLE is more than NONE, though not much more; SELDOM is more often than NEVER, though not much more often.

15. **(a)** BAD is to WORSE as WORSE is to WORST. Think carefully. Beginning with the initial pair: WORST, WORSE, BAD, good, better, best.

16. **(c)** This analogy has to do with the action of heat upon water. From ICE to WATER to STEAM.

17. **(c)** One who is DEMONIC is fiendish, much worse than NAUGHTY; RAGE is much more intense than simple ANGER.

18. **(c)** An HOUR is longer than a MINUTE; a MINUTE is longer than a SECOND. The fact that there are sixty minutes in an hour and sixty seconds in a minute is irrelevant to this analogy.

19. **(a)** To LAUGH is more intensive than to SMILE; to BATHE is more intensive than merely to WASH.

20. **(c)** RUN is greater than WALK; to MULTIPLY makes the total grow much more quickly than to ADD.

21. **(b)** GUSH is a much heavier, quicker flow than TRICKLE; TORRID is much hotter than TEPID.

22. **(c)** A WEEK is longer than a DAY; a DAY is longer than an HOUR.

23. **(c)** To RECOMMEND is stronger and more compelling than to SUGGEST; to CALCULATE is much more accurate and specific than to ESTIMATE.

24. **(d)** To DRONE is to speak languidly in a monotone; to DECLAIM is to make a fiery oration. To PRAISE is to say something nice; to EXTOL is to glorify.

25. **(d)** A QUART is more than a PINT; a GALLON is more than a QUART. A gallon is also more than a liter, but since the initial pair represents nonmetric measures, it is best to maintain the analogy in nonmetric.

26. **(b)** GRIEF is intensive and all-encompassing DISTRESS; to COVET is to WANT inordinately.

Test XIV. Grammatical

1. b	5. b	9. a	13. c	17. c	21. b	25. a
2. c	6. a	10. b	14. c	18. b	22. d	26. d
3. c	7. b	11. d	15. b	19. c	23. b	
4. a	8. d	12. c	16. b	20. a	24. d	

Explanatory Answers

1. **(b)** SPRING : SPRUNG :: LIE : LAIN :: present : participle.

2. **(c)** ROSE : RISE :: WENT : GO :: past : present.

3. **(c)** SHABBILY : HARMONIOUSLY :: SHABBY : HARMONIOUS :: adverb : adjective.

4. **(a)** INFAMY : INFAMOUS :: PLAUSIBILITY : PLAUSIBLE :: noun : adjective

5. **(b)** YOUR : THEIR :: BABIES' :: ITS. All are possessives.

6. **(a)** SHEEP : ALUMNUS :: EWE : ALUMNA :: male : female.

7. **(b)** RAT : RATS :: MOUSE : MICE :: singular : plural.

8. **(d)** I : WE :: MOOSE : MOOSE :: singular : plural.

9. **(a)** LIES : DRINKS :: LAIN : DRUNK :: present : participle.

10. **(b)** HIM : US :: HE : WE :: objective : subjective.

11. **(d)** FIRST : ONE :: THIRD : THREE : ordinal : cardinal

12. **(c)** SPOKE : SPEAK :: TOLD : TELL :: past : present.

13. **(c)** REVERT : REVERSION :: SYMPATHIZE : SYMPATHY :: verb : noun.

14. **(c)** LB. : CAPT. :: POUND : CAPTAIN :: abbreviation : word. The abbreviation for lawyer is LLB.

15. **(b)** DOWN : DOWNY :: AGE : OLD. Downy means covered with down. As an analogous statement, covered with age would be old. Aging involves a process which is not implied by the relationship of the first two terms. Historic imparts more meaning than necessary.

16. **(b)** REGRESS : STERILIZE :: REGRESSIVE : STERILE :: verb : adjective.

17. **(c)** MAN'S : MINE :: MAN : I :: possessive : subjective.

18. **(b)** LAY : ATE :: LIES : EATS :: past : present. In order to determine the tense of the word *lay,* it is imperative to look at it in conjunction with the term in the C position.

19. **(c)** WE'RE : THEY'RE :: NE'ER : E'ER :: we are : they are :: never : ever. On each side of the analogy there are parallel contractions.

20. **(a)** HIS : ITS :: MINE : YOURS. All four terms are possessives. A pronoun does not take an apostrophe in the possessive.

21. **(b)** RELIEF : BELIEVE :: RECEIVE : DECEIT :: ie : ie : ei : ei. All seven terms correctly follow the rule, "I before E except after C . . ." so the above interpretation is the only one possible.

22. **(d)** LEAF : LEAVES :: MEDIUM : MEDIA :: singular : plural.

23. **(b)** LIVES : LIFE :: BROTHERS-IN-LAW : BROTHER-IN-LAW :: plural : singular.

24. **(d)** BRING : BROUGHT :: WRITE : WROTE :: present : past. Avoid the temptation to choose a relationship based only upon sound before looking for meaningful relationships.

25. **(a)** RADII : ANALYSES :: RADIUS : ANALYSIS :: plural : singular.

26. **(d)** SIMPLEST : MOST :: SIMPLE : MANY :: superlative : positive.

Test XV. Miscellaneous

1. d	5. a	9. c	13. c	17. d	21. c	25. d
2. a	6. c	10. d	14. d	18. c	22. d	26. d
3. c	7. d	11. b	15. b	19. d	23. c	
4. b	8. a	12. a	16. a	20. a	24. a	

Explanatory Answers

1. **(d)** The analogy has to do with people's middle names. You might call this "completion." THOMAS ALVA Edison; FRANKLIN DELANO Roosevelt.

2. **(a)** The basis for this analogy is euphemisms. Today people who back certain REBEL groups prefer to call those groups FREEDOM FIGHTERS. Similarly, some people today prefer not to use the term RETARDED, substituting DISABLED in its place.

3. **(c)** This analogy is based on definition. A HAIKU is a poem of 3 lines; a SONNET is a poem of 14 lines.

4. **(b)** JENNY LIND and TOM THUMB were both introduced and promoted by P.T. Barnum; *THE GREATEST SHOW ON EARTH* and *THE TEN COMMANDMENTS* were both produced by Cecil B. DeMille. *Gone with the Wind* was produced by Daryl Zanuck. The other two distractors are related to all three capitalized terms but they do not serve to complete the analogy.

5. **(a)** FRANKLIN W. DIXON and CAROLYN KEENE are pseudonyms used by the single author of both the Hardy Boys series and the Nancy Drew series of young people's mysteries. ELLERY QUEEN, JR. and ELLERY QUEEN are both pseudonyms under which the same person, one Manfred Lepofsky, wrote many adult mysteries.

6. **(c)** LAX and JFK are official designations of airports, the one Los Angeles and the other Kennedy in New York. The FBI and CIA are both United States intelligence organizations, the first domestic and the second international. None of the other choices bears any meaningful relationship to the FBI.

7. **(d)** Rachel Carson's *THE SILENT SPRING* helped caused the nation to take notice of ENVIRONMENTAL EXPLOITATION. Harriet Beecher Stowe's *UNCLE TOM'S CABIN* caused people to consider more seriously the situation of BLACK EXPLOITATION.

8. **(a)** If you stretch, you may call this an analogy of degree. BOILing uses more water than STEAMing. Similarly, FRYing uses more oil than SAUTEing.

9. **(c)** You would have to call this an analogy based on identity, or, perhaps, sequence. MUHAMMAD ALI is CASSIUS CLAY. CASSIUS CLAY became MUHAMMAD ALI when he converted to the Black Muslim faith. KAREEM ABDUL JABBAR is LEW ALCINDOR. LEW ALCINDOR became KAREEM ABDUL JABBAR when he converted to the Black Muslim faith.

10. **(d)** πr^2 is the formula for calculating the area of a CIRCLE; $\frac{bh}{2}$ is the formula for calculating the area of a TRIANGLE.

11. **(b)** ACHILLES' downfall was the arrow which entered the unprotected area of his HEEL; SAMSON's downfall was the cutting of his hair. Delilah betrayed Samson by telling of his weakness, but Samson's hair, as a body part, is analogous to Achille's heel.

12. **(a)** This is an analogy of identity. In Britain, a LORRY is a TRUCK and BRACES are SUSPENDERS.

13. **(c)** ENGLAND and DENMARK are both constitutional monarchies; FRANCE and ISRAEL both have republican forms of government. The like forms of government on each side of the equation creates this analogy. Sweden is another constitutional monarchy; China is a Communist dictatorship; Namibia is occupied and governed by South Africa.

14. **(d)** Sometimes the trademark name of the earliest and most widely used entry into a field comes to be used by the public as the common name of the product itself. Thus, once it finds its way into the dessert dish, all GELATIN dessert tends to be called JELLO®; most office PHOTO-COPIERS tend to be called the XEROX® and their products Xeroxes.

15. **(b)** AK and MN are correct postal service abbreviations for Alaska and Minnesota; AZ and PA are correct postal service abbreviations for Arizona and Pennsylvania. The other choices are not correct postal service abbreviations.

16. **(a)** It is hard to get away from definition or, at least, association. ETYMOLOGY is the study of WORDS; HAGIOLOGY is the study of SAINTS.

17. **(d)** ZEUS and HERA are husband and wife, king and queen of the Greek gods; JUPITER and JUNO are husband and wife, the Roman counterparts of Zeus and Hera.

18. **(c)** Look for relationships without considering meanings whenever you encounter foreign words. You can always focus on meanings later if you find no simpler relationship. In this analogy, the first two terms are totally unrelated except that each comes from a different foreign language and each has been incorporated into the English language without translation. On the other side of the analogy, it is possible to choose two more such words that come from two additional foreign languages and have been incorporated into English. GESUNDHEIT is German and means "good health"; AL DENTE is Italian and means chewy, literally, "to the teeth"; CAVEAT EMPTOR is Latin and means "buyer beware"; SAVOIR FAIRE is French and means "social polish."

19. **(d)** This analogy is based upon the fact that the identical word has two entirely different, in fact practically opposite, meanings. To SANCTION is to give authoritative approval or consent. A SANCTION is an economic or military coercive measure with the aim of punishing and causing a change in behavior, usually of another country. The meanings of HEW have nothing to do with the meanings of SANCTION, but the two meanings of HEW are equally different from each other. To HEW is to cut as with an ax; to HEW is to adhere or to stick, as to the party line.

20. **(a)** The "PASTORALE" and "EROICA" are both symphonies, the first by Tchaikowsky and the second by Beethoven, though composers are irrelevant to this analogy. The "EMPEROR" and the "BRANDENBURG" are concerti, the first by Beethoven and the second by Bach. You could legitimately categorize this as a part to part analogy. The "Egmont" is an overture and the "Nutcracker" a suite.

21. **(c)** The TACTILE sense is to the FINGER as the OLFACTORY sense is to the NOSE.

22. **(d)** KOESTLER wrote *DARKNESS at Noon;* BEETHOVEN wrote the "MOONLIGHT Sonata." The analogy moves from literature into music, but the relationship is clear.

23. **(c)** The relationship hinges upon the relationship between grandparent and grandchild. MISS LILLIAN (Carter) was AMY (Carter)'s grandmother; ISAAC was grandfather of JOSEPH. The Biblical family progression is Abraham → Isaac → Jacob → Joseph.

24. **(a)** MILK and BROCCOLI are considered to be among the most nutritious and healthful foods; POTATO CHIPS and TWINKIES® fall into the category of junk foods.

25. **(d)** The first two countries, TANZANIA and the UNITED ARAB EMIRATES, have in common that they came into being through the voluntary alliance of two or more independent countries. KOREA and GERMANY have in common that they were once unitary countries that have now been divided into two separate countries.

26. **(d)** This analogy is based upon unselfish sacrifice. In Dicken's novel *A Tale of Two Cities*, Sidney CARTON goes to the guillotine in place of Charles DARNAY. According to legend, in ancient Syracuse PYTHIAS was sentenced to die, but his friend DAMON volunteered to serve as hostage so PYTHIAS could return home to say goodbye. Theoretically, if Pythias had not returned, Damon would have died in his place, so the analogy is complete and accurate. Actually, Pythias did return, and the king, Dionysus, was so impressed that he pardoned him rather than proceeding with the execution.

Part II

Seven Sample Exams
with Explanatory Answers

ANSWER SHEET
MILLER ANALOGIES SAMPLE TEST I

1 Ⓐ Ⓑ Ⓒ Ⓓ   21 Ⓐ Ⓑ Ⓒ Ⓓ   41 Ⓐ Ⓑ Ⓒ Ⓓ   61 Ⓐ Ⓑ Ⓒ Ⓓ   81 Ⓐ Ⓑ Ⓒ Ⓓ
2 Ⓐ Ⓑ Ⓒ Ⓓ   22 Ⓐ Ⓑ Ⓒ Ⓓ   42 Ⓐ Ⓑ Ⓒ Ⓓ   62 Ⓐ Ⓑ Ⓒ Ⓓ   82 Ⓐ Ⓑ Ⓒ Ⓓ
3 Ⓐ Ⓑ Ⓒ Ⓓ   23 Ⓐ Ⓑ Ⓒ Ⓓ   43 Ⓐ Ⓑ Ⓒ Ⓓ   63 Ⓐ Ⓑ Ⓒ Ⓓ   83 Ⓐ Ⓑ Ⓒ Ⓓ
4 Ⓐ Ⓑ Ⓒ Ⓓ   24 Ⓐ Ⓑ Ⓒ Ⓓ   44 Ⓐ Ⓑ Ⓒ Ⓓ   64 Ⓐ Ⓑ Ⓒ Ⓓ   84 Ⓐ Ⓑ Ⓒ Ⓓ
5 Ⓐ Ⓑ Ⓒ Ⓓ   25 Ⓐ Ⓑ Ⓒ Ⓓ   45 Ⓐ Ⓑ Ⓒ Ⓓ   65 Ⓐ Ⓑ Ⓒ Ⓓ   85 Ⓐ Ⓑ Ⓒ Ⓓ
6 Ⓐ Ⓑ Ⓒ Ⓓ   26 Ⓐ Ⓑ Ⓒ Ⓓ   46 Ⓐ Ⓑ Ⓒ Ⓓ   66 Ⓐ Ⓑ Ⓒ Ⓓ   86 Ⓐ Ⓑ Ⓒ Ⓓ
7 Ⓐ Ⓑ Ⓒ Ⓓ   27 Ⓐ Ⓑ Ⓒ Ⓓ   47 Ⓐ Ⓑ Ⓒ Ⓓ   67 Ⓐ Ⓑ Ⓒ Ⓓ   87 Ⓐ Ⓑ Ⓒ Ⓓ
8 Ⓐ Ⓑ Ⓒ Ⓓ   28 Ⓐ Ⓑ Ⓒ Ⓓ   48 Ⓐ Ⓑ Ⓒ Ⓓ   68 Ⓐ Ⓑ Ⓒ Ⓓ   88 Ⓐ Ⓑ Ⓒ Ⓓ
9 Ⓐ Ⓑ Ⓒ Ⓓ   29 Ⓐ Ⓑ Ⓒ Ⓓ   49 Ⓐ Ⓑ Ⓒ Ⓓ   69 Ⓐ Ⓑ Ⓒ Ⓓ   89 Ⓐ Ⓑ Ⓒ Ⓓ
10 Ⓐ Ⓑ Ⓒ Ⓓ   30 Ⓐ Ⓑ Ⓒ Ⓓ   50 Ⓐ Ⓑ Ⓒ Ⓓ   70 Ⓐ Ⓑ Ⓒ Ⓓ   90 Ⓐ Ⓑ Ⓒ Ⓓ
11 Ⓐ Ⓑ Ⓒ Ⓓ   31 Ⓐ Ⓑ Ⓒ Ⓓ   51 Ⓐ Ⓑ Ⓒ Ⓓ   71 Ⓐ Ⓑ Ⓒ Ⓓ   91 Ⓐ Ⓑ Ⓒ Ⓓ
12 Ⓐ Ⓑ Ⓒ Ⓓ   32 Ⓐ Ⓑ Ⓒ Ⓓ   52 Ⓐ Ⓑ Ⓒ Ⓓ   72 Ⓐ Ⓑ Ⓒ Ⓓ   92 Ⓐ Ⓑ Ⓒ Ⓓ
13 Ⓐ Ⓑ Ⓒ Ⓓ   33 Ⓐ Ⓑ Ⓒ Ⓓ   53 Ⓐ Ⓑ Ⓒ Ⓓ   73 Ⓐ Ⓑ Ⓒ Ⓓ   93 Ⓐ Ⓑ Ⓒ Ⓓ
14 Ⓐ Ⓑ Ⓒ Ⓓ   34 Ⓐ Ⓑ Ⓒ Ⓓ   54 Ⓐ Ⓑ Ⓒ Ⓓ   74 Ⓐ Ⓑ Ⓒ Ⓓ   94 Ⓐ Ⓑ Ⓒ Ⓓ
15 Ⓐ Ⓑ Ⓒ Ⓓ   35 Ⓐ Ⓑ Ⓒ Ⓓ   55 Ⓐ Ⓑ Ⓒ Ⓓ   75 Ⓐ Ⓑ Ⓒ Ⓓ   95 Ⓐ Ⓑ Ⓒ Ⓓ
16 Ⓐ Ⓑ Ⓒ Ⓓ   36 Ⓐ Ⓑ Ⓒ Ⓓ   56 Ⓐ Ⓑ Ⓒ Ⓓ   76 Ⓐ Ⓑ Ⓒ Ⓓ   96 Ⓐ Ⓑ Ⓒ Ⓓ
17 Ⓐ Ⓑ Ⓒ Ⓓ   37 Ⓐ Ⓑ Ⓒ Ⓓ   57 Ⓐ Ⓑ Ⓒ Ⓓ   77 Ⓐ Ⓑ Ⓒ Ⓓ   97 Ⓐ Ⓑ Ⓒ Ⓓ
18 Ⓐ Ⓑ Ⓒ Ⓓ   38 Ⓐ Ⓑ Ⓒ Ⓓ   58 Ⓐ Ⓑ Ⓒ Ⓓ   78 Ⓐ Ⓑ Ⓒ Ⓓ   98 Ⓐ Ⓑ Ⓒ Ⓓ
19 Ⓐ Ⓑ Ⓒ Ⓓ   39 Ⓐ Ⓑ Ⓒ Ⓓ   59 Ⓐ Ⓑ Ⓒ Ⓓ   79 Ⓐ Ⓑ Ⓒ Ⓓ   99 Ⓐ Ⓑ Ⓒ Ⓓ
20 Ⓐ Ⓑ Ⓒ Ⓓ   40 Ⓐ Ⓑ Ⓒ Ⓓ   60 Ⓐ Ⓑ Ⓒ Ⓓ   80 Ⓐ Ⓑ Ⓒ Ⓓ   100 Ⓐ Ⓑ Ⓒ Ⓓ

Tear Here

MILLER ANALOGIES
SAMPLE TEST I

Time: 50 Minutes. 100 Questions.

Directions: Each of these test questions consists of three CAPITALIZED words and four lettered words enclosed in parentheses. Two of the capitalized words are related in some way. Find the two related words and establish the nature of the relationship. Then study the four words lettered a, b, c, and d. Select the one lettered word which is related to the remaining capitalized word in the same way that the first two capitalized words are related. Mark the answer sheet for the letter preceding the word you select.

1. BALMY : MILD :: FAITHFUL : (a. explosive, b. docile, c. talkative, d. staunch)

2. BOLD : TIMID :: SQUANDER : (a. disperse, b. retrench, c. query, d. extinguish)

3. SEA : (a. fish, b. ocean, c. island, d. net) :: LAND : LAKE

4. BOTTLE : TIRE :: BRITTLE : (a. elastic, b. scarce, c. rubber, d. spheroid)

5. DIAMETER : RADIUS :: (a. 3, b. 8, c. 5, d. 6) : 4

6. GLABROUS : FACTITIOUS :: HIRSUTE : (a. authentic, b. fictional, c. fluent, d. replete)

7. PARANOIA : SCHIZOPHRENIA :: MEGALOMANIA : (a. melancholia, b. carcinoma, c. hepatitis, d. glaucoma)

8. (a. sales, b. investment, c. management, d. interest) : PROFIT :: LABOR : WAGES

9. HOBO : (a. knapsack, b. vagrant, c. park, d. slum) :: TRAVELER : TRUNK

10. DENIGRATE : DEFAMER :: MEDIATE : (a. mathematician, b. arbitrator, c. employer, d. laborer)

11. LAKE WOBEGON : (a. Minneapolis, b. Winesburg, c. Canterbury, d. Minnesota) :: MUDVILLE : CASTERBRIDGE

12. CORNET : OBOE :: (a. cello, b. drum, c. harpsichord, d. xylophone) : GUITAR

13. JANUARY : WEDNESDAY :: JANUS : (a. Thor, b. Apollo, c. Odin, d. Diana)

14. HORSE : (a. equestrian, b. hoofed, c. cabriolet, d. herbivorous) :: TIGER : CARNIVOROUS

15. GOOD : BETTER :: (a. terrible, b. worse, c. improvement, d. bad) : WORST

16. CLAN : FEUD :: NATION : (a. war, b. politics, c. armaments, d. retaliation)

17. ABUNDANCE : ABROGATE :: DEARTH : (a. deny, b. establish, c. abstain, d. absolve)

18. ONOMATOPOEIA : METAPHOR :: SOUND : (a. hiss, b. rhyme, c. saying, d. comparison)

19. SACRAMENTO : HELENA :: ALBANY : (a. New York, b. Little Rock, c. Houston, d. San Francisco)

20. (a. scan, b. feel, c. dear, d. seen) : READ :: REAP : PEAR

21. CAUTIOUS : CIRCUMSPECT :: PRECIPITOUS : (a. premonitory, b. profound, c. stealthy, d. steep)

22. SEISMOGRAPH : GEOLOGY :: ELECTROENCEPHALOGRAPH : (a. bacteriology, b. biology, c. neurology, d. cardiology)

23. ACUTE : VENERATE :: CHRONIC : (a. revere, b. actuate, c. flout, d. repent)

24. (a. toad, b. lion, c. shark, d. alligator) : TURTLE :: TIGER : MAN

25. INSTINCT : PLAN :: UNCONSCIOUS : (a. involuntary, b. intentional, c. spontaneous, d. imaginary)

26. INDIA : (a. Sri Lanka, b. Greece, c. Afghanistan, d. Pakistan) :: ITALY : SWITZERLAND

27. SWIM : SWAM :: BURST : (a. busted, b. bursted, c. burst, d. bust)

28. RAISIN : GRAPE :: PRUNE : (a. apricot, b. currant, c. plum, d. berry)

29. GRAM : OUNCE :: LITER : (a. deciliter, b. quart, c. kilogram, d. pound)

30. PESTLE : PHARMACIST :: STETHOSCOPE : (a. teacher, b. author, c. physician, d. doctor)

31. LIMPID : LUCID :: TURBID : (a. torpid, b. muddy, c. truculent, d. serene)

32. PEACH : (a. tomato, b. banana, c. cabbage, d. coconut) :: GRAPE : PLUM

33. .02 : .0004 :: .001 : (a. .000001, b. 0001, c. .0002, d. .000002)

34. SADNESS : PAIN :: FAILURE : (a. medication, b. palliation, c. pleasure, d. injury)

35. AMELIA EARHART : NELLIE BLY :: AVIATION : (a. medicine, b. journalism, c. law, d. prohibition)

36. ROMAN : MANOR :: (a. cleric, b. names, c. patrimony, d. estates) : MANSE

37. LACONIC : FLACCID :: REDUNDANT : (a. succinct, b. resilient, c. flimsy, d. swollen)

38. PNEUMATICS : (a. medicine, b. disease, c. physics, d. cars) :: ESKER : GEOLOGY

39. NECKLACE : MEDAL :: ADORNMENT : (a. jewel, b. metal, c. decoration, d. bronze)

40. RIVER : STREAM :: MOUNTAIN : (a. cliff, b. hill, c. canyon, d. peak)

41. HECKLE : NEEDLE :: (a. stock, b. deplete, c. book, d. stylus) : REPLENISH

42. (a. guerilla, b. terrorist, c. quash, d. mediate) : REBELLION :: NEGOTIATE : TREATY

43. BOTANIST : PLANTS :: GEOLOGIST : (a. trees, b. rocks, c. geography, d. gems)

44. CAT : FELINE :: OX : (a. equine, b. saturnine, c. bovine, d. canine)

45. WOLF : (a. wool, b. sheep, c. ewe, d. ram) :: DOG : CAT

46. (a. 5/16, b. 3/8, c. 2/6, d. 5/12) : 9/24 :: 4/11 : 12/33

47. FISHES : BIRDS :: (a. horses, b. cattle, c. wheat, d. mosses) : CEREALS

48. ROOM : CABIN :: HOUSE : (a. camp, b. cottage, c. hotel, d. ship)

49. BRASS : COPPER :: PEWTER : (a. lead, b. zinc, c. silver, d. bronze)

50. COWCATCHER : LOCOMOTIVE :: (a. coda, b. climax, c. epilogue, d. finale) : DENOUEMENT

51. PARIAH : OUTCAST :: ARCHON : (a. archivist, b. magistrate, c. martine, d. constable)

52. (a. capuccino, b. shamrock, c. wine, d. palm trees) : VODKA :: DEVALERA : STALIN

53. LANCET : CUT :: CHAMOIS : (a. polish, b. pliant, c. smooth, d. sheep)

54. (a. utter, b. elapse, c. exude, d. time) : EMIT :: STEP : PETS

55. SAFE : NECKLACE :: COMBINATION : (a. torque, b. bangle, c. circlet, d. clasp)

56. EXPERIMENT : (a. science, b. elucidation, c. hypothesis, d. investigation) :: EXAMINATION : ACHIEVEMENT

57. BOY : BULLET :: MAN : (a. gun, b. artillery shell, c. holster, d. trigger)

58. ENERVATE : (a. eradicate, b. invigorate, c. disconcert, d. propagate) :: MALICE : BENEVOLENCE

59. EVIDENCE : CONVICTION :: (a. oxygen, b. carbon dioxide, c. match, d. light) : COMBUSTION

60. EDIFICATION : AWARENESS :: EXACERBATION : (a. soreness, b. excitement, c. reduction, d. deliberation)

61. NEWTON : COPERNICUS :: SHAKESPEARE : (a. Fielding, b. Jonson, c. Dickens, d. Pope)

62. ST. AUGUSTINE : (a. Florida, b. Virginia, c. France, d. Spain) :: JAMESTOWN : ENGLAND

63. SNOW : DRIFT :: (a. hill, b. rain, c. sand, d. desert) : DUNE

64. CATAMARAN : TERMAGANT :: RAFT : (a. grisette, b. spinnaker, c. spinster, d. shrew)

65. 3^2 : 2^3 :: 9 : (a. 1, b. 6, c. 4, d. 8)

66. FICTION : NOVELIST :: FACTS : (a. legend, b. story, c. historian, d. research)

67. HARVARD : YALE :: SMITH : (a. Princeton, b. Purdue, c. Emory, d. Dartmouth)

68. CAT : WOLF :: (a. lion, b. dog, c. man, d. tiger) : DUCK

69. WHO : I :: WHOM : (a. we, b. me, c. whose, d. mine)

70. (a. obsequious, b. obstreperous, c. complacent, d. contume-lious) : SYCOPHANT :: CONTUMACIOUS : RENEGADE

71. DOWSER : ROD :: GEOMANCER : (a. stones, b. maps, c. plants, d. configurations)

72. JESUS : ATHENA :: (a. Mary, b. Pontius, c. Joseph, d. Luke) : ZEUS

73. (a. loss, b. victory, c. game, d. team) : WIN :: MEDICINE : CURE

74. SAFARI : SWAHILI :: SALAAM : (a. Arabic, b. shalom, c. peace, d. Africa)

75. ACID : ALKALI :: 6 : (a. 1, b. 4, c. 7, d. 8)

76. PEDESTAL : (a. column, b. sculpture, c. chandelier, d. stone) :: STALAGMITE : STALACTITE

77. BONA FIDE : IN TOTO :: CARTE BLANCHE : (a. eureka, b. status quo, c. avant-garde, d. ersatz)

78. SEA : COAST :: RIVER : (a. inlet, b. delta, c. stream, d. bank)

79. AMOUNT : NUMBER :: (a. lessen, b. augment, c. less, d. enumerate) : FEWER

80. VOLUME : CUBIC METER :: (a. area, b. length, c. capacity, d. mass) : LITER

81. (a. refrain, b. precede, c. sustain, d. foray) : FORBEAR :: ADUMBRATE : FORESHADOW

82. CHAMPION : CAUSE :: (a. signature, b. introduction, c. draft, d. ink) : LETTER

83. SHADOWS : CLOUDS :: SUN : (a. water, b. dark, c. rain, d. thunder)

84. WINTER : SUMMER :: BOSTON : (a. Miami, b. Madrid, c. São Paulo, d. San Diego)

85. CIRCLE : SPHERE :: (a. ice, b. angle, c. oval, d. square) : CUBE

86 KINETIC : MOTION :: PISCATORIAL : (a. pizza, b. painting, c. fish, d. picturesque)

87. RESPIRATION : CO_2 :: (a. hydrolysis, b. transpiration, c. oxidation, d. photosynthesis) : O_2

88. SAND : CLAY :: GLASS : (a. stone, b. hay, c. brick, d. dirt)

89. LOUISIANA PURCHASE : (a. Mexico, b. Spain, c. Great Britain, d. France) :: ALASKA : RUSSIA

90. X : M :: (a. V, b. X, c. L, d. I) : C

91. PUCCINI : OPERA :: (a. Pavlova, b. Verdi, c. "Giselle," d. Balanchine) : BALLET

92. POLTROON : TERROR :: PARANOIAC : (a. courage, b. shyness, c. persecution, d. paralysis)

93. DOOR : BOLT :: LETTER : (a. envelope, b. mail, c. seal, d. write)

94. AUTHOR : (a. royalties, b. charges, c. fees, d. contributions) :: AGENT : COMMISSIONS

95. OLD BAILEY : OLD VIC :: (a. Versailles, b. Bastille, c. Westminster, d. London) : LA SCALA

96. TRUDEAU : (a. Durant, b. De Toqueville, c. Malthus, d. Nast) :: ORWELL : HUXLEY

97. ORAL : AURAL :: SPEAK : (a. smell, b. see, c. sense, d. hear)

98. ACID : (a. NaHCO$_3$, b. H$_2$SO$_4$, c. NaCl, d. NaOH) :: ENZYME : AMYLASE

99. (a. sow, b. doe, c. vixen, d. bitch) : FOX :: DAM : SIRE

100. SALIVA : OIL :: MOUTH : (a. friction, b. comb, c. motor, d. cogwheel)

ANSWER KEY FOR MILLER ANALOGIES SAMPLE TEST I

1. d	21. d	41. a	61. b	81. a
2. b	22. c	42. c	62. d	82. c
3. c	23. c	43. b	63. c	83. a
4. a	24. d	44. c	64. d	84. c
5. b	25. b	45. b	65. d	85. d
6. a	26. d	46. b	66. c	86. c
7. a	27. c	47. d	67. d	87. d
8. c	28. c	48. d	68. c	88. c
9. a	29. b	49. a	69. b	89. d
10. b	30. c	50. b	70. a	90. d
11. b	31. b	51. b	71. d	91. d
12. a	32. a	52. b	72. a	92. c
13. c	33. a	53. a	73. c	93. c
14. d	34. d	54. d	74. a	94. a
15. b	35. b	55. d	75. d	95. b
16. a	36. b	56. c	76. c	96. d
17. b	37. b	57. b	77. c	97. d
18. d	38. c	58. b	78. d	98. b
19. b	39. c	59. a	79. c	99. c
20. c	40. b	60. a	80. c	100. c

Explanatory Answers for Miller Analogies Sample Test I

1. **(d)** BALMY and MILD are synonyms; therefore, the task is to look for a synonym for FAITHFUL, which in this case is STAUNCH.

2. **(b)** BOLD and TIMID are related as antonyms. SQUANDER, meaning to spend extravagantly, is the opposite of RETRENCH, meaning to curtail or economize.

3. **(c)** LAND and LAKE are related geographically in the same way as SEA and ISLAND; for as land surrounds a lake so does sea surround an island.

4. **(a)** A specific characteristic of a BOTTLE is that it is BRITTLE. Similarly, a specific characteristic of a TIRE is that it is ELASTIC.

5. **(b)** This is a mathematical relationship. A DIAMETER is twice the length of a RADIUS in a given circle; therefore, the missing term must be a number that is twice as great as 4. That, of course, is 8. In your own mind, you might say simply, "2 : 1 :: 2 : 1."

6. **(a)** GLABROUS (hairless) and HIRSUTE (hairy) are antonymns. The only antonym for FACTITIOUS (artificial) is AUTHENTIC.

7. **(a)** Every term in this analogy is a form of mental illness. PARANOIA, a psychosis characterized by delusions of persecution, and SCHIZOPHRE-NIA, a psychosis characterized by disintegration of the personality, are related by the fact that each is a form of mental illness. MEGALO-MANIA, a psychosis characterized by infantile feelings of personal om-nipotence, is also a form of mental illness. Therefore, the missing term must be MELANCHOLIA, a psychosis characterized by extreme depres-sion, because this is the only alternative that names a mental, rather than a physical, illness.

8. **(c)** LABOR is associated with WAGES in the same way that MANAGE-MENT is associated with PROFIT. In both cases the association is of people working for a reward. Sales, investment, and interest may each be said to yield a profit, but these do not parallel the relationship of people to their reward as established by the given word pair. In solving this anal-ogy, you must have the mental flexibility to think of *labor* and *manage-ment* as groups of people rather than as activities. If you think of labor as an activity, there are too many possible correct answers.

9. **(a)** This is an analogy of purpose. A TRAVELER uses a TRUNK in the same way that a HOBO uses a KNAPSACK.

10. **(b)** The relationship is one of action to actor. DENIGRATE (to belittle or to malign) is the action taken by the DEFAMER (one who injures by giv-ing misleading or false reports) in the same way that MEDIATE (to act as an intermediary agent) is the action taken by the ARBITRATOR (one chosen to settle differences between parties in dispute).

11. **(b)** MUDVILLE, the town in the poem "Casey at the Bat" and CAS-TERBRIDGE, the town in the Hardy novel *The Mayor of Casterbridge* are fictional places. Likewise, LAKE WOBEGON of Keillor's book *Lake Wobegon Days* and WINESBURG of Anderson's *Winesburg, Ohio,* are fictional places.

12. **(a)** This is a part-to-part analogy. CORNET and OBOE are each part of the larger category of wind instruments in the same way that GUITAR and CELLO are each part of the larger category of string instruments. Harp-sichord, too, belongs to the category of string instruments; however, be-cause it has internal, rather than external, strings, it is not as closely related to guitar as cello.

13. **(c)** JANUARY was named for JANUS, the guardian deity of gates in Roman mythology, as WEDNESDAY was named for ODIN, chief of the Scandinavian gods. The Anglo-Saxon version of Odin was Woden; hence Woden's Day became Wednesday.

14. **(d)** This is a characteristic relationship. A specific characteristic of a TIGER is that it is CARNIVOROUS (meat-eating) as a specific characteristic of a HORSE is that it is HERBIVOROUS (plant-eating).

15. **(b)** This is an analogy of degree. Adjectives such as good and bad have three degrees of comparison; positive, comparative, and superlative. In this question, GOOD, which is the positive degree, is less good than BETTER, the comparative degree, to the same extent as WORSE, the comparative, is less bad than WORST, the superlative degree.

16. **(a)** The relationship is one of object to action. Just as a CLAN may become involved in a FEUD, so may a NATION become involved in a WAR. If you solve this analogy via a A : C :: B : D model, the relationship becomes one of degree. A CLAN is smaller than a NATION, thus its conflict, a FEUD is smaller than a WAR.

17. **(b)** ABUNDANCE and DEARTH are antonyms. The opposite of ABROGATE (to nullify or cancel) is ESTABLISH.

18. **(d)** ONOMATOPOEIA (a word whose sound suggests its sense) is a figure of speech that makes a SOUND relationship. METAPHOR (an implied comparison between unlike things) is a figure of speech that makes a COMPARISON.

19. **(b)** SACRAMENTO and HELENA are related because each is a capital city. Sacramento is the capital of California and Helena the capital of Montana. Since ALBANY is also a state capital, it must be paired with LITTLE ROCK, the capital of Arkansas, to complete the analogy.

20. **(c)** This is a nonsemantic analogy. Transposing the first and last letters of REAP forms the word PEAR just as transposing the first and last letters of READ forms the word DEAR.

21. **(d)** CAUTIOUS and CIRCUMSPECT are related as synonyms. The only synonym offered for PRECIPITOUS is STEEP.

22. **(c)** This is an analogy of purpose. A SEISMOGRAPH, an instrument for recording vibrations within the earth, is used in GEOLOGY (the study of the earth) as an ELECTROENCEPHALOGRAPH, an instrument for recording brain waves, is used in NEUROLOGY (the scientific study of the nervous system).

23. **(c)** ACUTE and CHRONIC are related as antonyms. Acute means having a sudden onset, sharp rise and short course; chronic means marked by long duration or frequent recurrence. VENERATE, which means to honor,

must therefore be paired with its opposite, FLOUT, meaning to scoff or to treat with contemptuous disregard, in order to complete the analogy.

24. **(d)** This is a part-to-part analogy. TIGER and MAN are each part of the larger category of mammals. TURTLE, which is part of the larger category of reptiles, must therefore be paired with ALLIGATOR, the only reptile among the answer choices. A toad is an amphibian.

25. **(b)** An INSTINCT is an unreasoned or UNCONSCIOUS response to a stimulus. A PLAN is a reasoned or INTENTIONAL response to a stimulus.

26. **(d)** The relationship between ITALY and SWITZERLAND is that they share a common border, as do INDIA and PAKISTAN.

27. **(c)** The grammatical relationship between SWIM and SWAM is one of present tense to past tense; therefore, the task is to find the past tense of BURST, which is also BURST.

28. **(c)** The relationship is one of origin or sequence. A RAISIN is a dried GRAPE just as a PRUNE is a dried PLUM.

29. **(b)** A GRAM is a metric measure of weight. It is paired with an OUNCE which is an American measure of weight. A LITER is a metric measure of volume which must be paired with its near equivalent, an American QUART. In the American system of weights and measures, an ounce may also be a measure of volume, but it would be impossible to create an analogy with the necessary parallels with any interpretation other than that ounce is a measure of weight.

30. **(c)** This is an analogy of tool to its user or object to actor. A PESTLE is used by a PHARMACIST in the performance of his work as a STETHOSCOPE is used by a PHYSICIAN in the performance of his work. Choice (d) is incorrect because it is not as specific as (c); not all doctors are physicians.

31. **(b)** LIMPID and LUCID are synonyms meaning clear. A synonym for TURBID is MUDDY.

32. **(a)** The PEACH, TOMATO, GRAPE and PLUM are all juicy fruits that are grown in temperate climates.

33. **(a)** $(.02)^2 = .0004; (.001)^2 = .000001.$

34. **(d)** The relationship of the given word pair is one of cause and effect. SADNESS may be caused by FAILURE in the same way that PAIN may be caused by an INJURY.

35. **(b)** This is an analogy of the association of famous women to the field in which they pioneered. AMELIA EARHART achieved fame as one of the first women in AVIATION; NELLIE BLY, as one of the first women in JOURNALISM.

36. **(b)** ROMAN and MANOR are anagrams. So, too, are NAMES and MANSE.

37. **(b)** LACONIC (concise) and REDUNDANT (excessively wordy) are antonyms. Among the answer choices, the only antonym for FLACCID (flabby or limp) is RESILIENT (flexible).

38. **(c)** An ESKER (a ridge formed by a glacial stream) is part of the field of GEOLOGY as PNEUMATICS (the use of gas or air pressure) is part of the field of PHYSICS.

39. **(c)** A NECKLACE is used for ADORNMENT as a MEDAL is used for DECORATION.

40. **(b)** This is an analogy of degree. A RIVER is larger than a STREAM as a MOUNTAIN is larger than a HILL.

41. **(a)** HECKLE and NEEDLE are synonyms meaning to harass or badger. The only synonym offered for REPLENISH is STOCK.

42. **(c)** The relationship of the given word pair is action to object. One may NEGOTIATE (bring about by mutual agreement) a TREATY just as one may QUASH (crush) a REBELLION.

43. **(b)** The first word pair is related by the association of a scientist to his study. Of the choices offered, only the study of ROCKS is related to the GEOLOGIST as the study of PLANTS is related to the BOTANIST. To the extent that gemstones occur naturally among the rocks, the geologist will study them as well, but the primary concern of a geologist is rocks, their composition, and their history.

44. **(c)** FELINE means of or relating to the CAT family as BOVINE means of or relating to the OX or cow family.

45. **(b)** DOG and CAT are simply two different kinds of animal. WOLF and SHEEP are likewise two different kinds of animal. Gender is not a factor in the relationship of dog to cat, so it must not enter the analogy in relationship to wolf.

46. **(b)** Dividing numerator and denominator by 3, 12/33 can be reduced to 4/11. Similarly, dividing numerator and denominator by 3, 9/24 can be reduced to 3/8.

47. **(d)** This is an analogy of sequence. On the evolutionary scale, FISHES appeared long before BIRDS in the animal world; MOSSES, long before CEREALS in the plant world.

48. **(d)** A ROOM is a division of a HOUSE, specifically a living unit of a house. A CABIN is a living unit of a SHIP.

49. **(a)** BRASS is an alloy consisting essentially of COPPER and zinc. PEWTER is an alloy consisting of tin and LEAD.

50. **(b)** A COWCATCHER immediately precedes a LOCOMOTIVE as a CLIMAX (the point of highest dramatic tension) immediately precedes the DENOUEMENT (the unraveling or outcome of a sequence of events) in a story or a play.

51. **(b)** PARIAH and OUTCAST are synonyms. The only synonym offered for ARCHON is MAGISTRATE.

52. **(b)** Joseph STALIN was the leader of the Soviet Union which is intimately associated with VODKA. Eamon DEVALERA was the leader of Ireland which is intimately associated with the SHAMROCK.

53. **(a)** This is an analogy of purpose. A LANCET is a sharp surgical instrument used to CUT; a CHAMOIS is a soft, pliant leather prepared from the skin of the chamois or from sheepskin used to POLISH.

54. **(d)** This is a nonsemantic analogy. TIME spelled backwards is EMIT as STEP spelled backwards is PETS.

55. **(d)** A SAFE is opened by a COMBINATION; a NECKLACE by a CLASP.

56. **(c)** An EXPERIMENT tests a HYPOTHESIS as an EXAMINATION tests ACHIEVEMENT.

57. **(b)** The relationship is one of degree. A MAN is larger than a BOY; an ARTILLERY SHELL is larger and more effective than a BULLET.

58. **(b)** MALICE and BENEVOLENCE are antonyms. The only antonym offered for ENERVATE is INVIGORATE.

59. **(a)** EVIDENCE is necessary for CONVICTION in the judicial process just as OXYGEN is necessary for the chemical process of COMBUSTION. Heat is also necessary for combustion, but the source of heat may be other than a match.

60. **(a)** The relationship of the given word pair is one of cause and effect since EDIFICATION (enlightenment) results in AWARENESS. Similarly, EXACERBATION (aggravation) results in SORENESS.

61. **(b)** NEWTON and COPERNICUS are noted for their contributions to the field of science. Both SHAKESPEARE and JONSON are well-known for both drama and poetry. Notice that each of the alternatives names a figure from the field of literature; therefore, it is necessary to narrow the relationship to a particular area or areas of literature in order to answer this question correctly.

62. **(d)** JAMESTOWN was ENGLAND's first permanent settlement in the New World just as ST. AUGUSTINE was SPAIN's first permanent settlement.

63. **(c)** When blown by the wind, SNOW forms a DRIFT, and SAND forms a DUNE.

64. **(d)** CATAMARAN and RAFT are synonyms as are TERMAGANT and SHREW.

65. **(d)** $3^2 = 3 \times 3 = 9$
    $2^3 = 2 \times 2 \times 2 = 8$

66. **(c)** FICTION is the province of the NOVELIST as FACTS are the province of the HISTORIAN.

67. **(d)** The relationship between the terms of the given word pair is one of place. HARVARD and YALE are both located in New England as are SMITH and DARTMOUTH. Smith is a woman's college, but, since none of the four choices is a women's college, you must seek out another basis for the analogy.

68. **(c)** CAT and WOLF are related in that they are each members of the larger category of four-legged creatures. DUCK, which is a two-legged creature, must therefore be paired with the only other two-legged creature, which is MAN.

69. **(b)** This is a grammatical analogy. WHO is nominative and WHOM is objective. Likewise, I is nominative and ME is objective.

70. **(a)** The relationship between the words of the given pair is one of characteristic. CONTUMACIOUS (an adjective meaning rebellious) describes a RENEGADE (a noun meaning one who rejects lawful or conventional behavior). Similarly, OBSEQUIOUS (an adjective meaning subservient) describes a SYCOPHANT (a noun meaning servile flatterer or parasite).

71. **(d)** A DOWSER divines the presence of water or minerals by means of a ROD as a GEOMANCER divines by means of geographical features or CONFIGURATIONS.

72. **(a)** The relationship is that of child to parent. ATHENA was the child of ZEUS; JESUS was the child of MARY.

73. **(c)** The objective of a GAME is to WIN as the objective of MEDICINE is to CURE. The relationship is that of objective to action.

74. **(a)** SAFARI means journey in the SWAHILI language. SALAAM is an ARABIC greeting. This is an answer you should be able to get by elimination. Swahili is a language, and Arabic is the only language offered among the choices.

75. **(d)** Acidity and alkalinity are expressed on a pH scale whose values run from 0 to 14, with 7 representing neutrality. Numbers less than 7 indicate increasing acidity and numbers greater than 7 represent increasing alkalinity. Therefore, ACID : ALKALI :: 6 (a pH indicating mild acidity) : 8 (a pH indicating mild alkalinity).

76. **(c)** Stalagmites and stalactites are deposits of calcium carbonate formed by the dripping of calcareous water in a cave. A STALAGMITE grows up from the floor of the cave, while a STALACTITE hangs down from the ceiling of the cave. Similarly, a PEDESTAL is an architectural support or base that raises something up from the ground and a CHANDELIER is a lighting fixture that hangs down from the ceiling.

77. **(c)** BONA FIDE (meaning in good faith) and IN TOTO (meaning in full) are Latin words which have been borrowed intact for use in English. AVANT-GARDE (meaning pioneer) and CARTE BLANCHE (meaning blanket permission) are French words which have been borrowed intact for use in English. Eureka is borrowed from the Greek; status quo, from Latin; and ersatz, from German.

78. **(d)** This is an analogy of place or of whole to part. The land bordering the SEA is the COAST as the land bordering a RIVER is a BANK.

79. **(c)** In this grammatical analogy, AMOUNT refers to quantity or bulk while NUMBER refers to items that can be counted one by one. Similarly, LESS refers to quantity and FEWER to items that can be counted.

80. **(c)** The relationship expressed by the given word pair is one of measurement. VOLUME may be measured in CUBIC METERs as CAPACITY may be measured in LITERs.

81. **(a)** ADUMBRATE and FORESHADOW are synonyms. The only synonym offered for FORBEAR (meaning to hold back or abstain) is REFRAIN.

82. **(c)** This is an analogy of action to object. One may CHAMPION a CAUSE as one may DRAFT a LETTER. This is another of those analogy questions which require mental flexibility. If you insist upon thinking of *champion* as a noun, for indeed a champion may have a cause, you cannot find a parallel noun on the other side of the analogy. Once you switch your thinking and recognize that *champion* is being used as a verb, it is easy to find a parallel activity the object of which is a letter.

83. **(a)** SUN is necessary to the formation of SHADOWS as WATER is necessary to the formation of CLOUDS. C : A :: D : B.

84. **(c)** When it is WINTER in BOSTON, it is SUMMER in SÃO PAULO since the seasons are reversed in the northern and southern hemispheres.

85. **(d)** A CIRCLE is a plane figure; a SPHERE, the corresponding solid figure. A SQUARE is a plane figure and a CUBE the corresponding solid figure.

86. **(c)** KINETIC is an adjective meaning of or relating to MOTION as PISCATORIAL is an adjective meaning of or relating to FISH.

87. **(d)** During the process of RESPIRATION, living things take in oxygen and give off CO_2 and water. During the process of PHOTOSYNTHESIS, green plants take in carbon dioxide and water and give off O_2.

88. **(c)** The relationship existing between the terms of the given word pair is one of purpose since SAND is used to make GLASS. Similarly, CLAY is used to make BRICK.

89. **(d)** ALASKA was purchased from RUSSIA (in 1867) as the area known as the LOUISIANA PURCHASE was purchased from FRANCE (in 1803).

90. **(d)** The relationship between Roman numerals X (10) and M (1000) is 1 to 100. The same relationship exists between the Roman numerals I (1) and C (100).

91. **(d)** PUCCINI created OPERAS as BALANCHINE created BALLETS. Although Pavlova was a famous ballerina and "Giselle" is the name of a well-known ballet, only Balanchine (as a choreographer) stands in the same relationship to the ballet as Puccini (as a composer) stands in relationship to opera.

92. **(c)** A characteristic of a POLTROON (coward) is a feeling of TERROR as a characteristic of a PARANOIAC is a feeling of PERSECUTION.

93. **(c)** The relationship between the terms of the given word pair is one of object to action. However, three of the choices offered are actions one may take on the object letter. Therefore, it is necessary to narrow the relationship to the specific action of closing or securing. A DOOR is secured by a BOLT and a LETTER is secured by a SEAL.

94. **(a)** The relationship is one of an individual to his or her means of payment. An AGENT receives COMMISSIONS (a percentage of the total fees paid) for his or her part in a business transaction. An AUTHOR receives ROYALTIES (a percentage of the total payment made for a work) for his or her part in creating the work sold.

95. **(b)** The OLD VIC is a theater is London; LA SCALA is the Milan opera house. Both are houses in which performances take place. OLD BAILEY is a London court with prison attached; the BASTILLE was a Paris prison.

96. **(d)** Both George ORWELL and Aldous HUXLEY wrote novels with heavy political content set in the future. Both Garry TRUDEAU and Thomas NAST gained fame as political cartoonists.

97. **(d)** ORAL means uttered by the mouth or spoken. AURAL means of or relating to the ear or to the sense of hearing. Therefore, ORAL describes SPEAK as AURAL describes HEAR.

98. **(b)** The formula for a specific ACID is H_2SO_4 (sulphuric acid). The name for a specific ENZYME is AMYLASE.

99. **(c)** This analogy is one of female to male. VIXEN is a female animal and FOX is her male counterpart. DAM is a female animal parent and SIRE is the male counterpart.

100. **(c)** A characteristic of SALIVA is that it lubricates the MOUTH. A characteristic of OIL is that it lubricates a MOTOR.

ANSWER SHEET
MILLER ANALOGIES SAMPLE TEST II

1 Ⓐ Ⓑ Ⓒ Ⓓ   21 Ⓐ Ⓑ Ⓒ Ⓓ   41 Ⓐ Ⓑ Ⓒ Ⓓ   61 Ⓐ Ⓑ Ⓒ Ⓓ   81 Ⓐ Ⓑ Ⓒ Ⓓ
2 Ⓐ Ⓑ Ⓒ Ⓓ   22 Ⓐ Ⓑ Ⓒ Ⓓ   42 Ⓐ Ⓑ Ⓒ Ⓓ   62 Ⓐ Ⓑ Ⓒ Ⓓ   82 Ⓐ Ⓑ Ⓒ Ⓓ
3 Ⓐ Ⓑ Ⓒ Ⓓ   23 Ⓐ Ⓑ Ⓒ Ⓓ   43 Ⓐ Ⓑ Ⓒ Ⓓ   63 Ⓐ Ⓑ Ⓒ Ⓓ   83 Ⓐ Ⓑ Ⓒ Ⓓ
4 Ⓐ Ⓑ Ⓒ Ⓓ   24 Ⓐ Ⓑ Ⓒ Ⓓ   44 Ⓐ Ⓑ Ⓒ Ⓓ   64 Ⓐ Ⓑ Ⓒ Ⓓ   84 Ⓐ Ⓑ Ⓒ Ⓓ
5 Ⓐ Ⓑ Ⓒ Ⓓ   25 Ⓐ Ⓑ Ⓒ Ⓓ   45 Ⓐ Ⓑ Ⓒ Ⓓ   65 Ⓐ Ⓑ Ⓒ Ⓓ   85 Ⓐ Ⓑ Ⓒ Ⓓ
6 Ⓐ Ⓑ Ⓒ Ⓓ   26 Ⓐ Ⓑ Ⓒ Ⓓ   46 Ⓐ Ⓑ Ⓒ Ⓓ   66 Ⓐ Ⓑ Ⓒ Ⓓ   86 Ⓐ Ⓑ Ⓒ Ⓓ
7 Ⓐ Ⓑ Ⓒ Ⓓ   27 Ⓐ Ⓑ Ⓒ Ⓓ   47 Ⓐ Ⓑ Ⓒ Ⓓ   67 Ⓐ Ⓑ Ⓒ Ⓓ   87 Ⓐ Ⓑ Ⓒ Ⓓ
8 Ⓐ Ⓑ Ⓒ Ⓓ   28 Ⓐ Ⓑ Ⓒ Ⓓ   48 Ⓐ Ⓑ Ⓒ Ⓓ   68 Ⓐ Ⓑ Ⓒ Ⓓ   88 Ⓐ Ⓑ Ⓒ Ⓓ
9 Ⓐ Ⓑ Ⓒ Ⓓ   29 Ⓐ Ⓑ Ⓒ Ⓓ   49 Ⓐ Ⓑ Ⓒ Ⓓ   69 Ⓐ Ⓑ Ⓒ Ⓓ   89 Ⓐ Ⓑ Ⓒ Ⓓ
10 Ⓐ Ⓑ Ⓒ Ⓓ   30 Ⓐ Ⓑ Ⓒ Ⓓ   50 Ⓐ Ⓑ Ⓒ Ⓓ   70 Ⓐ Ⓑ Ⓒ Ⓓ   90 Ⓐ Ⓑ Ⓒ Ⓓ
11 Ⓐ Ⓑ Ⓒ Ⓓ   31 Ⓐ Ⓑ Ⓒ Ⓓ   51 Ⓐ Ⓑ Ⓒ Ⓓ   71 Ⓐ Ⓑ Ⓒ Ⓓ   91 Ⓐ Ⓑ Ⓒ Ⓓ
12 Ⓐ Ⓑ Ⓒ Ⓓ   32 Ⓐ Ⓑ Ⓒ Ⓓ   52 Ⓐ Ⓑ Ⓒ Ⓓ   72 Ⓐ Ⓑ Ⓒ Ⓓ   92 Ⓐ Ⓑ Ⓒ Ⓓ
13 Ⓐ Ⓑ Ⓒ Ⓓ   33 Ⓐ Ⓑ Ⓒ Ⓓ   53 Ⓐ Ⓑ Ⓒ Ⓓ   73 Ⓐ Ⓑ Ⓒ Ⓓ   93 Ⓐ Ⓑ Ⓒ Ⓓ
14 Ⓐ Ⓑ Ⓒ Ⓓ   34 Ⓐ Ⓑ Ⓒ Ⓓ   54 Ⓐ Ⓑ Ⓒ Ⓓ   74 Ⓐ Ⓑ Ⓒ Ⓓ   94 Ⓐ Ⓑ Ⓒ Ⓓ
15 Ⓐ Ⓑ Ⓒ Ⓓ   35 Ⓐ Ⓑ Ⓒ Ⓓ   55 Ⓐ Ⓑ Ⓒ Ⓓ   75 Ⓐ Ⓑ Ⓒ Ⓓ   95 Ⓐ Ⓑ Ⓒ Ⓓ
16 Ⓐ Ⓑ Ⓒ Ⓓ   36 Ⓐ Ⓑ Ⓒ Ⓓ   56 Ⓐ Ⓑ Ⓒ Ⓓ   76 Ⓐ Ⓑ Ⓒ Ⓓ   96 Ⓐ Ⓑ Ⓒ Ⓓ
17 Ⓐ Ⓑ Ⓒ Ⓓ   37 Ⓐ Ⓑ Ⓒ Ⓓ   57 Ⓐ Ⓑ Ⓒ Ⓓ   77 Ⓐ Ⓑ Ⓒ Ⓓ   97 Ⓐ Ⓑ Ⓒ Ⓓ
18 Ⓐ Ⓑ Ⓒ Ⓓ   38 Ⓐ Ⓑ Ⓒ Ⓓ   58 Ⓐ Ⓑ Ⓒ Ⓓ   78 Ⓐ Ⓑ Ⓒ Ⓓ   98 Ⓐ Ⓑ Ⓒ Ⓓ
19 Ⓐ Ⓑ Ⓒ Ⓓ   39 Ⓐ Ⓑ Ⓒ Ⓓ   59 Ⓐ Ⓑ Ⓒ Ⓓ   79 Ⓐ Ⓑ Ⓒ Ⓓ   99 Ⓐ Ⓑ Ⓒ Ⓓ
20 Ⓐ Ⓑ Ⓒ Ⓓ   40 Ⓐ Ⓑ Ⓒ Ⓓ   60 Ⓐ Ⓑ Ⓒ Ⓓ   80 Ⓐ Ⓑ Ⓒ Ⓓ   100 Ⓐ Ⓑ Ⓒ Ⓓ

Tear Here

MILLER ANALOGIES
SAMPLE TEST II

Time: 50 Minutes. 100 Questions.

Directions: Each of these test questions consists of three CAPITALIZED words and four lettered words enclosed in parentheses. Two of the capitalized words are related in some way. Find the two related words and establish the nature of the relationship. Then study the four words lettered a, b, c, and d. Select the one lettered word which is related to the remaining capitalized word in the same way that the first two capitalized words are related. Mark the answer sheet for the letter of the word you select.

1. CLOY : (a. collect, b. empty, c. glut, d. spoil) :: ARROGATE : USURP

2. ROBBERY : INCARCERATION :: (a. marking, b. singing, c. sleeping, d. embezzlement) : APPLAUSE

3. ICHTHYOLOGY : (a. insects, b. mammals, c. fish, d. invertebrates) :: ORNITHOLOGY : BIRDS

4. FIRST : PENULTIMATE :: JANUARY : (a. December, b. November, c. February, d. June)

5. HOPE : PLEASURE :: DESPONDENCY : (a. frolic, b. gratification, c. joy, d. anguish)

6. DICHOTOMY : DISSEMBLE :: DIVISION : (a. feign, b. assemble, c. resemble, d. return)

7. LONGFELLOW : WHITMAN :: (a. Tagore, b. Keats, c. Heine, d. Dickens) : TENNYSON

8. MITER : BISHOP :: (a. stole, b. cleric, c. robe, d. biretta) : PRIEST

9. OK : PA :: KS : (a. CT, b. AZ, c. W.V., d. NY)

10. SEED : BREED :: (a. origin, b. specimen, c. need, d. act) : DEED

11. (a. influence, b. compose, c. touch, d. infect) : RESULT :: AFFECT : EFFECT

12. SAUTÉING : COOKERY :: FAGOTING : (a. juggling, b. forestry, c. embroidery, d. medicine)

13. CAMPHOR : AROMATIC :: LILAC : (a. lavender, b. flower, c. fragrant, d. rose)

14. (a. skiers, b. winter, c. athletes, d. blades) : SKATES :: RUNNERS : SLEDS

15. LOCARNO : SWITZERLAND :: ARGONNE : (a. France, b. Quebec, c. Germany, d. Belgium)

16. ARMY : FOOD :: DEFENSE : (a. digestion, b. vegetation, c. nutrition, d. supply)

17. DAVID : (a. Matthew, b. Moses, c. Luke, d. Peter) :: RUTH : JEZEBEL

18. BENEFICENT : INIMICAL :: DELETERIOUS : (a. amicable, b. hostile, c. matchless, d. ordinary)

19. ANEMOMETER : (a. smell, b. texture, c. wind, d. pressure) :: ODOMETER : DISTANCE

20. WHIP : HORN :: CRACK : (a. blow, b. break, c. tattoo, d. march)

21. HILL : MOUNTAIN :: (a. depression, b. discomfort, c. headache, d. fear) : PAIN

22. (a. "The Merry Widow," b. "Naughty Marietta," c. "Iolanthe," d. "Carmen") : "MIKADO" :: "H.M.S. PINAFORE" : "GONDOLIERS"

23. BELL : HOLMES :: (a. Watson, b. Edison, c. Graham, d. Doyle) : WATSON

24. WHEEL : COG :: (a. heaven, b. ribbon, c. rim, d. bulb) : FILAMENT

25. POLICEMAN : (a. convict, b. justice, c. conduct, d. crime) :: DENTIST : CAVITY

26. ROUND : CHUCK :: (a. circle, b. flank, c. chipped, d. throw) : RIB

27. FRACTIOUS : SYSTEMATIC :: DEBILITATE : (a. invigorate, b. undermine, c. diverge, d. annul)

28. FOUR : TWENTY :: (a. two, b. five, c. three, d. seven) : FIFTEEN

29. GROUND CREW : SEMAPHORE :: PILOT : (a. radio, b. airplane, c. stewardess, d. copilot)

30. GLAND : ENDOCRINE :: MUSCLE : (a. hard, b. strong, c. dessicated, d. striated)

31. PROHIBITED : BANNED :: CANONICAL : (a. reputable, b. authoritative, c. referred, d. considered)

32. VIXEN : BACCHUS :: SEAMSTRESS : (a. Ceres, b. Neptune, c. Venus, d. Minerva)

33. ICE : STEAM :: BRICK : (a. straw, b. mortar, c. pole, d. stone)

34. BREATHING : (a. oxygen, b. lungs, c. carbon dioxide, d. nose) :: CRYING : TEARS

35. MARRY : REPENT :: HASTE : (a. contrition, b. delay, c. leisure, d. deliberate)

36. JAMES I : (a. James II, b. George I, c. Elizabeth I, d. Charles I) :: GEORGE V : EDWARD VIII

37. PLANS : ARCHITECT :: TREACHERY : (a. thief, b. traitor, c. cheater, d. killer)

38. LILY : ROSEMARY :: PURITY : (a. lamb, b. squalor, c. remembrance, d. thyme)

39. ANCHOR : KEY :: (a. dock, b. boat, c. prow, d. keel) : CHAIN

40. (a. Scopes, b. Darrow, c. Darwin, d. Jennings) : BRYAN :: SACCO : VANZETTI

41. (a. subterranean, b. subconscious, c. superb, d. advertised) : SUBLIMINAL :: PLETHORIC : SUPERFLUOUS

42. VICTORY : PYRRHIC :: FRUIT : (a. ripe, b. bitter, c. pie, d. tree)

43. TOUCH : DOWN :: (a. walk, b. river, c. home, d. stocking) : RUN

44. MITOSIS : DIVISION :: OSMOSIS : (a. diffusion, b. concentration, c. digestion, d. metamorphosis)

45. SUN : (a. summer, b. tan, c. parasol, d. beach) :: COLD : OVERCOAT

46. PHOEBUS : (a. Helius, b. Eos, c. Diana, d. Perseus) :: SUN : MOON

47. (a. equality, b. generous, c. wantonness, d. goodness) : LIBERTINE :: ADVOCACY : LAWYER

48. POUND : KILOGRAM :: WEIGHT : (a. weight, b. area, c. volume, d. capacity)

49. PRECARIOUS : ZEALOUS :: CERTAIN : (a. apathetic, b. ardent, c. indigent, d. sensitive)

50. PONDER : THOUGHT :: ARBITRATE : (a. endorsement, b. plan, c. argument, d. settlement)

51. OBSTRUCT : IMPENETRABLE :: IMPEDE : (a. forebearing, b. hidden, c. impervious, d. merciful)

52. OCTAVE : SESTET :: (a. scale, b. ending, c. quatrain, d. symphony) : COUPLET

53. NOVEL : (a. epic, b. drama, c. volume, d. story) :: *TOM SAWYER* : *AENEID*

54. PURSER : (a. bank, b. ship, c. race track, d. highway) :: BRAKEMAN : TRAIN

55. DRINK : SECURITY :: THIRST : (a. assuredness, b. stocks, c. fear, d. money)

56. CIRCLE : OVAL :: (a. figure, b. octagon, c. starfish, d. semicircle) : PARALLELOGRAM

57. RESILIENCY : RUBBER :: LAMBENCY : (a. oil, b. sheep, c. candlelight, d. lawn)

58. VIRTUOSO : (a. orchestra, b. home, c. prison, d. college) :: TEACHER : CLASSROOM

59. PLATEN : (a. newspaper, b. algae, c. ribbon, d. giant) :: COMB : COMPACT

60. (a. 4, b. 7, c. 9, d. 14) : 28 :: 11 : 44

61. CAPE : WADI :: PROMONTORY : (a. gully, b. waterfall, c. meadow, d. fen)

62. BINDING : BOOK :: WELDING : (a. box, b. tank, c. chair, d. wire)

63. SERFDOM : FEUDALISM :: ENTREPRENEURSHIP : (a. laissez-faire, b. captain, c. radical, d. capitalism)

64. (a. bassos, b. dynamos, c. heroes, d. solos) : EMBARGOES :: VOLCANOES : TOMATOES

65. FOAL : HORSE :: CYGNET : (a. ring, b. fish, c. swan, d. constellation)

66. FRANCHISE : (a. license, b. commerce, c. separate, d. freedom) :: TYRANNY : DISSENT

67. HOUSE : BUILD :: TRENCH : (a. dig, b. trap, c. obliterate, d. dry)

68. CELL : WORKER :: ORGANISM : (a. occupation, b. proletariat, c. product, d. nation)

69. ANGLO-SAXON : ENGLISH :: LATIN : (a. Roman, b. Greek, c. Italian, d. Mediterranean)

70. METRO : (a. Paris, b. Rome, c. Moscow, d. Tokyo) :: UNDERGROUND : LONDON

71. FETISH : TALISMAN :: FEALTY : (a. allegiance, b. faith, c. payment, d. real estate)

72. ACCELERATOR : (a. cylinder, b. inertia, c. motion, d. exhaust) :: CATALYST : CHANGE

73. INTELLIGENCE : UNDERSTANDING :: CONFUSION : (a. bemusement, b. pleasure, c. school, d. unhappiness)

74. TALKING : YELLING :: GIGGLING : (a. rejoicing, b. laughing, c. chuckling, d. sneering)

75. 49 : 7 :: (a. 98, b. 103, c. 94, d. 144) : 12

76. (a. Chrysler, b. mink, c. chauffeur, d. Boeing) : CADILLAC :: BEAVER : CHEVROLET

77. BREAK : BROKEN :: FLY : (a. flied, b. flew, c. flown, d. flying)

78. DEFALCATE : EXCULPATE :: EMBEZZLEMENT : (a. blame, b. uncover, c. exoneration, d. divulge)

79. SAW : (a. teeth, b. knife, c. board, d. blade) :: SCISSORS : CLOTH

80. PEDAL : PIANO :: BRIDGE : (a. case, b. tune, c. rosin, d. violin)

81. BUCOLIC : CIMMERIAN :: PEACEFUL : (a. warlike, b. tenebrous, c. doubtful, d. smirking)

82. FLATTERY : (a. praise, b. self-interest, c. honesty, d. openness) :: FLIGHT : SAFETY

83. PRAYER : (a. church, b. bible, c. religion, d. fulfillment) :: RESEARCH : DISCOVERY

84. PAYMENT : PREMIUM :: DEBT : (a. cracker, b. prize, c. insurance, d. scarcity)

85. SACRIFICE : HIT :: STEAL : (a. leave, b. slay, c. walk, d. rob)

86. (a. clap, b. play, c. doom, d. fork) : MOOD :: SLEEK : KEELS

87. DEMOLISH : BUILDING :: (a. sail, b. raze, c. dock, d. scuttle) : SHIP

88. LOGGIA : JALOUSIE :: GALLERY : (a. lintel, b. dowel, c. jamb, d. shutter)

89. PAGE : CUB :: (a. book, b. paper, c. herald, d. knight) : REPORTER

90. VIRGO : TAURUS :: SEPTEMBER : (a. May, b. January, c. June, d. November)

91. FELICITY : CONGENIAL :: BLISS : (a. clever, b. compatible, c. fierce, d. unfriendly)

92. WHEEL : FENDER :: (a. paper, b. heading, c. letter, d. health) : SALUTATION

93. REQUEST : VISIT :: DEMAND : (a. return, b. welcome, c. invasion, d. house)

94. DENOUEMENT : (a. climax, b. outcome, c. complication, d. untying) :: DEBIT : CREDIT

95. STRAIGHT : POKER :: SMASH : (a. hit, b. tennis, c. ruin, d. bat)

96. (a. miser, b. sandwich, c. surprise, d. tight) : SCROOGE :: LYNCH : GUILLOTINE

97. VALLEY : GORGE :: MOUNTAIN : (a. hill, b. cliff, c. acme, d. high)

98. ALPHA : OMEGA :: MERCURY : (a. Saturn, b. planet, c. Pluto, d. Venus)

99. CHIFFON : TWEED :: (a. synthetic, b. sheer, c. dark, d. textured) : ROUGH

100. SIDEREAL : (a. side, b. part, c. stars, d. planets) :: LUNAR : MOON

ANSWER KEY FOR MILLER ANALOGIES SAMPLE TEST II

1. c	21. b	41. b	61. a	81. b
2. b	22. c	42. b	62. b	82. b
3. c	23. a	43. c	63. d	83. d
4. b	24. d	44. a	64. c	84. c
5. d	25. d	45. c	65. c	85. c
6. a	26. b	46. c	66. d	86. c
7. b	27. a	47. c	67. a	87. d
8. d	28. c	48. a	68. b	88. d
9. d	29. a	49. a	69. c	89. d
10. c	30. d	50. d	70. a	90. a
11. a	31. b	51. c	71. a	91. b
12. c	32. b	52. c	72. c	92. b
13. c	33. a	53. a	73. a	93. c
14. d	34. c	54. b	74. b	94. c
15. a	35. c	55. c	75. d	95. b
16. c	36. d	56. b	76. b	96. b
17. b	37. b	57. c	77. c	97. b
18. a	38. c	58. a	78. c	98. c
19. c	39. b	59. c	79. c	99. b
20. a	40. b	60. b	80. d	100. c

EXPLANATORY ANSWERS FOR MILLER ANALOGIES SAMPLE TEST II

1. **(c)** ARROGATE and USURP, which both mean to sieze without justification, are related as synonyms; the only synonym for CLOY, meaning to satiate, is GLUT.

2. **(b)** This is a cause-and-effect analogy. ROBBERY can result in INCARCERATION, and SINGING can result in APPLAUSE.

3. **(c)** The relationship is one of classification. ICHTHYOLOGY is the study of FISH, and ORNITHOLOGY is the study of BIRDS.

4. **(b)** This is a sequence relationship. JANUARY is the FIRST month of a year, and NOVEMBER is the PENULTIMATE, or next to last, month of a year.

5. **(d)** HOPE and DESPONDENCY are contrasting concepts. The concept that contrasts with PLEASURE is ANGUISH.

6. **(a)** DICHOTOMY and DIVISION are synonyms; a synonym for DISSEMBLE (meaning to disguise) is FEIGN.

7. **(b)** The relationship between LONGFELLOW and WHITMAN is that both of them were American poets. Since TENNYSON was an English poet, the task is to determine who is another English poet. KEATS is the only choice. Dickens was an English novelist, Heine a German poet and philosopher, and Tagore a Hindu poet.

8. **(d)** The analogy is one of association. A MITER is a head ornament usually worn by a BISHOP; a BIRETTA is a cap characteristically worn by a PRIEST. A stole and a robe are also worn by a priest, but biretta more specifically completes the correspondence with miter as headgear.

9. **(d)** OK and KS are both proper post office abbreviations for states (Oklahoma and Kansas). Oklahoma is also on the southern border of Kansas; PA (Pennsylvania in post office abbreviation) is on the southern border of NY (New York). WV (West Virginia) also borders upon PA, but its geographic relationship to PA is the reverse of that of KS to OK. KS is to the north of OK; WV is to the south of PA.

10. **(c)** This is a nonsemantic analogy. SEED, BREED, DEED, and NEED all rhyme.

11. **(a)** This is an analogy of synonyms. AFFECT is a verb meaning to INFLUENCE. EFFECT as a noun means RESULT. (The verb *effect* means *to bring about*.)

12. **(c)** The relationship is one of action to object. Since SAUTÉING is one act or form of COOKERY, the task is to determine what FAGOTING is an act or form of. The correct answer is EMBROIDERY.

13. **(c)** AROMATIC is a characteristic of CAMPHOR; a characteristic of LILAC is FRAGRANT.

14. **(d)** This is a part-to-whole analogy. BLADES are parts of SKATES; RUNNERS are parts of SLEDS.

15. **(a)** The relationship is one of place. LOCARNO is located in SWITZERLAND; the ARGONNE, a region which saw fierce fighting during the First World War, is in FRANCE near the Belgian border.

16. **(c)** This is a purpose analogy. A purpose of an ARMY is to provide DEFENSE; a purpose of FOOD is to provide NUTRITION.

17. **(b)** RUTH and JEZEBEL were both women who figured in the Old Testament. Since DAVID was a man in the Old Testament, the task is to find another man who was mentioned in the Old Testament. MOSES is the correct choice.

18. **(a)** BENEFICENT (beneficial) and DELETERIOUS (harmful) are antonyms. The only available antonym for INIMICAL (hostile) is AMICABLE (friendly).

19. **(c)** The analogy is one of function. An ODOMETER measures DISTANCE; an ANEMOMETER measures the velocity of the WIND.

20. **(a)** The relationship is one of object to action. One may CRACK a WHIP; one may BLOW a HORN.

21. **(b)** In this analogy of degree, a HILL is a smaller version of a MOUNTAIN; DISCOMFORT is a lesser version of PAIN. Note that a headache and depression are specific types of pain or discomfort, not degrees.

22. **(c)** The relationship is one of classification or part to part. The "MIKADO," "H.M.S. PINAFORE" and "GONDOLIERS" are all operettas written by Gilbert and Sullivan. "IOLANTHE" is the only other Gilbert and Sullivan operetta offered among the choices.

23. **(a)** This analogy is based upon the relationship of an individual to his assistant. Sherlock HOLMES' name is often paired with that of his loyal and admiring assistant, WATSON. The first person to hear a message over the newly invented telephone was Alexander Graham BELL's assistant, WATSON.

24. **(d)** This is a part-to-whole relationship. A COG is part of a WHEEL just as a FILAMENT is a part of a light BULB.

25. **(d)** One characteristic of a DENTIST is that he fights a CAVITY. Similarly, a characteristic of a POLICEMAN is that he fights CRIME.

26. **(b)** Every term in this analogy, ROUND, CHUCK and RIB, is a cut of beefsteak. Therefore, the missing term must be FLANK.

27. **(a)** The given pair are related as antonyms since FRACTIOUS means wild or unruly, the opposite of SYSTEMATIC. DEBILITATE, which means to weaken, must be paired with its opposite, INVIGORATE, which means to strengthen.

28. **(c)** In this numerical analogy, the relationship between FOUR and TWENTY is a one-to-five ratio; the number with the same ratio to FIFTEEN is THREE. The sentence by which you solve this analogy question is: "Twenty divided by five equals four; fifteen divided by five equals three."

29. **(a)** The analogy is based upon actor and object or, better still, worker and tool. The GROUND CREW gives messages to the cockpit crew by way of SEMAPHORE flags or lights; the PILOT transmits messages by way of RADIO.

30. **(d)** ENDOCRINE is one type of GLAND; one type of MUSCLE is STRIATED.

31. **(b)** PROHIBITED and BANNED are related as synonyms; a synonym for CANONICAL is AUTHORITATIVE.

32. **(b)** The relationship between VIXEN and SEAMSTRESS is one of gender since both are female. Since BACCHUS is masculine (the Roman god of wine), the task is to find another male among the answer choices, and NEPTUNE (the Roman god of the sea) is the only possibility.

33. **(a)** This analogy has to do with characteristics. ICE is solid; STEAM has little substance. BRICK is solid; by comparison with brick, STRAW has little substance.

34. **(c)** The relationship is action to object since CRYING releases TEARS. The task, then, is to determine what BREATHING releases. The process of respiration involves the intake of oxygen and the release of CARBON DIOXIDE.

35. **(c)** In this adage analogy, the familiar saying is "MARRY in HASTE; REPENT at LEISURE."

36. **(d)** The relationship is one of sequence. The English king EDWARD VIII was followed by GEORGE V. To complete the analogy, you must choose CHARLES I, successor to JAMES I.

37. **(b)** The analogy is based upon association. PLANS are associated with an ARCHITECT as TREACHERY is associated with a TRAITOR.

38. **(c)** This analogy is based on symbolism or simple association. The LILY is a symbol of PURITY; ROSEMARY is for REMEMBRANCE.

39. **(b)** A KEY hangs from a CHAIN; an ANCHOR hangs from a BOAT.

40. **(b)** SACCO and VENZETTI are associated as co-defendants in a famous trial. BRYAN and DARROW are associated as opposing counsel in the famous trial of John Scopes who was tried for teaching the theory of evolution in defiance of Tennessee law.

41. **(b)** PLETHORIC and SUPERFLUOUS are synonyms for excess; a synonym for SUBLIMINAL is SUBCONSCIOUS, meaning outside the area of conscious awareness.

42. **(b)** A Pyrrhic victory is a bitter one since it means a victory gained at ruinous loss; therefore, PYRRHIC is an undesirable characteristic of VICTORY. A similar undesirable characteristic of FRUIT is BITTERNESS.

43. **(c)** The relationship between TOUCH and DOWN is grammatical since these words can be used by themselves and also as a common sports-

oriented compound word; therefore, the task is to determine which word can be used by itself and also as part of a common sports-oriented compound word with RUN. HOME is the correct choice.

44. **(a)** The relationship is one of part to whole. MITOSIS is one kind of DIVISION, specifically the series of processes that takes place in the nucleus of a dividing cell which results in the formation of two new nuclei each having the same number of chromosomes as the parent nucleus. OSMOSIS is one kind of DIFFUSION, specifically diffusion through a semipermeable membrane separating a solution of lesser solute concentration from one of greater concentration to equalize the concentration of the two solutions.

45. **(c)** The purpose or function of an OVERCOAT is to protect one from the COLD; a PARASOL protects one from the SUN.

46. **(c)** This is a mythological analogy. PHOEBUS is the god of the SUN; DIANA is the goddess of the MOON.

47. **(c)** The relationship is one of characteristic. One characteristic of a LAWYER is his ADVOCACY or support of his client; a characteristic of a LIBERTINE, or one who leads a dissolute life, is WANTONNESS.

48. **(a)** This is a descriptive analogy. A POUND is a measurement of WEIGHT; a KILOGRAM is also a measure of WEIGHT.

49. **(a)** PRECARIOUS and CERTAIN are antonyms; an antonym for ZEALOUS is APATHETIC.

50. **(d)** The correspondence is one of action to object. To PONDER aids THOUGHT: to ARBITRATE aids a SETTLEMENT.

51. **(c)** OBSTRUCT and IMPEDE are synonyms; a synonym for IMPENETRABLE is IMPERVIOUS.

52. **(c)** This is an analogy of parts. OCTAVE, SESTET, and COUPLET are all parts of a sonnet. Only QUATRAIN among the choices is also a part of a sonnet. If you know nothing about sonnets, you might notice that the three capitalized terms all have something to do with numbers—octave, 8; sestet, 6; couplet, 2—and so choose as the fourth term quatrain, 4.

53. **(a)** The relationship between *TOM SAWYER* and the *AENEID* is one of classification. *TOM SAWYER* is a NOVEL and the *AENEID* is an EPIC.

54. **(b)** The correspondence is one of association or place. A BRAKEMAN is associated with a TRAIN; a PURSER is associated with a SHIP.

55. **(c)** DRINK serves the function of relieving THIRST; SECURITY serves the function of relieving FEAR.

56. **(b)** CIRCLE and OVAL are both figures enclosed with one continuous curved side. Since a PARALLELOGRAM is a figure enclosed with straight sides, the task is to find another straight-sided figure. OCTAGON is the only available choice.

57. **(c)** RESILIENCY is a characteristic of RUBBER; LAMBENCY, which means brightness or flickering, is a characteristic of CANDLELIGHT.

58. **(a)** A TEACHER works in a CLASSROOM; therefore, the task is to determine where a VIRTUOSO works. Among the choices, an ORCHESTRA is the most likely place.

59. **(c)** In this part-to-part analogy, a COMB and COMPACT are usually parts of the contents of a purse; a PLATEN, or roller, and a RIBBON are parts of the typewriter.

60. **(b)** The numerical relationship between 11 and 44 is a ratio of 1 to 4; therefore, the task is to determine what number when paired with 28 is also in the ratio of 1 to 4. The answer is 7. The sentence is: "$44 \div 11 = 4$ just as $28 \div 7 = 4$."

61. **(a)** CAPE and PROMONTORY are synonyms meaning a point of land jutting into the sea; a synonym for WADI is GULLY.

62. **(b)** BINDING secures or holds together a BOOK; WELDING secures or holds together a TANK.

63. **(d)** SERFDOM is a characteristic of FEUDALISM; ENTREPRENEURSHIP is a characteristic of CAPITALISM. Laissez-faire may be an aspect of both entrepreneurship and of capitalism but in creating an analogy, *capitalism* forms a much better parallel with *feudalism*.

64. **(c)** The relationship between VOLCANOES and TOMATOES is grammatical. Each is a plural formed by adding *es*. Since EMBARGOES is also a plural formed by adding *es*, the task is to find another word that also forms its plural this way. HEROES is the correct choice.

65. **(c)** A FOAL is a young HORSE; a CYGNET is a young SWAN. The relationship is one of young to old or sequence.

66. **(d)** This analogy is one of cause and effect. TYRANNY often leads to DISSENT; a FRANCHISE, a right or immunity from some restriction, leads to FREEDOM to vote or to act. A very specific type of franchise, a right to market a product under a well-known name, leads to commerce. This specificity is not called for.

67. **(a)** The relationship is object to action. A HOUSE is something to BUILD; a TRENCH is something to DIG.

68. **(b)** The correspondence is one of part to whole. A CELL is part of an ORGANISM; a WORKER is part of the PROLETARIAT. A worker

may also be part of a nation, but PROLETARIAT is more specifically related to a WORKER.

69. **(c)** This is a sequence relationship. ANGLO-SAXON is an early form of ENGLISH; LATIN is an early form of ITALIAN.

70. **(a)** The subway in LONDON is called the UNDERGROUND; the subway in PARIS is called the METRO.

71. **(a)** FETISH and TALISMAN are synonyms; a synonym for FEALTY is ALLEGIANCE.

72. **(c)** The relationship is that of cause-and-effect as a CATALYST causes CHANGE, and an ACCELERATOR causes MOTION.

73. **(a)** UNDERSTANDING is a characteristic of INTELLIGENCE; a characteristic of confusion is BEMUSEMENT. Unhappiness could also be a characteristic, but BEMUSEMENT is more specifically connected to CONFUSION.

74. **(b)** YELLING is a greater degree of TALKING; a greater degree of GIGGLING is LAUGHING. Chuckling, while not exactly a synonym for giggling, is of the same degree. Rejoicing is more inclusive than laughing; it adds a dimension not called for in an analogy that begins "talking : yelling" and which offers a more specific choice.

75. **(d)** 7 squared is 49; 12 squared is 144.

76. **(b)** The correspondence is one of part to part. CHEVROLET and CADILLAC are both types of automobiles. Since a BEAVER is a type of animal, to complete the analogy another type of animal must be selected. MINK is the only available choice.

77. **(c)** In this grammatical analogy, the past participle of BREAK is BROKEN; the past participle of FLY is FLOWN.

78. **(c)** This is an action-to-object analogy. To DEFALCATE is an act of EMBEZZLEMENT; to EXCULPATE is an act of EXONERATION.

79. **(c)** The relationship is one of purpose since the purpose of SCISSORS is to cut CLOTH just as the purpose of a SAW is to cut a BOARD.

80. **(d)** A PEDAL is part of a PIANO; a BRIDGE is part of a VIOLIN.

81. **(b)** BUCOLIC and PEACEFUL are synonyms since BUCOLIC refers to pastoral and peaceful scenes; a synonym of CIMMERIAN, meaning shrouded in gloom and darkness, is TENEBROUS.

82. **(b)** A purpose of FLIGHT is SAFETY; a purpose of FLATTERY is SELF-INTEREST.

83. **(d)** The relationship is one of purpose since the aim of RESEARCH is DISCOVERY; the aim of PRAYER is FULFILLMENT.

84. **(c)** The correspondence is one of association since PAYMENT is the term applied to money expended to reduce a DEBT just as PREMIUM is the term applied to money expended to obtain INSURANCE.

85. **(c)** SACRIFICE, HIT, and STEAL are all plays in baseball games. Among the choices only WALK is another type of baseball play.

86. **(c)** The relationship is nonsemantic. SLEEK spelled backwards is KEELS; MOOD spelled backwards is DOOM. Actually, once you have ascertained that there is no meaningful nor grammatical relationship among the three capitalized terms, you need only note that all three contain double letters and that only one choice has double letters.

87. **(d)** The relationship is action to object. To destroy a BUILDING you can DEMOLISH it; to destroy a SHIP you can SCUTTLE it.

88. **(d)** LOGGIA and GALLERY are both types of porches; since JALOUSIE is a type of blind, the task is to find another type of blind, and SHUTTER is the correct choice.

89. **(d)** The relationship is one of degree. A CUB is a young REPORTER; a PAGE is a young KNIGHT.

90. **(a)** The zodiac sign VIRGO is associated with the month of SEPTEMBER; TAURUS is associated with MAY.

91. **(b)** FELICITY and BLISS are synonyms; a synonym for CONGENIAL is COMPATIBLE.

92. **(b)** Both WHEEL and FENDER are parts of a larger automotive unit; a SALUTATION and a HEADING are parts of a letter.

93. **(c)** The relationship is one of degree. REQUEST is a polite term, and a DEMAND can be an unpleasant request. VISIT is a polite term so the task is to find a word that denotes an unpleasant visit. INVASION is the correct choice.

94. **(c)** DEBIT and CREDIT are antonyms; an antonym for DENOUEMENT is COMPLICATION.

95. **(b)** A STRAIGHT is a characteristic of a POKER game; a SMASH is a characteristic stroke in a game of TENNIS.

96. **(b)** Every term in this analogy is a word derived from a person's name. SCROOGE comes from Dickens' Ebenezer Scrooge in *A Christmas Carol;* LYNCH, to put to death by mob action, comes from a Judge Lynch; a GUILLOTINE takes its name from Dr. Joseph Guillotin.

Among the choices only SANDWICH describes both a thing and a person from which it takes its name. The Earl of Sandwich is said to have been the first to put meat between slices of bread.

97. **(b)** A GORGE is a steep part of a VALLEY; a CLIFF is a steep part of a MOUNTAIN.

98. **(c)** The relationship is one of sequence. Just as ALPHA and OMEGA are the first and last letters in the Greek alphabet, MERCURY and PLUTO are respectively the planets closest to and farthest from the sun.

99. **(b)** This analogy is one of characteristic. A characteristic of TWEED is that it is ROUGH; a characteristic of CHIFFON is that it is SHEER.

100. **(c)** The relationship is one of association. LUNAR is associated with the MOON: SIDEREAL is related to the STARS.

ANSWER SHEET
MILLER ANALOGIES SAMPLE TEST III

1 Ⓐ Ⓑ Ⓒ Ⓓ   21 Ⓐ Ⓑ Ⓒ Ⓓ   41 Ⓐ Ⓑ Ⓒ Ⓓ   61 Ⓐ Ⓑ Ⓒ Ⓓ   81 Ⓐ Ⓑ Ⓒ Ⓓ

2 Ⓐ Ⓑ Ⓒ Ⓓ   22 Ⓐ Ⓑ Ⓒ Ⓓ   42 Ⓐ Ⓑ Ⓒ Ⓓ   62 Ⓐ Ⓑ Ⓒ Ⓓ   82 Ⓐ Ⓑ Ⓒ Ⓓ

3 Ⓐ Ⓑ Ⓒ Ⓓ   23 Ⓐ Ⓑ Ⓒ Ⓓ   43 Ⓐ Ⓑ Ⓒ Ⓓ   63 Ⓐ Ⓑ Ⓒ Ⓓ   83 Ⓐ Ⓑ Ⓒ Ⓓ

4 Ⓐ Ⓑ Ⓒ Ⓓ   24 Ⓐ Ⓑ Ⓒ Ⓓ   44 Ⓐ Ⓑ Ⓒ Ⓓ   64 Ⓐ Ⓑ Ⓒ Ⓓ   84 Ⓐ Ⓑ Ⓒ Ⓓ

5 Ⓐ Ⓑ Ⓒ Ⓓ   25 Ⓐ Ⓑ Ⓒ Ⓓ   45 Ⓐ Ⓑ Ⓒ Ⓓ   65 Ⓐ Ⓑ Ⓒ Ⓓ   85 Ⓐ Ⓑ Ⓒ Ⓓ

6 Ⓐ Ⓑ Ⓒ Ⓓ   26 Ⓐ Ⓑ Ⓒ Ⓓ   46 Ⓐ Ⓑ Ⓒ Ⓓ   66 Ⓐ Ⓑ Ⓒ Ⓓ   86 Ⓐ Ⓑ Ⓒ Ⓓ

7 Ⓐ Ⓑ Ⓒ Ⓓ   27 Ⓐ Ⓑ Ⓒ Ⓓ   47 Ⓐ Ⓑ Ⓒ Ⓓ   67 Ⓐ Ⓑ Ⓒ Ⓓ   87 Ⓐ Ⓑ Ⓒ Ⓓ

8 Ⓐ Ⓑ Ⓒ Ⓓ   28 Ⓐ Ⓑ Ⓒ Ⓓ   48 Ⓐ Ⓑ Ⓒ Ⓓ   68 Ⓐ Ⓑ Ⓒ Ⓓ   88 Ⓐ Ⓑ Ⓒ Ⓓ

9 Ⓐ Ⓑ Ⓒ Ⓓ   29 Ⓐ Ⓑ Ⓒ Ⓓ   49 Ⓐ Ⓑ Ⓒ Ⓓ   69 Ⓐ Ⓑ Ⓒ Ⓓ   89 Ⓐ Ⓑ Ⓒ Ⓓ

10 Ⓐ Ⓑ Ⓒ Ⓓ   30 Ⓐ Ⓑ Ⓒ Ⓓ   50 Ⓐ Ⓑ Ⓒ Ⓓ   70 Ⓐ Ⓑ Ⓒ Ⓓ   90 Ⓐ Ⓑ Ⓒ Ⓓ

11 Ⓐ Ⓑ Ⓒ Ⓓ   31 Ⓐ Ⓑ Ⓒ Ⓓ   51 Ⓐ Ⓑ Ⓒ Ⓓ   71 Ⓐ Ⓑ Ⓒ Ⓓ   91 Ⓐ Ⓑ Ⓒ Ⓓ

12 Ⓐ Ⓑ Ⓒ Ⓓ   32 Ⓐ Ⓑ Ⓒ Ⓓ   52 Ⓐ Ⓑ Ⓒ Ⓓ   72 Ⓐ Ⓑ Ⓒ Ⓓ   92 Ⓐ Ⓑ Ⓒ Ⓓ

13 Ⓐ Ⓑ Ⓒ Ⓓ   33 Ⓐ Ⓑ Ⓒ Ⓓ   53 Ⓐ Ⓑ Ⓒ Ⓓ   73 Ⓐ Ⓑ Ⓒ Ⓓ   93 Ⓐ Ⓑ Ⓒ Ⓓ

14 Ⓐ Ⓑ Ⓒ Ⓓ   34 Ⓐ Ⓑ Ⓒ Ⓓ   54 Ⓐ Ⓑ Ⓒ Ⓓ   74 Ⓐ Ⓑ Ⓒ Ⓓ   94 Ⓐ Ⓑ Ⓒ Ⓓ

15 Ⓐ Ⓑ Ⓒ Ⓓ   35 Ⓐ Ⓑ Ⓒ Ⓓ   55 Ⓐ Ⓑ Ⓒ Ⓓ   75 Ⓐ Ⓑ Ⓒ Ⓓ   95 Ⓐ Ⓑ Ⓒ Ⓓ

16 Ⓐ Ⓑ Ⓒ Ⓓ   36 Ⓐ Ⓑ Ⓒ Ⓓ   56 Ⓐ Ⓑ Ⓒ Ⓓ   76 Ⓐ Ⓑ Ⓒ Ⓓ   96 Ⓐ Ⓑ Ⓒ Ⓓ

17 Ⓐ Ⓑ Ⓒ Ⓓ   37 Ⓐ Ⓑ Ⓒ Ⓓ   57 Ⓐ Ⓑ Ⓒ Ⓓ   77 Ⓐ Ⓑ Ⓒ Ⓓ   97 Ⓐ Ⓑ Ⓒ Ⓓ

18 Ⓐ Ⓑ Ⓒ Ⓓ   38 Ⓐ Ⓑ Ⓒ Ⓓ   58 Ⓐ Ⓑ Ⓒ Ⓓ   78 Ⓐ Ⓑ Ⓒ Ⓓ   98 Ⓐ Ⓑ Ⓒ Ⓓ

19 Ⓐ Ⓑ Ⓒ Ⓓ   39 Ⓐ Ⓑ Ⓒ Ⓓ   59 Ⓐ Ⓑ Ⓒ Ⓓ   79 Ⓐ Ⓑ Ⓒ Ⓓ   99 Ⓐ Ⓑ Ⓒ Ⓓ

20 Ⓐ Ⓑ Ⓒ Ⓓ   40 Ⓐ Ⓑ Ⓒ Ⓓ   60 Ⓐ Ⓑ Ⓒ Ⓓ   80 Ⓐ Ⓑ Ⓒ Ⓓ   100 Ⓐ Ⓑ Ⓒ Ⓓ

Tear Here

MILLER ANALOGIES
SAMPLE TEST III

Time: 50 Minutes. 100 Questions.

Directions: Each of these test questions consists of three CAPITALIZED words and four lettered words enclosed in parentheses. Two of the capitalized words are related in some way. Find the two related words and establish the nature of the relationship. Then study the four words lettered a, b, c, and d. Select the one lettered word which is related to the remaining capitalized word in the same way that the first two capitalized words are related. Mark the answer sheet for the letter of the word you select.

1. SCEPTER : AUTHORITY :: SCALES : (a. weight, b. justice, c. commerce, d. greed)

2. STONEHENGE : EASTER ISLAND :: (a. yeti, b. dodo, c. nene, d. rhea) : NESSIE

3. WORM : MOUSE :: BIRD : (a. man, b. snake, c. rodent, d. cheese)

4. (a. artist, b. description, c. narration, d. personality) : CHARACTERIZATION :: PICTURE : PORTRAIT

5. (a. orate, b. sing, c. mumble, d. speak) : TALK :: SCRAWL : WRITE

6. LYNDON JOHNSON : JOHN F. KENNEDY :: ANDREW JOHNSON : (a. Ulysses S. Grant, b. Abraham Lincoln, c. Martin Van Buren, d. William Pierce)

7. 46 : 39 :: (a. 61, b. 42, c. 76, d. 39) : 54

8. STEAM : WATER :: (a. lake, b. cloud, c. salt, d. tide) : OCEAN

9. SODIUM : SALT :: OXYGEN : (a. acetylene, b. carbon tetrachloride, c. water, d. ammonia)

10. (a. theft, b. notoriety, c. police, d. jail) : CRIME :: CEMETERY : DEATH

11. GRASS : (a. cow, b. onion, c. lettuce, d. earth) :: SNOW : MILK

12. HAND : (a. girth, b. fingers, c. horse, d. glove) :: LIGHT-YEAR : SPACE

13. QUISLING : CHAMBERLAIN :: COLLABORATION : (a. appeasement, b. negotiation, c. rejection, d. diplomacy)

14. PICCOLO : (a. trumpet, b. trombone, c. horn, d. alto saxophone) :: VIOLIN : BASS

15. DIVULGE : DISCLOSE :: APPRAISAL : (a. revision, b. respite, c. continuation, d. estimate)

16. WEALTH : TANGIBLE :: (a. price, b. gold, c. success, d. gifts) : INTANGIBLE

17. HEMOGLOBIN : COACHES :: BLOOD : (a. train, b. whip, c. fuel, d. road)

18. SHELTER : (a. refuge, b. cave, c. mansion, d. protection) :: BREAD : CAKE

19. AFFLUENT : (a. charity, b. luck, c. misfortune, d. indifference) :: IMPOVERISHED : LAZINESS

20. INNING : BASEBALL :: (a. time, date, c. era, d. chronology) : HISTORY

21. BULWER : (a. Sackville, b. Sherlock, c. Scotland, d. London) :: LYTTON : WEST

22. (a. stifle, b. tell, c. joke, d. offer) : LAUGH :: THROW : JAVELIN

23. CHARLESTON : (a. Tucson, b. Jackson, c. Williamsburg, d. Chicago) :: BOSTON : PHILADELPHIA

24. VINTNER : MINER :: (a. vines, b. wine, c. liquid, d. grape) : ORE

25. (a. jaguar, b. mink, c. cougar, d. chinchilla) : GIRAFFE :: TIGER : ZEBRA

26. (a. Athena, b. Artemis, c. Hera, d. Medea) : FRIGGA :: ZEUS : ODIN

27. 5 : 8 :: 25 : (a. 29, b. 40, c. 60, d. 108)

28. LIMP : CANE :: (a. cell, b. muscle, c. heat, d. cold) : TISSUE

29. CONFESSOR : KINGMAKER :: EDWARD : (a. Warwick, b. Alfred, c. George, d. Gloucester)

30. (a. parchment, b. concrete, c. cardboard, d. timber) : ADOBE :: PAPER : PAPYRUS

31. HANDS : ARMS :: (a. Vulcan, b. crack, c. Diana, d. destiny) : MORPHEUS

32. HYMN : THEIR :: CELL : (a. score, b. peal, c. tree, d. mile)

33. DOG : SWAN :: (a. bark, b. noise, c. days, d. collie) : SONG

34. EINSTEIN : MALTHUS :: RELATIVITY : (a. population, b. religion, c. economy, d. democracy)

35. GALLEY : ROOKERY :: MEAL : (a. ship, b. seal, c. peal, d. chess)

36. PEACH : (a. apple, b. beet, c. grape, d. tomato) :: CHERRY : RADISH

37. LASSITUDE : (a. longitude, b. languor, c. purity, d. alacrity) :: PARSIMONY : BENEFACTION

38. THERMOSTAT : REGULATE :: (a. draft, b. windows, c. insulation, d. thermometer) : CONSERVE

39. MONGREL : PEDIGREE :: BOOR : (a. thoroughbred, b. manners, c. ancestry, d. lineage)

40. (a. earth, b. Venus, c. Sputnik, d. berry) : PLANET :: CANAL : RIVER

41. PIRAEUS : OSTIA :: (a. Athens, b. Florence, c. Milan, d. Crete) : ROME

42. (a. psychology, b. philology, c. philosophy, d. philately) : PHRENOLOGY :: ASTRONOMY : ASTROLOGY

43. ORACLE : LOGICIAN :: INTUITION : (a. guess, b. syllogism, c. faith, d. theory)

44. PELEE : (a. France, b. mountain, c. Martinique, d. island) :: ETNA : SICILY

45. GERONTOLOGY : GENEALOGY :: (a. families, b. aging, c. gerunds, d. birth) : LINEAGE

46. ROMAN : (a. Caesar, b. Rembrandt, c. gladiator, d. Van Dyke) :: NOSE : BEARD

47. HYDROGEN : 1 :: (a. carbon, b. oxygen, c. nitrogen, d. potassium) : 16

48. (a. protein, b. nucleus, c. neutron, d. vacuole) : PROTON :: ARCH : HEEL

49. 19 : 23 :: (a. 7, b. 11, c. 13, d. 17) : 13

50. PANORAMA : ABYSS :: CHURCH DOOR : (a. truth, b. bond, c. speck, d. ocean)

51. (a. Laos, b. Indonesia, c. Afganistan, d. Japan) : INDIA :: NEVADA : COLORADO

52. CONCISE : (a. refined, b. expanded, c. clear, d. blunt) :: REMOVE : OBLITERATE

53. TRAINING : ACUMEN :: (a. stupidity, b. experience, c. hunger, d. restlessness) : INANITION

54. BANTAM : (a. fly, b. chicken, c. fowl, d. small) :: WELTER : LIGHT

55. JACKET : (a. lapel, b. button, c. vest, d. dinner) :: PANTS : CUFF

56. (a. grave, b. aggravated, c. theft, d. first degree) : GRAND :: ASSAULT : LARCENY

57. (a. Athena, b. Ceres, c. Artemis, d. Aphrodite) : ZEUS :: EVE : ADAM

58. SERAPHIC : (a. Napoleonic, b. Mephistophelian, c. Alexandrine, d. euphoric) :: IMPROVIDENT : PRESCIENT

59. STRIPES : (a. bars, b. oak leaf, c. stars, d. general) :: SERGEANT : MAJOR

60. (a. precarious, b. deleterious, c. deterred, d. immortal) : CELEBRATED :: DEADLY : LIONIZED

61. MANET : REMBRANDT :: (a. Picasso, b. Dali, c. Pollock, d. Cezanne) : VAN GOGH

62. (a. glove, b. stocking, c. weakness, d. mitt) : GAUNTLET :: HAT : HELMET

63. STAPES : COCHLEA :: BRIM : (a. hat, b. derby, c. crown, d. head)

64. (a. rococo, b. severe, c. Etruscan, d. stylish) : ORNAMENTED :: SOGGY : MOIST

65. BURSAR : (a. funds, b. semester, c. accounts, d. purse) :: SEMINAR : IVY

66. NEW YORK : RHODES :: LIBERTY : (a. Apollo, b. scholar, c. tyranny, d. freedom)

67. RUBY : EMERALD :: TOMATO : (a. rose, b. onion, c. peach, d. lettuce)

68. SOLID : MELTING :: SOLUTION : (a. saturation, b. liquefaction, c. heating, d. mixing)

69. (a. royal, b. kingly, c. regal, d. princely) : LAGER :: TIME : EMIT

70. HENRY FIELDING : (a. Victorian, b. Romantic, c. Restoration, d. Augustan) :: BEN JONSON : ELIZABETHAN

71. ARKANSAS : FLORIDA :: NEW MEXICO : (a. Tennessee, b. Ohio, c. California, d. Illinois)

72. SIN : ATONEMENT :: (a. clemency, b. peace, c. war, d. virtue) : REPARATION

73. (a. solo, b. duet, c. trio, d. quartet) : QUINTET :: PRIZEFIGHT : BASKETBALL

74. PIPE : POT :: (a. scrub, b. ream, c. scourge, d. drain) : SCOUR

75. (a. echo, b. elephant, c. page, d. blue) : MEMORY :: DENIM : WALLPAPER

76. (a. Jupiter, b. Hippocrates, c. Cadmus, d. Ptolemy) : HANNIBAL :: CADUCEUS : SWORD

77. STYX : RUBICON :: ANATHEMA : (a. curse, b. pariah, c. parsee, d. song)

78. EPISTEMOLOGY : (a. letters, b. weapons, c. knowledge, d. roots) :: PALEONTOLOGY : FOSSILS

79. (a. ear, b. foundry, c. corps, d. fife) : FLINT :: DRUM : STEEL

80. CABER : (a. run, b. pass, c. mount, d. toss) :: EYE : BLINK

81. PLATO : (a. Socrates, b. Sophocles, c. Aristophanes, d. Aristotle) :: FREUD : JUNG

82. (a. law, b. book, c. band, d. wagon) : WAINWRIGHT :: DICTIONARY : LEXICOGRAPHER

83. 15 : 6 :: 23 : (a. 8, b. 7, c. 6, d. 5)

84. CONCERT : (a. andante, b. a cappella, c. opera, d. artistry) :: PERFORMANCE : PANTOMIME

85. (a. uniform, b. commander, c. platoon, d. sentry) : DOG :: GARRISON : FLOCK

86. PORTUGAL : IBERIA :: TOOTH : (a. dentist, b. cavity, c. nail, d. comb)

87. RADIUS : (a. circle, b. arc, c. chord, d. diameter) :: YARD : FATHOM

88. EMINENT : LOWLY :: FREQUENT : (a. often, b. frivolous, c. rare, d. soon)

89. FILIGREE : METAL :: (a. lace, b. linen, c. cotton, d. silk) : THREAD

90. INTAGLIO : (a. cameo, b. caviar, c. Machiavellian, d. harem) :: CONCAVE : CONVEX

91. MEZZANINE : (a. orchestra, b. stage, c. proscenium, d. second balcony) :: ABDOMEN : THORAX

92. BULBOUS : GAUNT :: (a. unruly, b. onerous, c. tractable, d. strong) : CONTUMACIOUS

93. GLACIER : MOLASSES :: (a. dirge, b. moth, c. spring, d. mountain) : TORTOISE

94. FOLD : (a. fell, b. hand, c. falls, d. boat) :: FORD : STREAM

95. VERDI : (a. *La Traviata*, b. *Fidelio*, c. *Aida*, d. *Rigoletto*) :: CHOPIN : *PARSIFAL*

96. SUBSTITUTE : TEAM :: UNDERSTUDY : (a. school, b. congregation, c. actor, d. cast)

97. PORT : (a. vintage, b. harbor, c. starboard, d. left) :: HEADLIGHTS : TRUNK

98. YORKTOWN : VICKSBURG :: CONCORD : (a. Philadelphia, b. Providence, c. Antietam, d. Valley Forge)

99. (a. fish, b. breath, c. pint, d. quart) : GILL :: OCTAVE : MONOTHEISM

100. ROOSTER : (a. crow, b. coop, c. egg, d. owl) :: EFFERVESCENT : EFFETE

Answer Key for Miller Analogies
Sample Test III

1. b	21. a	41. a	61. d	81. d
2. a	22. a	42. a	62. a	82. d
3. b	23. c	43. b	63. c	83. d
4. b	24. b	44. c	64. a	84. b
5. c	25. a	45. b	65. b	85. d
6. b	26. c	46. d	66. a	86. d
7. a	27. b	47. b	67. d	87. d
8. b	28. d	48. c	68. a	88. c
9. c	29. a	49. b	69. c	89. a
10. d	30. b	50. d	70. d	90. a
11. c	31. d	51. c	71. c	91. d
12. c	32. b	52. d	72. c	92. c
13. a	33. c	53. c	73. a	93. a
14. d	34. a	54. a	74. b	94. b
15. d	35. b	55. a	75. a	95. b
16. c	36. b	56. b	76. b	96. d
17. a	37. d	57. a	77. a	97. c
18. c	38. c	58. b	78. c	98. c
19. b	39. b	59. b	79. d	99. d
20. c	40. c	60. b	80. d	100. d

Explanatory Answers for Miller Analogies
Sample Test III

1. **(b)** A SCEPTER is a symbol of AUTHORITY; SCALES are a symbol of JUSTICE.

2. **(a)** The factor that all terms of this analogy have in common is that all concern mysteries. STONEHENGE and the statues at EASTER IS-LAND present mysteries as to their origin and purpose. The YETI, Abominable Snowman, and NESSIE, Loch Ness Monster, present mysteries as to their existence and nature. The dodo is an extinct bird presenting no mystery. Nene is a Hawaiian goose, and rhea is a South American bird somewhat akin to an ostrich.

3. **(b)** The relationship is that of object to actor or eaten to eater. A BIRD eats a WORM; a SNAKE eats a MOUSE.

4. **(b)** A PORTRAIT is a PICTURE of a person; a CHARACTERIZATION is a DESCRIPTION of the qualities or traits of a person.

5. **(c)** To MUMBLE is to TALK carelessly, thus making it difficult to be understood; to SCRAWL is to WRITE carelessly, thus making it difficult to be understood.

6. **(b)** LYNDON JOHNSON was a vice-president who succeeded JOHN F. KENNEDY following Kennedy's assassination. ANDREW JOHNSON was the vice-president under ABRAHAM LINCOLN who became president after Lincoln's assassination.

7. **(a)** In a mathematical analogy, always look first for the simplest relationship between two terms. The difference between 46 and 39 is 7. Since the number in choice (a) is 7 greater than the fourth term, your analogy is all set. $46 - 39 = 7$; $61 - 54 = 7$. Choice (d) is incorrect because it reverses the order of the relationship.

8. **(b)** This is an analogy of the gaseous to the liquid state of a substance. STEAM is the vapor form into which WATER is converted by heat. A CLOUD is the vapor form into which OCEAN water is converted by condensation.

9. **(c)** SODIUM is one of the elements of SALT; OXYGEN is one of the elements of WATER.

10. **(d)** In this analogy of cause and effect, a CRIME usually results in time spent in JAIL; DEATH usually results in burial in a CEMETERY.

11. **(c)** SNOW and MILK are related because they are both white; GRASS and LETTUCE are both green.

12. **(c)** This analogy is one of measurement. A LIGHT-YEAR is a unit of measurement in SPACE. A HAND is a unit of measurement (equal to four inches) used to determine the height of a HORSE.

13. **(a)** This analogy comes straight out of World War II. QUISLING was the Norwegian leader who quickly made common cause with the Nazis and became infamous for his COLLABORATION. CHAMBERLAIN was the British Prime Minister who thought that APPEASEMENT, giving Czechoslovakia to Hitler, would satisfy the Nazi hunger for conquest and would avert the war.

14. **(d)** A VIOLIN is a small high-pitched string instrument; a BASS is a large low-pitched string instrument. Since a PICCOLO is a small high-pitched wood-wind instrument, a large low-pitched wood-wind instrument must be selected to complete the analogy. An ALTO SAXOPHONE is the correct choice. Trumpet and trombone are brass, not woodwind instruments. An English horn is classified as a woodwind, but an unspecified horn is considered brass.

15. **(d)** DIVULGE and DISCLOSE are synonyms; a synonym for APPRAISAL is ESTIMATE.

16. **(c)** The correspondence is one of characteristic. WEALTH is usually measured in TANGIBLE units; SUCCESS is often measured in IN-TANGIBLE units.

17. **(a)** In this analogy of a part to a whole, HEMOGLOBIN is part of BLOOD; COACHES constitute parts of a TRAIN.

18. **(c)** BREAD and CAKE are related because the former is a necessity while the latter is a luxury; similarly a SHELTER is a necessity, and a MANSION is a luxury. It's a matter of degree.

19. **(b)** In this cause-and-effect analogy, LUCK may contribute to making one AFFLUENT; LAZINESS may contribute to making one IMPOVERISHED.

20. **(c)** The relationship is one of measurement. A division of a BASEBALL game is an INNING; a phase of HISTORY is called an ERA.

21. **(a)** The analogy hinges upon the hyphenated last names of certain English authors, namely, Edward BULWER-LYTTON and Vita SACK-VILLE-WEST.

22. **(a)** This is an action-to-object analogy. One may THROW a JAVELIN and one may STIFLE, or repress, a LAUGH. This question may prove puzzling because there is absolutely no meaningful relationship between throwing a javelin and stifling a laugh. However, the action-to-object relationship is real and legitimate.

23. **(c)** In this place analogy, CHARLESTON, BOSTON, and PHILADELPHIA are related because they were important colonial cities. Among the available choices, only WILLIAMSBURG was another colonial city.

24. **(b)** The relationship here is that of actor to the object of his/her actions. The MINER works to extract ORE from the earth; the VINTNER works to produce and to sell WINE. While the vintner uses grapes to produce the wine, the grapes serve as a tool rather than as an object of his/her activity.

25. **(a)** JAGUAR and GIRAFFE are related because both have spots; a TIGER and a ZEBRA are both striped.

26. **(c)** ZEUS was king of the gods in Greek mythology; HERA was his wife. ODIN was the supreme god in Norse mythology; FRIGGA was his wife.

27. **(b)** This analogy is based upon the clock. When the big hand points to 5, it is 25 minutes past the hour; similarly, when the big hand points to 8, it is 40 minutes past the hour.

28. **(d)** A person with a LIMP is likely to use a CANE; a person with a COLD is likely to use a TISSUE.

29. **(a)** The correspondence is one of association. EDWARD was known as the CONFESSOR; WARWICK was known as the KINGMAKER.

30. **(b)** This is an analogy of sequence. CONCRETE has replaced ADOBE as a building material; PAPER has replaced PAPYRUS as a writing material.

31. **(d)** Truly this is an analogy based upon association. In commonly used expressions the linkage is, ''in the ARMS of MORPHEUS'' and ''in the HANDS of DESTINY.''

32. **(b)** Each of the given terms in this analogy has a homophone, a word pronounced the same but spelled differently: HYMN (him); THEIR (there); and CELL (sell). Among the choices, only PEAL has a homophone (peel).

33. **(c)** The relationship is one of association. We speak of a SWAN SONG, that is, a farewell appearance or final act, and DOG DAYS, a period of hot, sultry weather or stagnation and inactivity. Swans do not sing, therefore, for purposes of this analogy, the barking of dogs is irrelevant.

34. **(a)** The correspondence is between a thinker and the theory with which he is associated. EINSTEIN developed the theory of RELATIVITY; MALTHUS is famous for his theory of POPULATION. Although Malthus was an economist, it is not his field but his theory that successfully completes this analogy. The relationship of Malthus to the economy would be analogous to the relationship of Einstein to physics.

35. **(b)** In this analogy of place, a GALLEY is where a MEAL is produced, usually on board a ship; a ROOKERY is the nesting place of a colony of seals, usually a rocky promontory or an isolated rock. It serves as the place where a baby SEAL is produced.

36. **(b)** PEACH and CHERRY are fruits that grow on trees; RADISH and BEET are root vegetables.

37. **(d)** The opposite of PARSIMONY, or stinginess, is BENEFACTION, which means charitable donation; an antonym for LASSITUDE, meaning listlessness, is ALACRITY, which means promptness of response.

38. **(c)** The purpose of a THERMOSTAT is to REGULATE room temperature; the purpose of INSULATION is to CONSERVE energy.

39. **(b)** A MONGREL has no PEDIGREE just as a BOOR has no MANNERS.

40. **(c)** The correspondence is between man-made and natural objects. SPUTNIK is a man-made object which orbits; a PLANET is a natural object which orbits. Similarly, a CANAL is a man-made waterway, and a RIVER is a natural waterway.

41. **(a)** In this place analogy, PIRAEUS is a port city near ATHENS; OSTIA was a port city near ROME.

42. **(a)** Since ASTRONOMY and ASTROLOGY both deal with the stars, with astronomy being the accepted science and astrology a disputed or questionable science, the task is to find an accepted science similar to the disputed science of PHRENOLOGY (which deals with the head). PSYCHOLOGY is the correct choice.

43. **(b)** The correspondence is one of thinker to tool. An ORACLE's prophecies are based on INTUITION; a LOGICIAN may reason by means of a SYLLOGISM, a formal scheme of deductive thinking.

44. **(c)** In this analogy of place or location, ETNA is a volcano located on the island of SICILY. PELEE is a volcano located on the island of MARTINIQUE.

45. **(b)** The relationship is one of classification. GERONTOLOGY is the study of AGING; GENEALOGY is the study of LINEAGE.

46. **(d)** We speak of a ROMAN NOSE and a VAN DYKE BEARD. The correspondence is one of association.

47. **(b)** HYDROGEN, the lightest element, has an atomic weight of 1. OXYGEN, with 8 protons and 8 neutrons in its nucleus, has an atomic weight of 16. Knowledge of chemistry is essential to this answer. Without such knowledge, you must guess.

48. **(c)** The relationship is one of part to part. An ARCH and a HEEL are parts of a foot; PROTONs and NEUTRONs are parts of the nucleus of an atom.

49. **(b)** A prime number is a number that is divisible by no other numbers except 1 and itself. All the terms in question 49, the given terms and the choices, are prime numbers, so you must base your answer on another relationship. 19 and 23 are prime numbers in sequence. Completing the analogy, 11 and 13 are prime numbers in sequence.

50. **(d)** A characteristic of both a PANORAMA and a CHURCH DOOR is that they are wide; an ABYSS and an OCEAN are characteristically deep.

51. **(c)** In this analogy of place, NEVADA, and COLORADO are states separated by another state, Utah. INDIA and AFGHANISTAN are countries separated by another country, Pakistan.

52. **(d)** REMOVE and OBLITERATE are synonyms, both resulting in elimination, but varying in intensity. One must, therefore, find another word for CONCISE that has the same result, yet varies in intensity. Concise means succinct or pithy; BLUNT is a synonym but has the stronger connotation of brusqueness or rudeness.

53. **(c)** In this cause-and-effect analogy, TRAINING results in ACUMEN or keenness of perception or discernment. Similarly, HUNGER results in INANITION, a loss of vitality from absence of food and water.

54. **(a)** BANTAM, WELTER, LIGHT, and FLY are all weight divisions in boxing.

55. **(a)** A LAPEL is a folded-over part of a JACKET; a CUFF is a folded-over part of a pair of PANTS.

56. **(b)** ASSAULT and LARCENY are both legal terms for crimes. GRAND corresponds to LARCENY, describing the degree of the crime. The term which indicates the degree of ASSAULT is AGGRAVATED.

57. **(a)** In this analogy of association of object to actor, ATHENA is said to have sprung from the head of ZEUS; EVE is said to have been made from the rib of ADAM.

58. **(b)** IMPROVIDENT and PRESCIENT are related as antonyms. The former relates to the inability and the latter to the ability to foresee the future. Similarly, the opposite of SERAPHIC, which means angelic, is MEPHISTOPHELIAN, which means devilish.

59. **(b)** In the army, STRIPES are associated with the rank of SERGEANT; an OAK LEAF is associated with the rank of MAJOR.

60. **(b)** In this cause-and-effect analogy, something that is DELETERIOUS (exceedingly harmful) may prove DEADLY; a person who is CELEBRATED (widely known) may be LIONIZED.

61. **(d)** REMBRANDT and VAN GOGH, the initial B : D related pair, were both Dutch painters. MANET and CEZANNE were both French painters. The painter paired with the French Manet must be a French painter because the painter paired with the Dutch Rembrandt is a Dutch painter. Picasso, while he spent much of his artistic life in France, was Spanish.

62. **(a)** A HAT is a head covering worn in peace and a HELMET is a head covering worn in war; since GAUNTLET is a hand covering worn in war, one must look for a hand covering that is worn in peace: a GLOVE.

63. **(c)** The STAPES and the COCHLEA are parts of an ear; a BRIM and a CROWN are parts of a hat. This is a part-to-part analogy. Avoid the part-to-whole temptation.

64. **(a)** The relationship is one of degree. ROCOCO means excessively ORNAMENTED; SOGGY means excessively MOIST.

65. **(d)** A BURSAR, SEMINAR, and IVY are all things associated with college. To complete the analogy another term associated with college must be selected; that term is SEMESTER.

66. **(a)** The Statue of LIBERTY is set at the entrance to the harbor of NEW YORK; a statue of APOLLO was set at the entrance to the harbor of ancient RHODES. The analogy is one of place or location, but you do need some knowledge of ancient history in order to answer it.

67. **(d)** A RUBY is a red gem and an EMERALD is green; a TOMATO is red and LETTUCE is green.

68. **(a)** In this measurement analogy, the MELTING point is an important measure of a SOLID; the SATURATION point is an important measurement of a SOLUTION.

69. **(c)** In this nonsemantic analogy, REGAL spelled backwards is LAGER; TIME spelled backwards is EMIT.

70. **(d)** The correspondence is one of association. BEN JONSON is associated with the ELIZABETHAN period, the last part of the sixteenth century. Similarly, the novelist and playwright HENRY FIELDING is associated with the AUGUSTAN or eighteenth-century period.

71. **(c)** In this place analogy, ARKANSAS and NEW MEXICO are interior states; FLORIDA and CALIFORNIA are related because they are coastal states.

72. **(c)** ATONEMENT is compensation made for an offense against moral or religious law (a SIN). REPARATION is compensation made by a defeated nation for losses sustained by another nation as a result of WAR between the two nations.

73. **(a)** A PRIZEFIGHT is fought by SOLO contestants, one on each side; a BASKETBALL team is a QUINTET, five players on each side.

74. **(b)** In this object-to-action analogy, to clean a POT thoroughly you need to SCOUR it; to clean a PIPE thoroughly you need to REAM it.

75. **(a)** MEMORY, DENIM, and WALLPAPER are all related because of a common characteristic. They all tend to fade. An ECHO also fades.

76. **(b)** In this association analogy, a SWORD is a symbol of warfare, associated with HANNIBAL, a great soldier; a CADUCEUS is a symbol for medicine and should be related to HIPPOCRATES, a famous physician.

77. **(a)** This analogy is based on synonyms. Both the STYX and the RUBICON represent points of no return. The Styx is the river which the dead cross into Hades; the Rubicon is a line which, once crossed, represents total commitment. An ANATHEMA is a CURSE.

78. **(c)** PALEONTOLOGY is concerned with the study of FOSSILS; EPISTEMOLOGY is concerned with the study of KNOWLEDGE.

79. **(d)** In this part-to-part analogy, a FIFE is used with a DRUM to make up a marching corps; a FLINT is used with STEEL to produce a fire.

80. **(d)** The correspondence is one of object to action. One can BLINK an EYE, and one can TOSS a CABER, a large pole which is thrown as a feat of strength in a Scottish sport.

81. **(d)** ARISTOTLE was a follower, albeit with modifications, of PLATO; JUNG was a follower, again with modifications, of FREUD.

82. **(d)** This analcgy is one of worker to the article created. A LEXICOG-RAPHER compiles a DICTIONARY; a WAINWRIGHT makes a WAGON.

83. **(d)** Think of this as a nonsemantic or configurational analogy utilizing numbers instead of words. $1 + 5 = 6$; $2 + 3 = 5$. In other words, the two digits of the first number added together create the next number.

84. **(b)** A CONCERT in which there is singing without musical accompaniment is A CAPELLA; a dramatic PERFORMANCE in which there is no dialogue is a PANTOMIME.

85. **(d)** A SENTRY guards a GARRISON; a sheep DOG guards a FLOCK.

86. **(d)** PORTUGAL is part of the peninsula of IBERIA; a TOOTH is part of a COMB. You must shift your thinking away from the mouth to arrive at the answer.

87. **(d)** A YARD (three feet) is half as long as a FATHOM (six feet). In a given circle, the RADIUS is half as long as the DIAMETER.

88. **(c)** EMINENT and LOWLY are antonyms; an antonym for FREQUENT is RARE.

89. **(a)** In this definition analogy, FILIGREE is delicate ornamental open-work made of METAL; LACE is delicate open-work fabric made from THREAD.

90. **(a)** CONCAVE means curving inward whereas CONVEX means curving outward. INTAGLIO is incised carving. It relates, therefore, to CONCAVE. A CAMEO, which is carved in relief, corresponds to CONVEX.

91. **(d)** The MEZZANINE is located directly below the SECOND BALCONY, just as the ABDOMEN is located below the THORAX.

92. **(c)** BULBOUS, which means rotund, is the opposite of GAUNT, which means thin. An antonym for CONTUMACIOUS, meaning disobedient or rebellious, is TRACTABLE, meaning docile or yielding.

93. **(a)** A GLACIER, MOLASSES, and a TORTOISE are all related because they move slowly. Among the choices given, only a DIRGE is also slow-moving.

94. **(b)** In this action-to-object analogy, one may FORD a STREAM, and one can FOLD a HAND in cards. Mental flexibility is a must in answering Miller Analogy questions.

95. **(b)** CHOPIN did not compose *PARSIFAL*. To complete the analogy, you must select what VERDI did not compose. The correct choice is *FIDELIO* which was composed by Beethoven.

96. **(d)** A SUBSTITUTE is used to replace someone on TEAM; an UNDERSTUDY is used to replace someone in a CAST.

97. **(c)** PORT and STARBOARD are opposite sides of a ship; the HEADLIGHTS and the TRUNK are at opposite ends of an automobile.

98. **(c)** In this place analogy, YORKTOWN was the site of a major battle in the Revolutionary War; VICKSBURG was the site of a major battle in the Civil War. Since CONCORD was also a site of a Revolutionary War battle, another Civil War battle site must be found to complete the analogy. ANTIETAM is the correct choice.

99. **(d)** The relationship is based upon an eight-to-one ratio. An OCTAVE is a series of eight; MONOTHEISM is belief in one God. There are eight GILLs in one QUART.

100. **(d)** Since EFFERVESCENT, meaning exuberant, and EFFETE, meaning exhausted, are opposites, the task is to find a contrast for ROOSTER. A rooster is associated with morning, whereas an OWL is a night bird.

ANSWER SHEET
MILLER ANALOGIES SAMPLE TEST IV

1 Ⓐ Ⓑ Ⓒ Ⓓ	21 Ⓐ Ⓑ Ⓒ Ⓓ	41 Ⓐ Ⓑ Ⓒ Ⓓ	61 Ⓐ Ⓑ Ⓒ Ⓓ	81 Ⓐ Ⓑ Ⓒ Ⓓ
2 Ⓐ Ⓑ Ⓒ Ⓓ	22 Ⓐ Ⓑ Ⓒ Ⓓ	42 Ⓐ Ⓑ Ⓒ Ⓓ	62 Ⓐ Ⓑ Ⓒ Ⓓ	82 Ⓐ Ⓑ Ⓒ Ⓓ
3 Ⓐ Ⓑ Ⓒ Ⓓ	23 Ⓐ Ⓑ Ⓒ Ⓓ	43 Ⓐ Ⓑ Ⓒ Ⓓ	63 Ⓐ Ⓑ Ⓒ Ⓓ	83 Ⓐ Ⓑ Ⓒ Ⓓ
4 Ⓐ Ⓑ Ⓒ Ⓓ	24 Ⓐ Ⓑ Ⓒ Ⓓ	44 Ⓐ Ⓑ Ⓒ Ⓓ	64 Ⓐ Ⓑ Ⓒ Ⓓ	84 Ⓐ Ⓑ Ⓒ Ⓓ
5 Ⓐ Ⓑ Ⓒ Ⓓ	25 Ⓐ Ⓑ Ⓒ Ⓓ	45 Ⓐ Ⓑ Ⓒ Ⓓ	65 Ⓐ Ⓑ Ⓒ Ⓓ	85 Ⓐ Ⓑ Ⓒ Ⓓ
6 Ⓐ Ⓑ Ⓒ Ⓓ	26 Ⓐ Ⓑ Ⓒ Ⓓ	46 Ⓐ Ⓑ Ⓒ Ⓓ	66 Ⓐ Ⓑ Ⓒ Ⓓ	86 Ⓐ Ⓑ Ⓒ Ⓓ
7 Ⓐ Ⓑ Ⓒ Ⓓ	27 Ⓐ Ⓑ Ⓒ Ⓓ	47 Ⓐ Ⓑ Ⓒ Ⓓ	67 Ⓐ Ⓑ Ⓒ Ⓓ	87 Ⓐ Ⓑ Ⓒ Ⓓ
8 Ⓐ Ⓑ Ⓒ Ⓓ	28 Ⓐ Ⓑ Ⓒ Ⓓ	48 Ⓐ Ⓑ Ⓒ Ⓓ	68 Ⓐ Ⓑ Ⓒ Ⓓ	88 Ⓐ Ⓑ Ⓒ Ⓓ
9 Ⓐ Ⓑ Ⓒ Ⓓ	29 Ⓐ Ⓑ Ⓒ Ⓓ	49 Ⓐ Ⓑ Ⓒ Ⓓ	69 Ⓐ Ⓑ Ⓒ Ⓓ	89 Ⓐ Ⓑ Ⓒ Ⓓ
10 Ⓐ Ⓑ Ⓒ Ⓓ	30 Ⓐ Ⓑ Ⓒ Ⓓ	50 Ⓐ Ⓑ Ⓒ Ⓓ	70 Ⓐ Ⓑ Ⓒ Ⓓ	90 Ⓐ Ⓑ Ⓒ Ⓓ
11 Ⓐ Ⓑ Ⓒ Ⓓ	31 Ⓐ Ⓑ Ⓒ Ⓓ	51 Ⓐ Ⓑ Ⓒ Ⓓ	71 Ⓐ Ⓑ Ⓒ Ⓓ	91 Ⓐ Ⓑ Ⓒ Ⓓ
12 Ⓐ Ⓑ Ⓒ Ⓓ	32 Ⓐ Ⓑ Ⓒ Ⓓ	52 Ⓐ Ⓑ Ⓒ Ⓓ	72 Ⓐ Ⓑ Ⓒ Ⓓ	92 Ⓐ Ⓑ Ⓒ Ⓓ
13 Ⓐ Ⓑ Ⓒ Ⓓ	33 Ⓐ Ⓑ Ⓒ Ⓓ	53 Ⓐ Ⓑ Ⓒ Ⓓ	73 Ⓐ Ⓑ Ⓒ Ⓓ	93 Ⓐ Ⓑ Ⓒ Ⓓ
14 Ⓐ Ⓑ Ⓒ Ⓓ	34 Ⓐ Ⓑ Ⓒ Ⓓ	54 Ⓐ Ⓑ Ⓒ Ⓓ	74 Ⓐ Ⓑ Ⓒ Ⓓ	94 Ⓐ Ⓑ Ⓒ Ⓓ
15 Ⓐ Ⓑ Ⓒ Ⓓ	35 Ⓐ Ⓑ Ⓒ Ⓓ	55 Ⓐ Ⓑ Ⓒ Ⓓ	75 Ⓐ Ⓑ Ⓒ Ⓓ	95 Ⓐ Ⓑ Ⓒ Ⓓ
16 Ⓐ Ⓑ Ⓒ Ⓓ	36 Ⓐ Ⓑ Ⓒ Ⓓ	56 Ⓐ Ⓑ Ⓒ Ⓓ	76 Ⓐ Ⓑ Ⓒ Ⓓ	96 Ⓐ Ⓑ Ⓒ Ⓓ
17 Ⓐ Ⓑ Ⓒ Ⓓ	37 Ⓐ Ⓑ Ⓒ Ⓓ	57 Ⓐ Ⓑ Ⓒ Ⓓ	77 Ⓐ Ⓑ Ⓒ Ⓓ	97 Ⓐ Ⓑ Ⓒ Ⓓ
18 Ⓐ Ⓑ Ⓒ Ⓓ	38 Ⓐ Ⓑ Ⓒ Ⓓ	58 Ⓐ Ⓑ Ⓒ Ⓓ	78 Ⓐ Ⓑ Ⓒ Ⓓ	98 Ⓐ Ⓑ Ⓒ Ⓓ
19 Ⓐ Ⓑ Ⓒ Ⓓ	39 Ⓐ Ⓑ Ⓒ Ⓓ	59 Ⓐ Ⓑ Ⓒ Ⓓ	79 Ⓐ Ⓑ Ⓒ Ⓓ	99 Ⓐ Ⓑ Ⓒ Ⓓ
20 Ⓐ Ⓑ Ⓒ Ⓓ	40 Ⓐ Ⓑ Ⓒ Ⓓ	60 Ⓐ Ⓑ Ⓒ Ⓓ	80 Ⓐ Ⓑ Ⓒ Ⓓ	100 Ⓐ Ⓑ Ⓒ Ⓓ

Tear Here

MILLER ANALOGIES
SAMPLE TEST IV

Time: 50 Minutes. 100 Questions.

Directions: Each of these test questions consists of three CAPITALIZED words and four lettered words enclosed in parentheses. Two of the capitalized words are related in some way. Find the two related words and establish the nature of the relationship. Then study the four words lettered a, b, c, and d. Select the one lettered word which is related to the remaining capitalized word in the same way that the first two capitalized words are related. Mark the answer sheet for the letter of the word you select.

1. NEEDLE : (a. thread, b. pen, c. eye, d. hole) :: GLOBE : ORANGE

2. ARCHIPELAGO : ISLAND :: GALAXY : (a. universe, b. space, c. star, d. Milky Way)

3. DUCTILE : (a. malleable, b. adamant, c. regal, d. channel) :: LATENT : COVERT

4. NEWSPRINT : (a. paper, b. linotype, c. newsstand, d. tree) :: STEEL : ORE

5. EXPERIMENTATION : MATRICULATION :: DISCOVERY : (a. mothering, b. molding, c. learning, d. wedding)

6. BUTTER : GUNS :: (a. plowshares, b. margarine, c. fig trees, d. pruning hooks) : SWORDS

7. MAINE : (a. Miami, b. Cuba, c. Puerto Rico, d. Quebec) :: ARIZONA : HAWAII

8. (a. *Plaza Suite*, b. *Manhattan*, c. *Brighton Beach Memoirs*, d. *Auntie Mame*) : BILOXI BLUES :: ANNIE HALL : RADIO DAYS

9. MANTISSA : LOGARITHM :: SINE : (a. cosine, b. ration, c. exponent, d. trigonometry)

10. BOXER : BOER :: (a. England, b. China, c. Chinaman, d. Empress) : SOUTH AFRICA

11. (a. Bartók, b. Mozart, c. Fauré, d. Beethoven) : WAGNER :: TCHAIKOVSKY : PROKOFIEV

12. (a. grind, b. thresh, c. harvest, d. grow) : WHEAT :: DISTILL : WATER

13. BRAGGADOCIO : RETICENCE :: MISERLINESS : (a. profligacy, b. ecstasy, c. obloquy, d. falsity)

14. 625 : (a. 5^5, b. 6^4, c. 7^4, d. 12^3) :: 5^4 : 2401

15. SANDHURST : ENGLAND :: (a. Harvard, b. Pittsburgh, c. West Point, d. M.I.T.) : UNITED STATES

16. AURICLE : VENTRICLE :: (a. sinus, b. epiglottis, c. thalamus, d. esophagus) : CEREBELLUM

17. (a. trees, b. circus, c. merry-go-round, d. scooter) : STILTS :: BUS : AUDITORIUM

18. PARIS : (a. London, b. Priam, c. Achilles, d. Helen) :: ACHILLES : HECTOR

19. GENEROUS : LAVISH :: TIMOROUS : (a. tumid, b. craven, c. courageous, d. foolhardy)

20. MECCA : BENARES :: MOSLEM : (a. Islam, b. India, c. Hindu, d. Buddhist)

21. POLO : ROLLS :: (a. mansion, b. mallet, c. race, d. swimming) : YACHT

22. (a. barber, b. bristle, c. comb, d. stroke) : BRUSH :: CRUISER : FLEET

23. HUDSON : BUICK :: PACKARD : (a. Stutz, b. Locomobile, c. Maxwell, d. Oldsmobile)

24. IMBROGLIO : SYMMETRY :: (a. dentures, b. savory, c. distasteful, d. cavernous) : TOOTHSOME

25. (a. Galen, b. Magyar, c. Bede, d. Pericles) : LUKE :: SCHWEITZER : SALK

26. ASSAYER : ORE :: TRENCHERMAN : (a. ditch, b. food, c. dikes, d. security)

27. BRAZIL : (a. Portugal, b. Spain, c. Venezuela, d. Surinam) :: GUYANA : FRENCH GUIANA

28. (a. lunch, b. meal, c. breakfast, d. brunch) : SUPPER :: SMOG : HAZE

29. APPRAISAL : REVENUE :: (a. defrosting, b. clear, c. hiding, d. sun) : VISIBILITY

30. F : X :: 1 : (a. 4, b. 8, c. 2, d. 6)

31. RUPEE : (a. shah, b. guilder, c. rizal, d. krone) :: INDIA : NETHER-LANDS

32. (a. servile, b. kowtow, c. refractory, d. inhibited) : OBSEQUI-OUS :: IMPRECATORY : EULOGISTIC

33. BLUE : ORANGE :: (a. indigo, b. yellow, c. purple, d. red) : GREEN

34. CHEETAH : SPEED :: (a. blade, b. cleavage, c. bird, d. incision) : KEENNESS

35. (a. hock, b. jockey, c. stable, d. hand) : HORSE :: TONGUE : BELL

36. EPILOGUE : NOVEL :: (a. cheers, b. curtain call, c. performance, d. introduction) : APPLAUSE

37. (a. Nantucket, b. Puerto Rico, c. Hawaii, d. Long Island) : UNITED STATES :: TASMANIA : AUSTRALIA

38. ANCHISES : (a. Troilus, b. Achilles, c. Ajax, d. Aeneas) :: JO-CASTA : OEDIPUS

39. LEES : DREGS :: SYBARITIC : (a. sensual, b. moderate, c. cultish, d. servile)

40. ISRAEL : VIETNAM :: JORDAN : (a. Cambodia, b. Korea, c. Burma, d. France)

41. MAP : (a. explorer, b. geography, c. legend, d. atlas) :: TEXT : FOOTNOTE

42. (a. clock, b. watch, c. time, d. hour) : TELL :: GUM : CHEW

43. "YANKEE DOODLE" : DUSTER :: PILLOW : (a. coop, b. macaroni, c. blanket, d. broom)

44. COOPER : (a. lithographer, b. cartographer, c. photographer, d. biographer) :: BARREL : MAP

45. PUPA : (a. tadpole, b. larva, c. cocoon, d. bumblebee) :: FETUS : CHILD

46. DEALING : STOCK EXCHANGE :: (a. preserving, b. selling, c. buying, d. copying) : LANDMARK

47. UPRISING : (a. revolution, b. settlement, c. quarrel, d. disquiet) :: FIB : LIE

48. (a. Crete, b. Malta, c. Sicily, d. Corsica) : SARDINIA :: BOLIVIA : ARGENTINA

49. EVIL : EXORCISE :: BREAD : (a. carbohydrate, b. break, c. sandwich, d. shred)

50. COWARD : (a. loser, b. lily-livered, c. hero, d. villain) :: YOLK : ALBUMEN

51. (a. humid, b. speedy, c. piquant, d. moist) : VAPID :: OBDURATE : COMPASSIONATE

52. CUCUMBER : WATERMELON :: CANTALOUPE : (a. squash, b. radish, c. cherry, d. plum)

53. (a. head, b. nose, c. ear, d. limbs) : MAN :: STRINGS : VIOLIN

54. ILLNESS : (a. debility, b. hospital, c. doctor, d. panacea) :: VIBRATION : SOUND

55. VERDUN : DUNKIRK :: YPRES : (a. Bateau Woods, b. El Alamein, c. San Juan Hill, d. Marne)

56. (a. gain, b. reward, c. loot, d. profit) : ROBBERY :: REVENGE : VENDETTA

57. ANALYSIS : FREUD :: (a. manipulation, b. illness, c. sex, d. stimulation) : OSTEOPATHY

58. CLAUSTROPHOBIA : CLOSETS :: AGORAPHOBIA : (a. ships, b. sheep, c. plants, d. plains)

59. SEARCH : FIND :: FIGHT : (a. win, b. lose, c. seek, d. contend)

60. (a. sympathy, b. encouragement, c. blasphemy, d. oblivion) : FRACAS :: APHRODITE : MARS

61. H : S :: (a. M, b. L, c. I, d. P) : W

62. HASTILY : DESPONDENTLY :: CIRCUMSPECTLY : (a. quick, b. circuit, c. rate, d. slowly)

63. BOXER : TABBY :: LABRADOR : (a. fighter, b. poodle, c. calico, d. nanny)

64. CROESUS : (a. boat, b. wealth, c. pleats, d. loyalty) :: ODYSSEUS : CRAFT

65. LUCERNE : MICHIGAN :: GENEVA : (a. United States, b. Victoria, c. Okeechobee, d. Switzerland)

66. (a. tally, b. game, c. concert, d. run) : SCORE :: PLAY : SCRIPT

67. CLEAVER : (a. ice, b. field, c. knife, d. writer) :: CONNELLY : PASTURES

68. DOG : INTRUDER :: (a. burglar, b. cat, c. knight, d. maiden) : DRAGON

69. REND : CLEAVE :: STICK : (a. stone, b. glue, c. cleave, d. branch)

70. PARTRIDGE : RABBIT :: (a. quail, b. pen, c. birds, d. covey) : WARREN

71. LAPIDARY : (a. ruby, b. wood, c. lick, d. food) :: SCULP-TOR : ALABASTER

72. WOOF : FILE :: WARP : (a. grade, b. rank, c. fold, d. twist)

73. MANY : MUCH :: FEW : (a. less, b. more, c. small, d. little)

74. FORSOOK : DRANK :: FROZEN : (a. swum, b. wrote, c. sang, d. chose)

75. SANDAL : BOOT :: (a. hammer, b. hatchet, c. shoemaker, d. blade) : AX

76. HORSE : (a. man, b. goat, c. archer, d. bull) :: CENTAUR : SATYR

77. (a. anode, b. bird, c. purchase, d. battery) : CELL :: ARROW : SHAFT

78. FELONY : MISDEMEANOR :: SIN : (a. piccalilli, b. picayune, c. peccadillo, d. picador)

79. NOVEMBER : APRIL :: (a. May, b. June, c. July, d. August) : SEPTEMBER

80. ALBANIA : POLAND :: CHINA : (a. Czechoslovakia, b. Russia, c. Yugoslavia, d. India)

81. WASTEFUL : (a. parsimonious, b. neglectful, c. vast, d. prodigal) :: DISINTERESTED : IMPARTIAL

82. SCHOONER : ZIGGURAT :: CRUISER : (a. cutter, b. campanile, c. viking, d. tug)

83. (a. pine, b. cedar, c. ash, d. willow) : OAK :: MOURNFUL : STURDY

84. ADVISE : EXHORT :: (a. force, b. tempt, c. prohibit, d. prevent) : ENTICE

85. STEEL : WELD :: LIPS : (a. frown, b. purse, c. fold, d. smirk)

86. TESTIMONY : (a. confession, b. judge, c. witness, d. trial) :: BIO-GRAPHY : AUTOBIOGRAPHY

87. STRATUM : SYLLABUS :: (a. strati, b. stratums, c. stratus, d. strata) : SYLLABI

88. LAMB : DEER :: (a. rabbit, b. peacock, c. horse, d. pig) : LION

89. VELOCITY : (a. wind, b. earth, c. vibration, d. destruction) :: BEAU-FORT : RICHTER

90. (a. distance, b. program, c. station, d. tube) : TELEVISION :: LEADER : ANARCHY

91. TATTOO : VESPERS :: (a. painting, b. needle, c. revelry, d. reveille) : MATINS

92. PROSTRATE : (a. dazzling, b. stealing, c. yielding, d. dehydrated) :: SUPINE : SLEEPING

93. MAHATMA GANDHI : WAR :: CARRY NATION : (a. suffrage, b. alcohol, c. temperance, d. employment)

94. 2/7 : (a. 1/16, b. 3/28, c. 3/21, d. 1/14) :: 4/7 : 1/7

95. (a. roc, b. canary, c. albatross, d. condor) : VULTURE :: PHOENIX : EAGLE

96. TINE : FORK : (a. car, b. gearshift, c. flange, d. wheelwright) : WHEEL

97. (a. tie, b. appearance, c. shoes, d. decoration) : ATTIRE :: WIT : COMMUNICATION

98. HUSK : (a. fat, b. chops, c. gristle, d. filet) :: GRAIN : MEAT

99. STARTLED : (a. interested, b. astounded, c. expected, d. unknown) :: WORK : TOIL

100. INEBRIOUS : (a. intoxicated, b. dull, c. sincere, d. abstemious) :: SPARTAN : GARRULOUS

ANSWER KEY FOR MILLER ANALOGIES
SAMPLE TEST IV

1. b	21. a	41. c	61. b	81. d
2. c	22. b	42. c	62. d	82. b
3. a	23. d	43. a	63. c	83. d
4. d	24. c	44. b	64. b	84. b
5. c	25. a	45. d	65. c	85. b
6. a	26. b	46. a	66. c	86. a
7. b	27. d	47. a	67. a	87. d
8. c	28. d	48. d	68. c	88. b
9. d	29. a	49. b	69. c	89. c
10. b	30. a	50. c	70. d	90. a
11. d	31. b	51. c	71. a	91. d
12. b	32. c	52. a	72. b	92. c
13. a	33. d	53. d	73. d	93. b
14. c	34. a	54. a	74. a	94. d
15. c	35. a	55. b	75. b	95. a
16. c	36. b	56. c	76. b	96. c
17. d	37. c	57. a	77. d	97. d
18. c	38. d	58. d	78. c	98. c
19. b	39. a	59. a	79. b	99. b
20. c	40. a	60. a	80. a	100. d

EXPLANATORY ANSWERS FOR
MILLER ANALOGIES SAMPLE TEST IV

1. **(b)** A GLOBE and an ORANGE are related because they are both round; a NEEDLE and a PEN are both pointed.

2. **(c)** This a whole-to-part analogy. An ARCHIPELAGO is made up of ISLANDs; a GALAXY is made up of STARs. A galaxy is part of the universe; the order of the relationship is the reverse of that between archipelago and island. The Milky Way is a galaxy.

3. **(a)** LATENT and COVERT are synonyms meaning hidden or concealed. A synonym for DUCTILE, which means easily influenced or altered, is MALLEABLE.

4. **(d)** In this analogy, the relationship is one of source to product. An original source of STEEL is ORE; an original source of NEWSPRINT is a TREE.

5. **(c)** In this purpose analogy, a purpose of EXPERIMENTATION is DISCOVERY; a purpose of MATRICULATION is LEARNING.

6. **(a)** The implication of the saying "BUTTER is better than GUNS" is that peace is better than war. The passage from Isaiah, "They shall bend their SWORDS into PLOWSHARES . . ." has the same implication. Pruning hooks are paired with spears.

7. **(b)** The opening blow of Japan's involvement in the Second World War was the sinking of the battleship *ARIZONA* in Honolulu harbor in HAWAII. The Spanish American war began with the sinking of the battleship *MAINE* in Havana harbor, CUBA.

8. **(c)** *ANNIE HALL* and *RADIO DAYS* are movies by Woody Allen in which he draws heavily upon his childhood experiences. *BRIGHTON BEACH MEMOIRS* and *BILOXI BLUES* are autobiographical Neil Simon plays.

9. **(d)** This analogy from the language of mathematics is based on a part-to-whole relationship. A MANTISSA is the decimal part of a LOGARITHM. SINE is a function in TRIGONOMETRY.

10. **(b)** This is an analogy involving history and place. The BOER War took place in SOUTH AFRICA; the BOXER rebellion occurred in CHINA.

11. **(d)** TCHAIKOVSKY and PROKOFIEV are related because they both are composers from Russia; therefore, to complete the analogy, WAGNER, a composer from GERMANY, must be paired with BEETHOVEN, another German composer.

12. **(b)** In this action-to-object analogy, you DISTILL WATER to remove unwanted substances from the refined water; similarly, you THRESH WHEAT to separate the grains from the unwanted chaff.

13. **(a)** BRAGGADOCIO, which means boastfulness, is opposite to RETICENCE; an antonym for MISERLINESS, which means stinginess, is PROFLIGACY, meaning reckless wastefulness.

14. **(c)** The nature of the relationship should be clear: synonyms. If need be, a bit of trial and error will yield the answer. $5^4 = 625 :: 7^4 = 2401$.

15. **(c)** SANDHURST is a school in ENGLAND which trains future military officers; WEST POINT has the same function in the UNITED STATES.

16. **(c)** In this part to part analogy, the AURICLE and VENTRICLE are both parts of the heart; the CEREBELLUM and THALAMUS are parts of the brain.

17. **(d)** A BUS and an AUDITORIUM are related because they are intended to serve more than one person; STILTS and a SCOOTER are usually intended for one person alone.

18. **(c)** In Homer's *Iliad,* ACHILLES slew HECTOR, and later PARIS slew ACHILLES.

19. **(b)** A person who is extremely GENEROUS is LAVISH; a person who is extremely TIMOROUS is CRAVEN, or cowardly.

20. **(c)** In this place analogy, MECCA is the sacred city of the MOSLEMs; BENARES is the sacred city of the HINDUs.

21. **(a)** POLO, a ROLLS Royce, and a YACHT are all things associated with rich people. Among the choices, MANSION is also associated with the wealthy.

22. **(b)** In this analogy of a part to a whole, a BRISTLE is part of a BRUSH; a CRUISER is part of a FLEET.

23. **(d)** HUDSON and PACKARD are names of cars that are no longer made; BUICK and OLDSMOBILE are names of popular current cars.

24. **(c)** IMBROGLIO, which means disorder, is opposite in meaning to SYMMETRY. An antonym for TOOTHSOME, which means palatable, is DISTASTEFUL.

25. **(a)** GALEN, LUKE, SCHWEITZER, and SALK are all related as physicians.

26. **(b)** In this analogy of association, an ASSAYER's job is to analyze ORE; a TRENCHERMAN's avocation is the enjoyment of FOOD.

27. **(d)** GUYANA, FRENCH GUIANA, BRAZIL, and SURINAM are all related in that they are the four South American countries in which Spanish is not the major language. Respectively, the languages spoken: English, French, Portuguese, and Dutch.

28. **(d)** There is a two-to-one relationship in this analogy since BRUNCH combines two meals, breakfast and lunch, and SUPPER is just one meal. Similarly, SMOG is a combination of two atmospheric conditions, smoke and fog, and HAZE is one atmospheric condition.

29. **(a)** This is a purpose analogy. The purpose of the APPRAISAL of a house is to gain tax REVENUE; the purpose of DEFROSTING a windshield is to increase VISIBILITY. Note that the sun is a cause of visibility, not the purpose of it.

30. **(a)** The correspondence is mathematical. F is the sixth letter of the alphabet and X is the twenty-fourth. Their ratio is 1 : 4. Upon seeing the "X," you might have expected this analogy to be based upon Roman numerals, but you should have shifted gears very quickly upon the realization that "F" is not a Roman numeral.

31. **(b)** The RUPEE is the basic unit of currency in INDIA. The basic unit of currency in the NETHERLANDS is the GUILDER.

32. **(c)** IMPRECATORY, which means damning, is opposite to EULOGISTIC, meaning full of praise. Similarly, an antonym of OBSEQUIOUS, meaning compliant, is REFRACTORY, which means unruly.

33. **(d)** BLUE and ORANGE are related as complementary colors; RED and GREEN are also complementary colors.

34. **(a)** In this characteristic analogy, a CHEETAH is known for its SPEED; a BLADE is proverbially known for its KEENNESS.

35. **(a)** The correspondence is one of part to whole. A HOCK is part of a HORSE, the joint of the hind leg; a TONGUE is part of a BELL.

36. **(b)** In this sequence analogy, an EPILOGUE follows the main action of a NOVEL. A CURTAIN CALL follows APPLAUSE in a performance.

37. **(c)** TASMANIA is an island state of AUSTRALIA; HAWAII is an island state of the UNITED STATES.

38. **(d)** JOCASTA was the mother of OEDIPUS; ANCHISES was the father of AENEAS.

39. **(a)** LEES is a synonym for DREGS. Similarly, a synonym for SYBARITIC, devoted to pleasure of luxury, is SENSUAL.

40. **(a)** ISRAEL and JORDAN are countries which were both once part of the land of Palestine. VIETNAM and CAMBODIA were both once parts of French Indochina.

41. **(c)** A FOOTNOTE is an explanatory reference in a TEXT; a LEGEND is an explanatory list of symbols used on a MAP.

42. **(c)** In this action-to-object analogy, one can TELL TIME and one can CHEW GUM.

43. **(a)** "YANKEE DOODLE," a DUSTER, and a PILLOW are related because each is associated with feathers. To complete the analogy, you must select another term associated with feathers, and a chicken COOP is the correct choice.

44. **(b)** The correspondence is one of worker to the thing created. A COOPER makes a BARREL; a CARTOGRAPHER makes a MAP.

45. **(d)** In this sequence analogy, the PUPA is the last stage of development before the birth of a BUMBLEBEE just as the FETUS is the last stage of development before the birth of a CHILD.

46. **(a)** The correspondence is one of action to situation. DEALING is an activity related to the STOCK EXCHANGE. PRESERVING is a typical activity associated with a LANDMARK.

47. **(a)** In this analogy of degree, a FIB is not quite telling a LIE; an UPRISING may not quite be a REVOLUTION.

48. **(d)** The relationship is one of geographical location. BOLIVIA is a country directly north of ARGENTINA. CORSICA is an island located directly north of the island of SARDINIA.

49. **(b)** The correspondence is one of object to action. One may EXORCISE EVIL; one may BREAK BREAD.

50. **(c)** The YOLK is the yellow part of an egg and the ALBUMEN is part of the egg white. A COWARD is associated with the color yellow; a HERO is associated with the color white.

51. **(c)** OBDURATE, meaning hardened in feelings, and COMPASSIONATE, meaning sympathetic to the distress of others, are antonyms. PIQUANT, meaning pungent or savory, and VAPID, meaning insipid or flat, are also antonyms.

52. **(a)** CUCUMBER, WATERMELON, CANTALOUPE, and SQUASH are all related because they have many seeds and grow on vines.

53. **(d)** In this part-to-whole analogy, a VIOLIN has four STRINGS and a MAN has four LIMBS.

54. **(a)** The correspondence is one of cause and effect. VIBRATION causes SOUND; ILLNESS causes DEBILITY.

55. **(b)** VERDUN and YPRES were battles fought in World War I; DUNKIRK and EL ALAMEIN were famous battles of World War II.

56. **(c)** REVENGE is the object of a VENDETTA; LOOT is the object of a ROBBERY. Gain or profit might also be objects of robbery, but loot is a more specific and characteristic object.

57. **(a)** FREUD attempted to relieve mental disorders through ANALYSIS; OSTEOPATHY attempts to relieve physical disorders through MANIPULATION of affected parts.

58. **(d)** A person suffering from CLAUSTROPHOBIA (a fear of closed spaces) would fear CLOSETS; a person suffering from AGORAPHOBIA (fear of open spaces) would fear PLAINS.

59. **(a)** A positive result of a SEARCH is to FIND what you are looking for; a positive result of a FIGHT is to WIN.

60. **(a)** In mythology, MARS, as the god of war, would encourage a FRACAS; as the goddess of love, APHRODITE would encourage SYMPATHY.

61. **(b)** In this sequence analogy, the difference between H, the eighth letter in the alphabet, and S, the nineteenth, is eleven. The letter with the same relation to W, the twenty-third letter, is L, the twelfth letter in the alphabet.

62. **(d)** The correspondence here is grammatical. HASTILY, DESPONDENTLY, and CIRCUMSPECTLY are all related as adverbs. Among the choices given, only SLOWLY is also an adverb.

63. **(c)** BOXER and LABRADOR are both breeds of dog; TABBY and CALICO are both descriptive terms applied to cat markings.

64. **(b)** In this characteristic analogy, CROESUS was known for his great WEALTH; ODYSSEUS was known for his great CRAFT.

65. **(c)** In this place analogy, Lake LUCERNE and Lake GENEVA are in Switzerland; Lake MICHIGAN and Lake OKEECHOBEE are in the United States.

66. **(c)** The SCRIPT is the written text of a PLAY; the SCORE is the written version of the music to be played at a CONCERT.

67. **(a)** Marc CONNELLY wrote a famous play with the word PASTURES in the title. The play was the Pulitzer Prize-winning *The Green Pastures*. Eldridge CLEAVER wrote a famous book with the word ICE in the title. The book was *Soul on Ice*.

68. **(c)** Call this one actor to object. The DOG attacks the INTRUDER; the KNIGHT attacks the DRAGON.

69. **(c)** The word *cleave* has two meanings. It can mean both *to cut* and *to adhere*. This analogy question draws upon the two meanings of the word *cleave* and their synonyms. On the left, to REND is to tear is to CLEAVE; on the right, to STICK is to adhere is to CLEAVE.

70. **(d)** RABBITs congregate in a WARREN; PARTRIDGEs congregate in a COVEY.

71. **(a)** The relationship is one of worker to his material. A LAPIDARY (an engraver of precious stones) may work with a RUBY; a SCULPTOR may work with ALABASTER.

72. **(b)** The correspondence is one of association of words. We speak of WARP and WOOF and also of RANK and FILE.

73. **(d)** The analogy is based upon the grammatical distinction between number and amount. Make up a parallel sentence to choose the best answer.

"MANY (in number) raindrops make MUCH (in amount) water; FEW (in number) raindrops make LITTLE (in amount) water." *Less* makes a reasonable and correct sentence but not a parallel completion of the analogy.

74. (a) In this grammatical analogy, FORSOOK and DRANK are simple past tenses; FROZEN and SWUM are past participles.

75. (b) This relationship is one of degree. A SANDAL is a lighter version of footwear than a BOOT; a HATCHET is a smaller version of a sharp-edged instrument than an AX.

76. (b) In this mythological analogy, a CENTAUR is half HORSE, half man; a SATYR is half GOAT, half man.

77. (d) The correspondence is one of whole to part. A CELL is part of a BATTERY; a SHAFT is part of an ARROW.

78. (c) In this degree analogy, a FELONY is a more serious offense than a MISDEMEANOR; similarly, a SIN is a more serious offense than a PECCADILLO (a slight offense).

79. (b) In the words of the well-known mnemonic rhyme, "Thirty days hath SEPTEMBER, APRIL, JUNE, and NOVEMBER."

80. (a) This analogy has to do with political alignments in the Communist world. ALBANIA and CHINA have Communist governments that are entirely outside the sphere of influence of the Soviet Union. POLAND and CZECHOSLOVAKIA are very much under Soviet domination.

81. (d) DISINTERESTED is a synonym for IMPARTIAL; a synonym for WASTEFUL is PRODIGAL.

82. (b) A SCHOONER and a CRUISER are both types of ships. A ZIGGURAT and a CAMPANILE are both types of towers.

83. (d) In this analogy of characteristics, we speak of the mighty (STURDY) OAK and the weeping (MOURNFUL) WILLOW.

84. (b) The relationship is one of degree. EXHORT means to urge on, which is a stronger degree of ADVISE; ENTICE is a stronger degree of TEMPT.

85. (b) In this action-to-object analogy, you WELD two pieces of STEEL to join or hold them together; you PURSE your LIPS by holding or pressing them together.

86. (a) TESTIMONY is a statement about someone else; a CONFESSION is a statement about oneself. A BIOGRAPHY is the written history of another person's life; an AUTOBIOGRAPHY is the written history of one's own life.

87. **(d)** The relationship in this analogy is grammatical. The plural of SYLLABUS is SYLLABI; the plural of STRATUM is STRATA.

88. **(b)** A LAMB and a DEER are related because they are both considered timid; a PEACOCK and a LION are related because they are both considered proud.

89. **(c)** The BEAUFORT Scale (invented by Sir Francis Beaufort) indicates VELOCITY of the wind in numbers from 10 to 12. The RICHTER Scale (named after Charles Richter) indicates the magnitude of a seismic VIBRATION or earthquake.

90. **(a)** The Greek root *tele* in TELEVISION means DISTANCE; the Greek root *arch* in ANARCHY means LEADER.

91. **(d)** A TATOO is an evening military signal, and VESPERS are evening prayers; REVEILLE is a morning military signal, and MATINS are morning prayers.

92. **(c)** In this situation-to-action analogy, a person who is PROSTRATE is in a position for YIELDING; a person who is SUPINE is in a position for SLEEPING.

93. **(b)** MAHATMA GANDHI was opposed to all forms of violence including WAR as CARRY NATION was opposed to the use of any kind of ALCOHOL.

94. **(d)** In this mathematical analogy, 1/4 of 4/7 is 1/7; 1/4 of 2/7 is 1/14.

95. **(a)** The relationship is one of real to imaginary. A PHOENIX is an imaginary bird and an EAGLE is an actual bird. Similarly, a ROC is imaginary and a VULTURE is real.

96. **(a)** A TINE is part of a FORK; a FLANGE is part of a WHEEL.

97. **(d)** One's ATTIRE is brightened with some DECORATION; one's COMMUNICATION is brightened with WIT.

98. **(c)** In this analogy, the relationship is one of discardable to usable. The HUSK is the discardable part of GRAIN; GRISTLE is the discardable part of MEAT. Note that fat may be discarded or used.

99. **(b)** The correspondence is one of degree. WORK is a milder form of TOIL; STARTLED is a milder form of ASTOUNDED.

100. **(d)** SPARTAN, meaning terse in speech, is the opposite of GARRULOUS: INEBRIOUS, which means drunken, is the opposite of ABSTEMIOUS, or temperate.

ANSWER SHEET
MILLER ANALOGIES SAMPLE TEST V

1 Ⓐ Ⓑ Ⓒ Ⓓ	21 Ⓐ Ⓑ Ⓒ Ⓓ	41 Ⓐ Ⓑ Ⓒ Ⓓ	61 Ⓐ Ⓑ Ⓒ Ⓓ	81 Ⓐ Ⓑ Ⓒ Ⓓ
2 Ⓐ Ⓑ Ⓒ Ⓓ	22 Ⓐ Ⓑ Ⓒ Ⓓ	42 Ⓐ Ⓑ Ⓒ Ⓓ	62 Ⓐ Ⓑ Ⓒ Ⓓ	82 Ⓐ Ⓑ Ⓒ Ⓓ
3 Ⓐ Ⓑ Ⓒ Ⓓ	23 Ⓐ Ⓑ Ⓒ Ⓓ	43 Ⓐ Ⓑ Ⓒ Ⓓ	63 Ⓐ Ⓑ Ⓒ Ⓓ	83 Ⓐ Ⓑ Ⓒ Ⓓ
4 Ⓐ Ⓑ Ⓒ Ⓓ	24 Ⓐ Ⓑ Ⓒ Ⓓ	44 Ⓐ Ⓑ Ⓒ Ⓓ	64 Ⓐ Ⓑ Ⓒ Ⓓ	84 Ⓐ Ⓑ Ⓒ Ⓓ
5 Ⓐ Ⓑ Ⓒ Ⓓ	25 Ⓐ Ⓑ Ⓒ Ⓓ	45 Ⓐ Ⓑ Ⓒ Ⓓ	65 Ⓐ Ⓑ Ⓒ Ⓓ	85 Ⓐ Ⓑ Ⓒ Ⓓ
6 Ⓐ Ⓑ Ⓒ Ⓓ	26 Ⓐ Ⓑ Ⓒ Ⓓ	46 Ⓐ Ⓑ Ⓒ Ⓓ	66 Ⓐ Ⓑ Ⓒ Ⓓ	86 Ⓐ Ⓑ Ⓒ Ⓓ
7 Ⓐ Ⓑ Ⓒ Ⓓ	27 Ⓐ Ⓑ Ⓒ Ⓓ	47 Ⓐ Ⓑ Ⓒ Ⓓ	67 Ⓐ Ⓑ Ⓒ Ⓓ	87 Ⓐ Ⓑ Ⓒ Ⓓ
8 Ⓐ Ⓑ Ⓒ Ⓓ	28 Ⓐ Ⓑ Ⓒ Ⓓ	48 Ⓐ Ⓑ Ⓒ Ⓓ	68 Ⓐ Ⓑ Ⓒ Ⓓ	88 Ⓐ Ⓑ Ⓒ Ⓓ
9 Ⓐ Ⓑ Ⓒ Ⓓ	29 Ⓐ Ⓑ Ⓒ Ⓓ	49 Ⓐ Ⓑ Ⓒ Ⓓ	69 Ⓐ Ⓑ Ⓒ Ⓓ	89 Ⓐ Ⓑ Ⓒ Ⓓ
10 Ⓐ Ⓑ Ⓒ Ⓓ	30 Ⓐ Ⓑ Ⓒ Ⓓ	50 Ⓐ Ⓑ Ⓒ Ⓓ	70 Ⓐ Ⓑ Ⓒ Ⓓ	90 Ⓐ Ⓑ Ⓒ Ⓓ
11 Ⓐ Ⓑ Ⓒ Ⓓ	31 Ⓐ Ⓑ Ⓒ Ⓓ	51 Ⓐ Ⓑ Ⓒ Ⓓ	71 Ⓐ Ⓑ Ⓒ Ⓓ	91 Ⓐ Ⓑ Ⓒ Ⓓ
12 Ⓐ Ⓑ Ⓒ Ⓓ	32 Ⓐ Ⓑ Ⓒ Ⓓ	52 Ⓐ Ⓑ Ⓒ Ⓓ	72 Ⓐ Ⓑ Ⓒ Ⓓ	92 Ⓐ Ⓑ Ⓒ Ⓓ
13 Ⓐ Ⓑ Ⓒ Ⓓ	33 Ⓐ Ⓑ Ⓒ Ⓓ	53 Ⓐ Ⓑ Ⓒ Ⓓ	73 Ⓐ Ⓑ Ⓒ Ⓓ	93 Ⓐ Ⓑ Ⓒ Ⓓ
14 Ⓐ Ⓑ Ⓒ Ⓓ	34 Ⓐ Ⓑ Ⓒ Ⓓ	54 Ⓐ Ⓑ Ⓒ Ⓓ	74 Ⓐ Ⓑ Ⓒ Ⓓ	94 Ⓐ Ⓑ Ⓒ Ⓓ
15 Ⓐ Ⓑ Ⓒ Ⓓ	35 Ⓐ Ⓑ Ⓒ Ⓓ	55 Ⓐ Ⓑ Ⓒ Ⓓ	75 Ⓐ Ⓑ Ⓒ Ⓓ	95 Ⓐ Ⓑ Ⓒ Ⓓ
16 Ⓐ Ⓑ Ⓒ Ⓓ	36 Ⓐ Ⓑ Ⓒ Ⓓ	56 Ⓐ Ⓑ Ⓒ Ⓓ	76 Ⓐ Ⓑ Ⓒ Ⓓ	96 Ⓐ Ⓑ Ⓒ Ⓓ
17 Ⓐ Ⓑ Ⓒ Ⓓ	37 Ⓐ Ⓑ Ⓒ Ⓓ	57 Ⓐ Ⓑ Ⓒ Ⓓ	77 Ⓐ Ⓑ Ⓒ Ⓓ	97 Ⓐ Ⓑ Ⓒ Ⓓ
18 Ⓐ Ⓑ Ⓒ Ⓓ	38 Ⓐ Ⓑ Ⓒ Ⓓ	58 Ⓐ Ⓑ Ⓒ Ⓓ	78 Ⓐ Ⓑ Ⓒ Ⓓ	98 Ⓐ Ⓑ Ⓒ Ⓓ
19 Ⓐ Ⓑ Ⓒ Ⓓ	39 Ⓐ Ⓑ Ⓒ Ⓓ	59 Ⓐ Ⓑ Ⓒ Ⓓ	79 Ⓐ Ⓑ Ⓒ Ⓓ	99 Ⓐ Ⓑ Ⓒ Ⓓ
20 Ⓐ Ⓑ Ⓒ Ⓓ	40 Ⓐ Ⓑ Ⓒ Ⓓ	60 Ⓐ Ⓑ Ⓒ Ⓓ	80 Ⓐ Ⓑ Ⓒ Ⓓ	100 Ⓐ Ⓑ Ⓒ Ⓓ

FINANCING YOUR GRADUATE EDUCATION

E ducation is expensive, and the higher the level of education, the greater the cost. As you contemplate going on to graduate or professional school, you must face the awesome question, "How am I going to pay for this?"

With the possible exceptions of a winning lottery ticket, a windfall inheritance or a very wealthy family, no single source of funds will be adequate to cover tuition, other educational costs, and living expenses during your years of graduate study. While the funding task is daunting, it is not impossible. With patience and hard work, you can piece together your own financial package.

CONSIDER DEFERRING YOUR APPLICATION

Y ou might consider putting off applications for a few years while you work at the highest paying job you can find and accumulate some funds. A few years' savings will not cover the entire bill, but they can help. A real effort to earn your own way is a show of sincerity and good faith when you approach funders, too. You are probably better off delaying your applications altogether rather than applying and deferring your entry once you have been accepted. Deferral, if permitted, is generally limited to one year, and one year may not be sufficient to build your tuition fund.

If you cannot find a really high-paying job, you might seek a position or series of positions closely related to your field for the years between undergraduate and graduate or professional school. A year or more of exposure and involvement can help you to focus your interest. Experience in the field shows up as an asset on your graduate admissions applications and on your applications for fellowships. The more crystallized your interests, the better essays and personal statements you can write to support your requests.

Another benefit to deferral is the opportunity to establish residence. As you research the various graduate programs, you are likely to discover that some of the most exciting programs in your field of interest are being offered at state universities. State universities tend to have lower tuition rates than do private universities. Furthermore, the tuition charged to bona fide residents

2 ■ FINANCING YOUR GRADUATE EDUCATION

is considerably lower than that charged to out-of-state residents. The requirements for establishing residence vary from state to state; make it a point to inquire about the possibility of in-state tuition at each state university you are considering. The suggestion that you delay application until you are nearly ready to enter graduate school does not hold with regard to delay for purposes of establishing residence. Since you can only establish residence in one state, you want to apply and be accepted before you select your new home state. Most universities will cooperate and will allow you to move to the state, find employment, and defer enrollment until you qualify for in-state tuition.

WORKING PART-TIME

Another possible way to pay—this one hard on you but possible at many, though not at all, institutions—is to be a part-time student and a full- or part-time wage earner. Again, there are a number of options. You might find a totally unrelated but high-paying job. You will have to be creative in your search. Sanitation workers, for instance, tend to have hours like 7 am to 3 pm which leaves afternoon and evening for classes and study. The job of the sanitation worker is physically exhausting but makes no mental demands and in most localities is quite well paid. Another job which does not take too much thought is working for a courier service like United Parcel. Such delivery services operate twenty-four hours a day. During the night, packages are off-loaded from big interstate trucks and from bulk deliveries from individual shippers and are sorted and loaded onto delivery trucks for route drivers the next day. There is usually plenty of turnover among these night workers, and most parcel service employees are unionized, so the hourly rate is attractive. An alternative to physical labor might be seeking a job in a field related to your studies. Such a job could reinforce your learning and contribute to the job experience section of your resume. If you are earning a degree in computer science, you might find computer-related employment. If you are entering law school, you might work as a paralegal.

GETTING HELP FROM YOUR EMPLOYER

If you both defer application and enter a related field, you may be fortunate enough to find an employer who will pay for a part or even all of your graduate education. This option is most viable if the advanced degree is to be in business or law, but some corporations will finance a master's degree or even a doctorate if the further training will make the employee more valuable to them. Employers cannot require that you continue your employment for any specified number of years after earning your degree. Rather they rely on your gratitude and good will.

The programs under which employers help pay for education are as varied as the number of employers and the graduate programs. Many banks, insurance companies, and brokerage houses offer tuition rebates as part of their benefits packages. These companies rebate part or all of the tuition for courses successfully completed by their employees. Sometimes the rate of reimbursement is tied to the grade earned in the course. Some large law firms will advance part of the law school tuition for promising paralegals after a number of years of service. If these students successfully complete law school and return to the firm for summers and a certain number of years afterwards, the balance of the tuition may be reimbursed. And some industrial corporations will cover the cost of part-time study which enhances the skills of employees, thus making them still more useful to the organization. Such corporations may permit these employees to work a shortened work-week at full-time pay while they study. Some companies even give the employee a year's leave, without salary but with tuition paid, and with a guarantee that the employee will have a job at the end of the leave. This guaranteed position at the end of the leave is worth a lot. It offers peace of mind and freedom to concentrate on research and writing and assures that you will immediately begin earning money with which to repay supplementary graduate loans and leftover undergraduate loans.

If you have been working for the same employer for a year or more, you might do well to inquire about a tuition rebate program. If you are a valuable employee, your employer may be willing to make an investment in you.

THE MILITARY OPTION

If you are heavily burdened with loans from your undergraduate years and are willing to serve for three years in the armed forces, the government will pay off a large portion of your college loans for you. Without the undergraduate debt, you will be eligible for larger loans for your graduate study, and you will not have so many years of high repayment bills to face. After your three years of service, you will be eligible for GI Bill benefits so that you will not need to incur such hefty loans for graduate school. While you are actually in the service, you can attend graduate school part time and have 75% of the cost paid for you. Funding for medical school and law school is even more attractive. From the point of view of footing the bill for graduate studies, the military option sounds too good to be true. Of course there are strings attached. You must serve in the armed forces. You are subject to military rules and military discipline. You may find that a transfer of location totally disrupts your studies if you are trying to attend part time. And, in case of war or other military emergency, you must serve and quite possibly face physical danger. This is the trade-off. If the advantages of having the government pay your education bills outweigh the drawbacks in your eyes, by all means explore the military option. Check with more than one branch of the services; programs vary and change frequently. Ask lots of questions. Be certain that you fully understand all of your obligations, and insist that the funding commitment be in writing. You cannot change your mind and just quit the armed forces, so you must be certain that this route is right for you before you sign up.

If full-time military service is out of the question for you, but having the government underwrite your education is still attractive, consider the National Guard or the Reserves. The all-volunteer standing armed forces are not adequate for all national security needs, so efforts are constantly being made to increase the appeal of the Guard and the Reserves. The benefits offered are frequently readjusted, so you must make your own inquiries about loan repayments and funding of ongoing education while you are in service. Life in the Guard or the Reserves is not nearly so restrictive on a daily basis as life in the regular armed forces, but both Guard members and Reservists are subject to call-up in times of need, and if you are called, you must serve. Circumstances of a call-up may include dangerous assignment, severe economic difficulties, or service that you find morally repugnant (such as strike-breaking if you are a member of a Guard unit called by the governor). If these contingencies do not upset you, this form of long-term, part-time military service can relieve you of much of the cost of your advanced degree.

NEED-BASED FUNDING

The need-based funding picture for graduate studies is quite different from its counterpart at the undergraduate level. Most undergraduate funding is need-based; most graduate funding is not. All universities have a mechanism for distributing need-based funding, in grant/loan/self-help packages similar to undergraduate packages, but the funds are more limited. Your application information packet will tell you how to apply for need-based funding.

Basically you will have to fill out a university financial aid application, a U.S. Department of Education approved multi-data entry form (FFS, the family financial statement of American College Testing service; FAF, the financial aid form of the Educational Testing Service; or GAPS-FAS, the graduate and professional school financial aid service of the Educational Testing Service in California), and whatever other forms the university requires. The university will coordinate its need-based package with department sponsored merit funding and with any outside funding you can gather. Plan to look beyond university need-based funding. It will be top-heavy toward loans and will not be adequate for all your needs.

The following information distributed to all graduate school applicants by a leading large state university is specific to that university yet, at the same time, is representative of the need-based funding situation nationwide.

ASSISTANCE THROUGH THE OFFICE OF STUDENT FINANCIAL AID (OSFA)

You may be eligible for financial aid if you are enrolled at least half-time (five semester hours during the academic year, or three semester hours during the summer session) as a graduate student in a program leading to a degree. Students admitted as Special Nondegree Students may also be eligible for some of the programs listed below.

How to Apply

Specific information and application materials may be obtained from OSFA. To determine your eligibility for aid through the OSFA, you must provide information about your financial situation by submitting either the Financial Aid Form (FAF) to the College Scholarship Service (CSS) or the Family Financial Statement (FFS) to American College Testing (ACT). This University does not accept the Graduate and Professional School Financial Aid Service (GAPSFAS) form.

OSFA will process your financial aid application as soon as your file becomes complete. Some financial aid programs are subject to the availability of funds (first-come, first-served) and others are not. To be considered for all limited funds, be sure to submit your materials as soon as possible after January 1 for the upcoming academic year.

Financial need is an eligibility requirement for all of the following sources of assistance except the Supplemental Loans for Students (SLS) program and part-time jobs.

- Graduate Tuition Grants are based on exceptional need. These institutional grant funds are very limited. Approximately 200 students are awarded tuition grants early in the March prior to the academic year in which they plan to enroll.
- Educational Opportunity Program (EOP) Grants are institutional grants for minority students who demonstrate exceptional need.
- The College Work-Study Program is an employment program subsidized by the federal government and the state.
- Perkins Loans are long-term federal loans based on exceptional need.
- Stafford Loans (formerly Guaranteed Student Loans—GSL) are long-term federal loans based on need and arranged with a bank, credit union, or savings and loan.

■ Supplemental Loans for Students (SLS) are arranged with a bank, credit union or savings and loan and are available to students with or without need.

In addition, part-time jobs (not to be confused with College Work-Study jobs) available throughout the campus and community are posted daily on bulletin boards outside of the OSFA.

Special Note to Assistantship/Fellowship Recipients

Since most assistantship income is classified as "wages," it will not affect your academic year financial aid award (which is usually based on your previous year's income, according to the federal formula for determining financial aid eligibility). However, fellowship income classified as "scholarship" rather than "wages" will be treated as "scholarship resources" in your financial aid package, and thus may affect your eligibility for other financial aid programs.

Nonresident financial aid awardees who receive assistantships that allow resident classification for tuition purposes may have their need-based aid decreased due to the decrease in their educational cost.

Outside need-based funding in the form of grants is confined mainly to special populations. Since these grants are limited in number, they too are based on a combination of merit and need, not merely upon demonstrated need. Some of these special population grants are targeted toward bringing minority students into the professions, such as those sponsored by the Black Lawyers' Associations of various states. Others aim to develop academic talent among Native Americans and Hispanics. Others, such as Business and Professional Women's Foundation Scholarships, are earmarked for mature women reentering the academic world in search of advanced degrees. Grant and fellowship directories tend to index grants by specialty, by region of the country, by point in the studies and time span of funding, and by targeted population. When you consult these directories, you must consider your own identity along every possible dimension in order to locate all funding which could apply to you.

Much outside funding comes in the form of loans. Although helpful and often necessary, loans are still a last resort. For this reason, we shall defer our discussion of loans until the end of this chapter.

FELLOWSHIPS AND ASSISTANTSHIPS

By far the greatest source of funding for graduate study is the graduate department or program itself. Most departments dispense a mixed bag of fellowships, teaching assistantships and research assistantships. Some of these may be allocated to the department by the university; still others are foundation fellowships for which the department nominates its most promising candidates. In most cases, the amount of money attached to the various fellowships and assistantships varies greatly—from tuition abatement alone, to tuition abatement plus stipend (also of varying sums), to stipend alone. Some of the fellowships and assistantships are specifically earmarked for only the first year of graduate study. Others are annually renewable upon application and evidence of satisfactory work in the previous year. Still others are guaranteed for a specified number of years—through three years of coursework, for one year of research or fieldwork, or a stipend to pay living costs during the year of writing a dissertation, for example.

The information below describes graduate student funding only at the University of Iowa. It is presented here to open the array of possibilities. The information provided by other universities is similar, but each is unique.

SUPPORT FROM THE GRADUATE COLLEGE AND YOUR DEPARTMENT OR PROGRAM

The following awards and appointments are the primary sources of financial assistance available to graduate students through their department or program.

- Teaching and Research Assistantships available in most departments, offer stipends typically ranging from $9,000 to $10,000 for half-time appointments. In accordance with general University policy, assistantship holders (quarter-time or more) are classified as residents for fee purposes for the terms during which their appointments are held and any adjacent summer sessions in which they are enrolled. Students on an appointment of half-time or more may have to carry a reduced academic load.

- Iowa Fellowships for first-year graduate students entering doctoral programs carry a minimum stipend of $14,500 plus full tuition for four years on a year-round basis (academic year and summer session). For two of the four years and all summers, recipients have no assignments and are free to pursue their own studies, research and writing.

- Graduate College Block Allocation Fellowships carry a stipend of $8,000 for the academic year.

- Graduate Opportunity Fellowships for first-year graduate students from underrepresented ethnic minority groups carry a one-year stipend of $8,000 for the academic year.

- Scholarships, traineeships, and part-time employment are offered by many graduate departments and programs. Funds are received from both public and private agencies, individuals, corporations, and philanthropic organizations. In general, submission of the *Application for Graduate Awards and Appointments* places eligible applicants in consideration for these awards.

How to Apply

Submit your *Application for Graduate Awards and Appointments* to your department or program by February 1 if you wish to be considered for the following fall. These non-need-based awards are made on the basis of academic merit. Only students admitted to a graduate department or program are eligible to apply. Fellowship and assistantship recipients are also eligible to apply for tuition scholarships awarded in amounts up to full-time tuition and fees. Contact your program or department for more specific information.

Surprisingly, the overall wealth of the institution is not necessarily reflected in the graduate funding it offers. Some universities choose to devote the bulk of their discretionary funds to undergraduate need-based aid. Others offer a greater share to graduate students. Some graduate departments in some universities have separate endowments apart from the university endowment as a whole. A department with its own source of funds can dispense these funds as it wishes, within the restrictions of the endowment, of course.

The case of Clark University in Worcester, Massachusetts, is illustrative of the ways a particular department funds its students. Clark is a relatively small, financially strapped institution. University-based funding for undergraduates is severely limited. Yet, every doctoral candidate in the geography department is equally funded; each receives tuition abatement and an equal stipend in return for teaching or research assistance. The funding is guaranteed for three years of course work. How can this be? The geography department at Clark has, over the years, developed an extremely high reputation. It is considered one of the premier geography departments in the United States. The university considers investment in its geography department to be one of its priorities because maintaining the reputation of its flagship department enhances the reputation of the university as a whole. Leading professors are eager to be associated with leading departments, so the Clark geography faculty includes some luminaries in its ranks. These faculty members in turn attract research funds. Research funds are used in part to pay for the services of research assistants. Publication of results of the research attracts further grants. These funds cover a number of graduate students. The reputation of the department also leads it to draw the best and the brightest among its doctoral candidates. These highly qualified students often draw outside fellowships on the basis of their own merit. Students who bring in their own funding release department funds for other students. And because of its reputation and the reputed caliber of its students, the department is often offered the opportunity to nominate its students to compete for private fellowships. Money entering the department in this way releases still more of the limited funds for student support. In a good year, there may even be funds to help some students at the beginning of their dissertation research. The situation at Clark, while it is Clark's alone, indicates that it may be possible to find funding even in a small, struggling school. Graduate aid is not monolithic. You must ask about the special features in each department and in each program. Do not limit your research to the overall university bulletin!

Sometimes a university will offer some departments the opportunity to nominate candidates for outside fellowships open to students of certain specified departments or to students of the university at large. For example, the MacArthur Foundation funds a number of interdisciplinary fellowships in peace studies at a few selected universities. Each participating university is allocated a number of fellowships to dispense at its discretion. The university then opens the competition to appropriate departments, and the departments in turn nominate candidates from among their most promising applicants. The departments choose nominees on the basis of personal statements submitted at the time of application and on the basis of those applicants' credentials and background experiences. They then solicit the nominees to prepare additional application materials and essays and supply additional recommendations to support application for the fellowship. Having MacArthur fellows among its students brings both money and prestige to the department. Each department studies credentials and statements carefully before soliciting applicants. However, the department could overlook someone. If you have not been invited to apply for a fellowship which you think you qualify for, you can suggest to the department—diplomatically, of course—that you consider yourself a likely candidate.

Few individuals are awarded any one fellowship, but each person who does win one is assured a comfortable source of funding. And someone has to win. It might as well be you. Those who win the named fellowships are removed from the competition for other merit-based or need-based funding, thus increasing the chance of other applicants to win any remaining funds.

Most foundation-funded fellowships, especially those for entering graduate students, are channelled through the department or program. To be considered for these fellowships you must be recommended by the department. There are some fellowships out there, however, for which you must apply as an individual. Some of these are regional, and some are targeted at a specific population. Some are tied to a field such as economics or philosophy, and others have a specific purpose in mind such as studies aimed at improving the welfare of the homeless. Of the privately funded fellowships some are for the first year only, some for the full graduate career, some for the last year of course work only, and still others to support the dissertation at a specific stage or throughout research and writing. Some are relatively small awards; others are so generous that they provide total financial security to the student. The sources of these fellowships range from your local Rotary Club to Rotary International, to AAUW (American Association of University Women) fellowships, to the prestigious Rhodes Scholarships.

FUNDING POSSIBILITIES FROM PRIVATE FOUNDATIONS

The names of some of the philanthropic foundations that give grants for graduate study are almost household words—Dana, Mellon, Ford, Sloan, Rockefeller, Guggenheim, MacArthur, Fulbright, Woodrow Wilson are but a few. These foundations, and others like them, offer funding at many levels of study and for a variety of purposes.

The National Science Foundation offers funding for the full graduate program in science and engineering for minority students as well as for the general population. Other National Science Foundation fellowships specifically fund the research and writing of doctoral dissertations. The U.S. Department of Education Jacob K. Javits Fellowships fund full doctoral programs in the arts, humanities and social sciences. The National Research Council Howard Hughes Medical Institute Doctoral Fellowships offer tuition and a $10,000 per year stipend for three to five years of doctoral work in biology or the health sciences. The Eisenhower Memorial Scholarship Foundation offers a number of $3,000 per year scholarships. The Mellon and Ford Foundations both fund ABD (all but dissertation) fellowships for minority Ph.D. candidates. Under the terms of the ABD fellowships, candidates teach one course per term at a liberal arts college and receive a healthy stipend while writing their dissertations. This program has the double-barreled purpose of assisting minority students while developing teaching talent.

The AAUW (American Association of University Women) is very active in disbursing funds to women for graduate study. Local units give small gifts to undergraduates. Larger grants are made by the AAUW through its Educational Foundation Programs office. In some years the AAUW supports as many as fifty women at the dissertation stage. The Business and Professional Women's Foundation gives scholarships to mature women entering graduate programs. Some of these scholarships are earmarked for women over the age of 35. The American Women in Selected Professions Fellowships fund women in their last year of law or graduate studies in sums ranging from $3,500 to $9,000 apiece.

Other funding for doctoral dissertations comes from the Woodrow Wilson National Fellowship Foundation (in social sciences and humanities), from the Social Science Research Council, and the Guggenheim Foundation. Some foundation funding is reserved for study abroad. Rhodes Scholarships, in particular, support students studying at Oxford. Various Fulbrights, Wilsons, Marshalls, and MacArthurs, among others, support research in foreign universities and at field sites.

The above listing is far from exhaustive. In fact, this is only a tiny sampling of the funding possibilities from private foundations. Even so, the number of grants available is far exceeded by the the number of graduate students who would like to have them. You must work hard to identify and to earn the grants for which you qualify.

FINDING SOURCES OF FINANCIAL AID

There are a number of directories that list these prizes, scholarships, and fellowships one by one. The directories give the name of the sponsor, who to contact, addresses, phone numbers, and deadlines. They also tell something of the purpose of the grants, the number of grants awarded, specific qualification requirements, and the dollar amounts. If the grants are awarded to support research, the directories may give representative titles of projects funded. One of the most useful features of the directories is their cross-indexing. When you consult a grants directory you can look up sources under ethnic designations, geographic designations, subject of study, purpose of research, duration of funding, etc. These directories are very useful as a starting point in the search for outside funding.

Consult the list of directories in the bibliography at the end of this chapter. With list in hand, go to a college library, large public library, or the financial aid office of your current institution and sit down with a directory and pad of paper. Give yourself many hours to find all the grants for which you qualify and to photocopy or write down the important details of each. Immediately call or write each sponsor requesting application materials. Do not rely on deadlines printed in the directories and put off requesting materials. Deadlines change. Do not discount grants or prizes with low dollar amounts attached. A small grant may not be adequate to see you through even a semester of study, but it will do much to enhance your resume. The fact that you were able to compete successfully for any prize makes you a more attractive candidate for the higher-tagged fellowships you apply for next year. If a grant cannot be combined, you may have to decline it, but the fact of having won is already in your favor. Most often, small grants can be combined with other sources of funding, so even small ones help.

APPLYING FOR A GRANT

The procedure for applying for grants and fellowships for your coursework years is similar for both university-administered and private foundation sources. The best advice is to start early. Everything takes longer than you expect, and deadlines tend to be inviolate. Everyone with money to give away is besieged by applicants. There is no need to extend deadlines.

Once you receive application material, begin immediately to accumulate the specified documentation. Each sponsor has different requirements, so read carefully. You will probably need official transcripts from every college you ever attended, even if you took only one course over the summer. You are likely to be asked for official copies of test scores, too. Letters of recommendation are always required. Think about them carefully. You want to request letters from people who have known you as a scholar—professors with whom you have worked closely or authors for whom you have done research or fact checking. You want your letters to be written by people whom you believe have admired your work and who express themselves well. And, consider the reliability of the people from whom you request letters of recommendation. Your application can be seriously jeopardized or even torpedoed if your recommendations do not come through on time. Choose carefully. Consider asking for one extra recommendation just in case someone lets you down. Having recommendations sent to you and then forwarding them in their sealed envelopes is the best way to keep track of what has come in if this procedure is permitted by the sponsor. Be aware that you may have to make a pest of yourself to get transcripts and letters in on time.

You are more in control of the other documents you are likely to be asked for in support of your application. The first of these is a "personal goals statement." This is a carefully reasoned, clear statement of your interests, the reasons for your choice of program, personal growth goals, and career goals. Ideally you should prepare this statement on a word processor so that you can retain the basic exposition but tailor each statement to the needs and interests of the specific sponsor. Try to tie in your statement with the special strengths of the program and with the advantages offered by a particular sponsor. Be sincere and enthusiastic. Adhere to the page limits or word count specified in the application instructions. And remember, neatness counts.

You may also be asked for your resume, samples of scholarly writing or summaries of research you have done. If the grant you seek is meant to finance research or dissertation, you may have to go into detail about the scope of your research, methodology, purpose, expected final results and even proposed budget. Give thought before you write. Then follow the sponsor's instructions, providing all the information that is requested, but not so much more as to overwhelm or bore the reader.

One caveat: Read the requirements carefully before you apply. If you do not fully qualify, do not apply. There are ample qualified applicants for every grant. Requirements will not be waived. The application process is an exacting one and requires you to impose upon others. Do not waste their time or your own.

EMPLOYMENT OPPORTUNITIES ON CAMPUS

While your department is clearly the best university-based source for fellowships, teaching assistantships, and research assistantships, do not totally discount the university as a whole. If you have an area of expertise outside of your own graduate department, by all means build upon it. If you are bilingual in a language taught at the university, you may be able to teach in the language department. Your best chance for a teaching assistantship outside of your department is in a university with relatively few graduate programs. Departments must favor their own graduate students, but if a department has no qualified students of its own, it may be delighted to acquire the services of a graduate student from another department. Some universities even have a formalized mechanism for allocating teaching assistants where they are needed. To return to the example of Clark, where all graduate students must serve as research or teaching assistants, often there are not as many openings for assistants in the undergraduate geography department as there are students. Clark has relatively few graduate programs, and geography students tend to have strong backgrounds in political science, economics and ecology. The graduate geography department and the undergraduate deans readily cooperate to place geography students where they are most needed. In universities with less defined needs for teaching assistants, you may have to be your own advocate. Regardless of your current department, if you can document your ability to assist in another department, you should pursue opportunities there. Do not be shy; let your area of special competence be well known.

Another possible source of university employment is as a residence advisor or freshman advisor. At some colleges and universities, residence advisors are undergraduates. At other institutions, older students—graduate students or students in one of the professional schools—are preferred. If you took peer- counseling training while in high school, consider yourself a candidate. If you were successful in a counseling function during your own undergraduate years, you should be a natural. In very large universities with big freshmen dormitories, a few graduate students with experience in residence advising may be taken on to coordinate and supervise the senior undergraduates who serve as floor or wing advisors. Obviously there are not many such coordinator positions available, but if you qualify, you may get the job.

There are a number of possible advantages to being appointed to a major university-based position such as teaching assistant or residence advisor. One is that, at a state university, you will become eligible instantly for in-state tuition. The reduced tuition is a valuable, non-taxable benefit. Another possibility is that you will be classified as an employee of the university. Policies vary, of course, but at many institutions employees of the university are eligible for reduced tuition or even for total remission of tuition. In addition, assistants generally receive a stipend which even if it does not totally cover living expenses is certainly a big help. Residence hall advisors may get free room along with tuition abatement, and residence hall advisors generally get choice accommodations.

If you were a member of a fraternity or sorority as an undergraduate, you may fulfill a role similar to that of residence advisor in your fraternity or sorority house. As an employee of the fraternity or sorority rather than of the university, you will not be eligible for employee-of-the-university benefits, but you will have free housing and, quite possibly, a salary or stipend as well. Fraternity employment will count toward self-help in a need-based package, but it should have no adverse effect on your winning a merit-based fellowship as well. Be aware, though, that if you are holding what is in effect two jobs, you may have to carry a lighter course load.

Students who work part time in the library, equipment and facilities departments, or in food service will probably not qualify for the perquisites of employees of the university (though depending on the institution and the number of hours worked they might). Campus-based hourly work tends not to be very well paid, but it does offer certain advantages such as elimination of travel time and costs and exemption from FICA (social security) deductions from your paycheck. Exemption from FICA is at the option of the institution, but is permitted by the federal tax code. The contribution which is not deducted has the effect of adding more than 7% to your salary.

ALL LOANS ARE NOT ALIKE

Finally loans come in to fill the financing gap. If you are already saddled with loans from your undergraduate education, you may cringe at the prospect of accumulating further debt. Don't panic. Not all loans are alike, and not all repayment schedules are equally onerous.

In particular, members of minority groups find creative financing routes available to them. The Consortium on the Financing of Higher Education (C.O.F.H.E.), a group of thirty-one universities and colleges including the Ivies and Sister colleges, is making a concerted effort to encourage minority students to pursue advanced degrees. The Kluge Foundation program at Columbia University is only one response to the funding problem. Because Columbia University is an expensive private university, its undergraduates often find themselves heavily indebted to the university by commencement. Under the terms of the Kluge grant, minority alumni of Columbia who successfully complete doctoral programs at accredited universities will have their undergraduate indebtedness wiped out by the Kluge funds. The Minority Issues Task Force of the Council of Graduate Schools is working on the funding problems of minority students, many of whom have very few resources. The funding picture is in constant flux. Be sure that you have the most current information at the moment you are ready to begin applying.

The loan forgiveness possibilities for members of the armed forces have already been touched upon. If military service is not for you, there are other loan forgiveness programs you may find attractive. With the shortage of highly-qualified, highly-motivated public school teachers, there has been a concerted effort to attract liberal arts graduates, even without full teaching credentials, into public school teaching. Liberal arts graduates who enter the public school teaching force under certain programs can have their undergraduate loans written off. If you enter public school teaching after receiving a graduate degree, you may still receive considerable help with those undergraduate loans. Paying off your own graduate school loans, then, will not be so overwhelming.

Most of the loan forgiveness programs for graduate loans apply to professional studies—medicine, dentistry, law, social work—rather than to straight academic disciplines. If your graduate studies will lead to a professional degree, you should not discount loan forgiveness programs out of hand.

A doctor who forgoes a lucrative suburban practice in favor of practicing for a number of years in an underserved area, be it poverty-ridden inner city or isolated rural community, may have a good portion of his or her loans paid off by the government or by private foundations or forgiven by the medical school itself. The doctor may find that the challenges of this practice and the gratitude of the population served are so satisfying that he or she will choose to make this practice a lifelong career. If not, the experience will certainly have been valuable as the doctor moves in new directions. Similarly, a number of prestigious law schools will wipe out the loans of their graduates who enter public service law instead of high-paying corporate law firms. And schools of social work or professional associations of social workers may help to pay off the loans of social workers who utilize their advanced degrees in certain aspects of social work or in highly underserved areas. If your ideals encourage using your educational opportunities to help others, you may find this assistance with your loan payments to give you the best of all possible worlds. The time commitment tends to only be a few years, after which you can move into the private sector with excellent experience to further your applications. Or, you may find that you really enjoy the work you have taken on and build a satisfying career in public service.

There are a number of other loan programs which, while they entail repayment, offer attractive features. The Hattie M. Strong Foundation, for instance, offers interest-free loans for the final year of graduate school or law school on the assumption that without money worries the student can earn higher grades in the final year and obtain a better position after graduation.

From your undergraduate days, you are probably aware of Stafford loans, formerly known as GSLs or Guaranteed Student Loans. At the graduate level the annual cap is $7,500 per year up to a borrowing limit of $54,750. The Stafford loan carries a lower rate of interest than most other loans. More important, repayment need not begin until six months after receipt of the degree, and the government pays the interest in the interim. There is a means test attached to the Stafford loan. Not every applicant is automatically eligible. However, many graduate students who are no longer dependent on parental income or assets do qualify for Stafford loans even though they did not as undergraduates.

University sponsored loans tend to be heavily need-based and to come as parts of total financial aid packages with grants, assistantships and jobs. And even need-based loans are often earmarked for specific underrepresented populations. If you think that you qualify, ask for the information and forms.

Everything that has been said about private foundation funding applies equally to loans as to grants and fellowships. The same directories which can lead you to grants and fellowships can lead you to foundation loans. Again, some of these require evidence of need; others are strictly merit-based. Some apply to the early years of graduate study; others are geared to the dissertation years. Some carry no or low rates of interest, and some have forgiveness provisions if certain conditions are met. In general, foundation loans are less painful than commercial loans. Do not limit your search through the grant directories to high-paying grants. Give equal attention to the smaller prizes and to the loan programs.

Most other loan programs are unrestricted as to income or assets but tend to have restrictions related to total debt with which the student is already burdened and to security or cosigners for the loan. The financial aid office of your current institution or the school to which you have been accepted can help you find your way through the maze of acronymic loan programs: SLS, PLUS, ALAS, TERI, Sallie Mae, Nellie Mae, and the Law Access Program administered by the Law School Admission Service. These last four are non-profit loan agencies which allow for greater flexibility than do the first three. In general the rates are tied to prime + 2 which is better than commercial rates. Repayment schedules, loan consolidation arrangements, co-signing requirements, etc. are all considered on a case-by-case basis.

GETTING INTO GRADUATE SCHOOL

Now that you know it is possible to pay for your graduate education, you must move toward securing admission and funding.

You have already taken a step toward graduate school because you have in hand a preparation book for a graduate school admission exam. Presumably you are about to take or have already taken one or more of these exams. A good score on the exam is an important component of the picture of competence and capability that you present to graduate programs and funding sponsors. If your grades and achievements have been impressive, a high score confirms you as an all-around good candidate. If either grades or achievements are mediocre, then high scores are imperative to bolster your cause. If you have not already taken the exam, study hard; prepare well. If you did not achieve a competitive score on a previous administration, it might be worthwhile to prepare further and try again.

The next thing to do is to begin to investigate which schools have the right programs for you. If you are still in college or out only a year or two, consult with professors who know you well, who are familiar not only with your interests but with your style of working. Professors may suggest programs that suit your needs, universities that offer emphasis in your areas of interest, and faculty members with whom you might work especially well. Your professors may have inside information about contemplated changes in program, focus or personnel at various institutions. This information can supplement the information in university bulletins and help you to decide which schools to apply to. If you have been out of school for several years, you may have to rely more on information bulletins. But do not stop there. Ask for advice and suggestions from people in the field, from present employers if your job is related to your career goals, and from the current faculty and advising staff at your undergraduate school. While the current personnel may not be familiar with you and your learning style, they will have up-to-date information on programs and faculties.

Send for university and departmental literature. Read everything you can about programs offered. Then study the statements on aid, both need-based and merit-based. Be sure that you are completely clear as to the process—criteria, forms required, other supporting documents, and deadlines. If any step of the process seems ambiguous, make phone calls. You can't afford to miss out on possible funding because you misinterpreted the application directions.

DON'T MISS DEADLINES

It's a good idea to prepare a master calendar dedicated to graduate school. Note the deadlines for each step of the process for every school, for every foundation, for every possible source of funds. Consult the master calendar daily. Anticipate deadlines, record actions taken by you and by others, follow up, keep on top of it. Do not just let events happen. Be proactive every step of the way.

The university, graduate school, and departmental bulletins will inform you about need-based aid and about any merit-based funding—teaching assistantships, research assistantships, no-strings fellowships, and private foundation fellowships—administered by the university or any of its divisions. This information will be complete for the funding to which it applies. It will include all procedures, documentation required, and deadlines. None of the literature you receive from the university, however, will tell you about fellowships or other funding for which you must apply directly. You must consult grants directories, foundation directories, and other source books to find the prizes, awards, scholarships, grants and fellowships for which you might qualify.

The following bibliography is an eclectic list of directories. The directories are listed by title and publisher without dates of publication. Most directories are updated frequently. Whenever you ask for a directory, look at the copyright date. If the directory appears to be more than a year old, ask the librarian if there is a newer edition available. Consult the most recent edition you can find. No matter how frequently a directory is updated, you should never rely on deadline dates given for grants. Write or call the sponsor of each grant that you are considering, and request the most current literature. Make certain that names and addresses have not changed. Verify dates for each step of the process. The information in the directory is a valuable starting point, but it is just that: a starting point.

Most of the directories listed below apply to more than one population. Use the index and the list of categories to find which portions of the book apply to you. Disregard any categories into which you do not fit. Concentrate in those areas where you do.

Aside from their copious cross-referencing, most directories also include bibliographies listing other information sources. Do not neglect these lists. One may send you to the perfect source for you.

BIBLIOGRAPHY

GENERAL DIRECTORIES

American Legion Education Program. Need a Lift? To Educational Opportunities, Careers, Loans, Scholarships, Employment. American Legion: Indianapolis, IN

Annual Register of Grant Support. Marquis: Chicago, IL

Catalog of Federal Domestic Assistance. U.S. Office of Management and Budget: Washington, D.C.

Chronicle Student Aid Annual. Chronicle Guidance Publication: Moravia, NY

*The College Blue Book,*Vol entitled *Scholarships, Fellowships, Grants & Loans.* Macmillan, NY

Directory of Financial Aids for Minorities. Reference Service Press: Santa Barbara, CA

Directory of Financial Aids for Women. Reference Service Press: Santa Barbara, CA

DRG: Directory of Research Grants. Oryx Press: Scottsdale, AZ

A Foreign Student's Selected Guide to Financial Assistance for Study and Research in the United States. Adelphi University Press: Garden City, NY

Foundation Directory. The Foundation Center: New York

Foundation Grants to Individuals. The Foundation Center: New York

The Graduate Scholarship Book, by Daniel J. Cassidy. Prentice Hall: New York.

Grants for Graduate Students, edited by John J. Wells and Amy J. Goldstein. Petersons: Princeton, NJ

The Grants Register. St. Martins: New York

Scholarships, Fellowships and Loans, Vols. VI-VIII. Bellman Publishing Co.: Arlington, MA

Selected List of Fellowship Opportunities and Aids to Advanced Education for United States Citizens and Foreign Nationals. National Science Foundation: Washington, D.C.

Taft Corporate Giving Directory: Comprehensive Profiles & Analyses of Major Corporate Philanthropic Programs. The Taft Group

---

FIELD AND SUBJECT DIRECTORIES

American Art Directory. R.R. Bowker: New York

American Mathematical Society Notices: "Assistantships and Fellowships in the Mathematical Sciences." December issue, each year.

American Philosophical Association. Proceedings and Addresses: "Grants and Fellowships of Interest to Philosophers." June each year.

Graduate Study in Psychology and Associated Fields. American Psychological Association: Washington, D.C.

Grants for the Arts, by Virginia P. White. Plenum Press: New York.

Grants and Awards Available to American Writers. PEN American Center: New York

Grants, Fellowships and Prizes of Interest to Historians. American Historical Association: Washington, D.C.

Grants in the Humanities: A Scholar's Guide to Funding Sources. Neal-Schuman: New York.

Journalism Career and Scholarship Guide. The Newspaper Fund: Princeton, NJ

Money for Artists: A Guide to Grants and Awards for Individual Artists. ACA Books: New York.

Music Industry Directory. Marquis: Chicago

Scholarships and Loans for Nursing Education. National League for Nursing: New York

WHERE TO LOOK

The best bibliography is of no use if you cannot locate the books that you seek. If you are in college, start with your college library and with the library of the office which promotes graduate study. The dean of the college may have a selection of directories on a bookshelf in the Dean's Office. Ask around. Financial aid offices may also have directories of foundation grants on their shelves. If your college is small or if you are no longer affiliated with a college, you might try the libraries of larger colleges and universities in your vicinity. Call before you go. The libraries of some large universities in major cities are restricted to students with ID cards and are closed to the public even for reference purposes. If the library is open to the public, a kind library assistant may tell you which directories are available so that you may make your trip to the most fruitful library.

One of the most helpful organizations in terms of well-stocked library of directories and general assistance in the search for grants is The Foundation Center. The Foundation Center is the publisher of a number of the directories listed. The Center also operates libraries and cooperating collections throughout the country. The center has four full scale libraries. These are at:

79 Fifth Avenue
(at 16th Street)
New York, NY 10003-3050
212-620-4230

312 Sutter St.
San Francisco, CA 94108
415-397-0902

1001 Connecticut Ave., N.W.
Suite 938
Washington, DC 20036
202-331-1400

1442 Hanna Building
1422 Euclid Ave.
Cleveland, OH 44115
216-861-1934

If any of these is convenient for you, call for current hours. The Center also operates a network of over 180 Cooperating Collections located in host nonprofit organizations in all 50 states, Australia, Canada, Mexico, Puerto Rico, the Virgin Islands, Great Britain and Japan. All contain a core collection of the Center's reference works and are staffed by professionals trained to direct grantseekers to appropriate funding information resources. Many host organizations also have other books and reports on funders and private foundations within their state.

Call toll-free 1-800-424-9836 for a complete address list.

If you have exhausted all other funding possibilities—need-based aid; university or department administered merit-based grants, fellowships and assistantships; privately sponsored grants, fellowships and loans; and government guaranteed loans—you may need to look into non-profit lending organizations. Start by contacting:

The Education Resources Institute
    (TERI)
330 Stuart Street
Boston, MA 02116
617-426-0681

New England Educational Loan Marketing Corp.
    (Nellie Mae)
25 Braintree Hill Park
Braintree, MA 02184
617-849-1325

Student Loan Marketing Association
    (Sallie Mae)
1050 Jefferson Street, NW
Washington, DC 20007
202-333-8000

Law School Admission Services
    (for law school loans, only)
P.O. Box 2000
Newtown, PA 18940-0998
215-968-1001

MILLER ANALOGIES
SAMPLE TEST V

Time: 50 Minutes. 100 Questions.

Directions: Each of these test questions consists of three CAPITALIZED words and four lettered words enclosed in parentheses. Two of the capitalized words are related in some way. Find the two related words and establish the nature of the relationship. Then study the four words lettered a, b, c, and d. Select the one lettered word which is related to the remaining capitalized word in the same way that the first two capitalized words are related. Mark the answer sheet for the letter of the word you select.

1. FEAST : MEAL :: VELLUM : (a. paper, b. fur, c. cotton, d. forest)

2. (a. leave, b. audition, c. divide, d. correct) : APPLY :: PART : POSITION

3. OXEN : STRENGTH :: (a. furnace, b. animal, c. cattle, d. ants) : INDUSTRY

4. ASSIDUOUS : EGREGIOUS :: (a. leafy, b. desultory, c. diligent, d. bitter) : FLAGRANT

5. SHIP : (a. crow's nest, b. deck, c. prow, d. mast) :: COLUMN : CAPITAL

6. DAVID COPPERFIELD : TINY TIM :: (a. Joseph Andrews, b. Ahab, c. Becky Sharp, d. Little Nell) : OLIVER TWIST

7. CLEOPATRA : (a. Caesar, b. poison, c. Anthony, d. beauty) :: GOLIATH : STONE

8. (a. circle, b. heart, c. dissemination, d. artery) : CIRCULATE :: DITCH : IRRIGATE

9. BRIGHT : GAUDY :: (a. urged, b. implied, c. prevented, d. acquiesced) : COMPELLED

10. (a. dissidence, b. deficiency, c. irreverence, d. deference) : DISRESPECT :: IMBUE : EXTRACT

11. EGO : ID :: SELF : (a. desire, b. society, c. conscience, d. morality)

12. HIGH GEAR : (a. automobile, b. driver, c. speed, d. brake) :: PROGRESS : RECESSION

13. (a. gem, b. spore, c. illegitimacy, d. superficiality) : SPURIOUS :: MONEY : COUNTERFEIT

14. AMIN : (a. Elizabeth II, b. Waldheim, c. Qaddafi, d. Adenauer) :: KING : BUNCHE

15. 225 : AREA :: (a. 2744, b. 3375, c. 38,416, d. 50,625) : VOLUME

16. QUEUE : (a. borough, b. tail, c. line, d. broom) :: CUE : BROUGHAM

17. COLONEL : REGIMENT :: (a. major, b. captain, c. private, d. general) : BATTALION

18. DILETTANTE : (a. thorough, b. painstaking, c. diplomatic, d. superficial) :: HOYDEN : CAREFREE

19. RECEIVER : DIAL :: KEYBOARD : (a. sound, b. chip, c. music, d. remport)

20. (a. rectify, b. make, c. find, d. realize) : MISTAKE :: REGAIN : LOSS

21. INDEX : FRONTISPIECE :: MATURITY : (a. adolescence, b. infancy, c. puberty, d. adulthood)

22. TAUTOLOGICAL : REDUNDANT :: (a. mature, b. incipient, c. obnoxious, d. late) : INCHOATE

23. SQUARE : (a. triangle, b. triplet, c. poem, d. duet) :: QUADRUPLET : COUPLET

24. MAY : (a. horn, b. charity, c. tempest, d. despair) :: FEAR : COD

25. (a. m, b. p, c. l, d. t) : H :: W : S

26. CHOLERIC : PHLEGMATIC :: (a. timid, b. blind, c. mute, d. temerarious) : CIRCUMSPECT

27. IRON : (a. hard, b. strong, c. steel, d. pig) :: OIL : CRUDE

28. (a. astronomy, b. play, c. symphony, d. heavens) : STAR :: CONCERT : SOLOIST

29. SALUTE : (a. motto, b. reveille, c. mess, d. orders) :: TROOP : EAGLE

30. PROVISIONS : QUARTERMASTER :: (a. cup, b. knife, c. saddle, d. manuscript) : SCRIVENER

31. ATLANTIS : (a. Pompeii, b. Xanadu, c. Byzantium, d. Zanzibar) :: SHANGRI-LA : EL DORADO

32. WIND : DEFICIT :: EROSION : (a. spending, b. appreciation, c. borrowing, d. employment)

33. (a. slot, b. note, c. band, d. harmony) : VALVE :: HARMONICA :: TRUMPET

34. FLAUNT : (a. destructively, b. stupidly, c. willingly, d. boastfully) :: BETRAY : DECEPTIVELY

35. HOUYHNHNM : YAHOO :: REASON : (a. learning, b. intelligence, c. ignorance, d. genius)

36. DEFIED : ASTRIDE :: EARTH : (a. geography, b. zoology, c. birth, d. life)

37. ISTANBUL : CONSTANTINOPLE :: (a. Stalingrad, b. Leningrad, c. Moscow, d. Odessa) : ST. PETERSBURG

38. (a. 1899, b. 1900, c. 1901, d. 1902) : 1910 :: 1950 : 1959

39. ADVOCATE : (a. impute, b. allude, c. imply, d. impugn) :: AMELIORATE : IMPAIR

40. HENRY MOORE : (a. Rodin, b. Pavlov, c. Van Gogh, d. Gertrude Stein) :: DONATELLO : BERNINI

41. HO CHI MINH : GANDHI :: FRANCE : (a. Indochina, b. Great Britain, c. Vietnam, d. India)

42. HEDGER : SHRUBBERY :: (a. snuffer, b. cougher, c. whittler, d. stickler) : STICK

43. MAN : (a. bird, b. centipede, c. elephant, d. Adam) :: WHEELBARROW : BICYCLE

44. (a. velocity, b. viscosity, c. temperature, d. density) : FLUID :: FRICTION : SOLID

45. CANTON : COUNTY :: (a. Ohio, b. Japan, c. Switzerland, d. China) : IRELAND

46. PECK : PINT :: 1 : (a. 4, b. 16, c. 8, d. 2)

47. TWEEZERS : BLEACH :: (a. steel, b. light, c. adding machine, d. eraser) : PICKPOCKET

48. JAWBONING : (a. persuade, b. filet, c. cleaning, d. arbitrate) :: FILIBUSTERING : OBSTRUCT

49. SHERRY : BEER :: PORT : (a. champagne, b. sauterne, c. claret, d. muscatel)

50. HONOR : GOVERNOR :: (a. Excellency, b. Majesty, c. Highness, d. Grace) : DUKE

51. ANDIRON : PEDESTAL :: (a. log, b. bucket, c. anvil, d. skillet) : STATUE

52. GENERAL : STARS :: COLONEL :: (a. oak, b. silver, c. gold, d. eagle)

53. (a. insist, b. reply, c. demur, d. demand) : REFUSE :: LAZY : INERT

54. HEART : HEAD :: VENERY : (a. ribaldry, b. flesh, c. mortality, d. restraint)

55. CALORIE : (a. energy, b. weight, c. metabolism, d. food) :: CENTURY : TIME

56. FLORIDA : SAUDI ARABIA :: (a. Louisiana, b. Georgia, c. Arkansas, d. Iraq) : IRAN

57. *KING LEAR* : *DIE FLEDERMAUS* :: *MACBETH* : (a. *Tosca*, b. *Othello*, c. *Ruddigore*, d. *Les Miserables*)

58. BOARDWALK : (a. Park Place, b. Atlantic City, c. display, d. escalator) :: STRAND : STORE

59. (a. Parliament, b. Congress, c. Great Britain, d. Senate) : LORDS :: HOUSE : COMMONS

60. 1789 : (a. Germany, b. France, c. England, d. Russia) :: 1776 : UNITED STATES

61. MALLARD : CANVASBACK :: (a. snow, b. north, c. drake, d. gander) : CANADA

62. WELL-FED : (a. penurious, b. healthy, c. wealthy, d. miserly) :: HUNGRY : IMPECUNIOUS

63. LAERTES : (a. Odysseus, b. Polonius, c. Claudius, d. Ophelia) :: ICARUS : DAEDALUS

64. SYRACUSE : (a. Oneonta, b. Geneva, c. Raleigh, d. Goshen) :: CARTHAGE : ALEXANDRIA

65. PALL : CLOY :: (a. obbligato, b. innuendo, c. declaration, d. crescendo) : INSINUATION

66. ORGANISM : (a. plant, b. animal, c. bacteria, d. cell) :: LIGHT : WAVE

67. KOLN : WIEN :: COLOGNE : (a. Vienna, b. Prague, c. Warsaw, d. Hamburg)

68. DCX : MDCCCXXX :: (a. CLX, b. XLI, c. LCD, d. LXVII) : CXXIII

69. WISDOM : (a. lion, b. owl, c. fox, d. deer) :: SPRING : ROBIN

70. BUTTERFLY : (a. insect, b. silkworm, c. wings, d. summer) :: CHRYSALIS : COCOON

71. ICELAND : NORWAY :: (a. winter, b. queen, c. president, d. sovereign) : KING

72. (a. Algeria, b. Hungary, c. Rumania, d. Belgium) : FRANCE :: DENMARK : ITALY

73. CYLINDER : LOCK :: MOTOR : (a. shaft, b. canal, c. tackle, d. escape)

74. BANANA : (a. sapphire, b. saltcellar, c. stone, d. tree) :: BUTTER : SKY

75. GNASH : TEETH :: (a. fold, b. clasp, c. gnarl, d. wring) : HANDS

76. (a. opossum, b. fox, c. beaver, d. lady) : KANGAROO :: CHICKEN : COCKROACH

77. APHRODITE : VENUS :: ARES : (a. Mercury, b. Mars, c. Apollo, d. Hermes)

78. METAPHYSICS : (a. humanities, b. medicine, c. logic, d. art) :: EPISTEMOLOGY : ETHICS

79. CLARINET : PIANO :: WIND : (a. reed, b. wood, c. percussion, d. pianist)

80. ELEVATOR : SKYSCRAPER :: (a. gangplank, b. companionway, c. bulkhead, d. bridge) : SHIP

81. PROPENSITY : (a. riches, b. weight, c. bias, d. thought) :: CLUB : MACE

82. SALZBURG : STRATFORD :: (a. Goethe, b. Avon, c. Mozart, d. Brahms) : SHAKESPEARE

83. FLAMMABLE : INFLAMMABLE :: PERTINENT : (a. impertinent, b. inopportune, c. incoherent, d. relevant)

84. (a. revolution, b. dance, c. torque, d. axis) : ROTATE :: FRICTION : RESIST

85. PRISM : (a. spectrum, b. reflection, c. light, d. binoculars) :: FAMINE : WANT

86. LOOP : HUB :: BEEF : (a. corn, b. beans, c. tobacco, d. cotton)

87. JANUARY : (a. Cleveland, b. June, c. Washington, d. Hermes) :: SUNDAY : MERCURY

88. LIFT : ELEVATOR :: (a. oil, b. grease, c. gas, d. petrol) : GASOLINE

89. (a. 1/6, b. 4/5, c. 2/5, d. 2/10) : 1/10 :: 3/4 : 3/16

90. TORT : LITIGATION :: CONTRACT : (a. signature, b. obligation, c. clause, d. equity)

91. BULL : (a. wolf, b. turtle, c. fish, d. snail) :: CRAB : LION

92. EQUINOX : SOLSTICE :: SEPTEMBER : (a. November, b. January, c. June, d. March)

93. (a. hand, b. brow, c. rose, d. soon) : KNIT :: DICTATION : TAKE

94. GARROTING : DEATH :: CANVASSING : (a. painting, b. shelter, c. votes, d. fight)

95. PUSILLANIMOUS : INVIDIOUS :: (a. paronomasia, b. slather, c. melodramatically, d. perfunctory) : SANCTIMONIOUS

96. SICKLE : RUSSIA :: (a. scythe, b. crescent, c. Caspian, d. hammer) : TURKEY

97. CICERO : DEMOSTHENES :: ROOSEVELT : (a. MacArthur, b. Hemingway, c. Shaw, d. Churchill)

98. TYRO : (a. tyrant, b. master, c. amateur, d. dabbler) :: TURPITUDE : PROBITY

99. COKE : COAL :: (a. oil, b. planks, c. saw, d. lumberjack) : TIMBER

100. SHOE : (a. fly, b. cobbler, c. pair, d. bell) :: SAW : GEAR

ANSWER KEY FOR
MILLER ANALOGIES SAMPLE TEST V

1. a	21. b	41. b	61. a	81. c
2. b	22. b	42. c	62. c	82. c
3. d	23. d	43. c	63. b	83. d
4. c	24. a	44. b	64. d	84. c
5. a	25. c	45. c	65. b	85. a
6. d	26. d	46. b	66. d	86. b
7. b	27. d	47. d	67. a	87. c
8. d	28. b	48. a	68. b	88. d
9. a	29. a	49. a	69. b	89. c
10. d	30. d	50. d	70. b	90. b
11. a	31. b	51. a	71. c	91. c
12. d	32. c	52. d	72. d	92. c
13. a	33. a	53. c	73. b	93. b
14. c	34. d	54. d	74. a	94. c
15. b	35. c	55. a	75. d	95. d
16. d	36. c	56. a	76. a	96. b
17. a	37. b	57. c	77. b	97. d
18. d	38. c	58. d	78. c	98. b
19. b	39. d	59. d	79. c	99. b
20. a	40. a	60. b	80. b	100. d

EXPLANATORY ANSWERS FOR
MILLER ANALOGIES SAMPLE TEST V

1. **(a)** In this analogy of degree, a FEAST is a rich and expensive MEAL; VELLUM is a rich and expensive kind of PAPER.

2. **(b)** The correspondence is one of action to object. You APPLY for a POSITION of employment; you AUDITION for a PART in a play.

3. **(d)** In this association analogy, OXEN are associated with STRENGTH; ANTS are associated with INDUSTRY.

4. **(c)** In this synonym analogy, another word for EGREGIOUS is FLAGRANT. A synonym for ASSIDUOUS is DILIGENT.

5. **(a)** A CROW'S NEST is a small observation platform near the top of the mast of a SHIP; a CAPITAL is the uppermost part of a COLUMN.

6. **(d)** The relationship among DAVID COPPERFIELD, TINY TIM and OLIVER TWIST is that they are all fictional characters created by Charles Dickens. To complete the analogy, another Dickens character must be selected, and LITTLE NELL is the correct choice.

7. **(b)** GOLIATH was killed by a STONE; CLEOPATRA was killed by the POISON of an asp by which she was bitten.

8. **(d)** In this object-to-action analogy, a DITCH is the channel through which water flows to IRRIGATE; an ARTERY is the vessel or channel through which blood may CIRCULATE.

9. **(a)** The relationship is one of degree since GAUDY is excessively BRIGHT; COMPELLED is excessively URGED.

10. **(d)** IMBUE, meaning to permeate, is the opposite of EXTRACT, meaning to draw out. The opposite of DISRESPECT is DEFERENCE.

11. **(a)** EGO is a psychological term for SELF; ID is a psychological term for DESIRE. The psychological term for conscience is superego.

12. **(d)** A HIGH GEAR and a BRAKE have opposite functions; similarly, PROGRESS and RECESSION are opposite in meaning.

13. **(a)** A GEM is worthless when it is SPURIOUS, that is, false; MONEY is worthless when it is COUNTERFEIT.

14. **(c)** Martin Luther KING and Ralph BUNCHE were both very reliable men working for peace. Idi AMIN and Muammar el-QADDAFI are known for tyranny, ruthlessness, and erratic behavior. While Kurt Waldheim's behavior has also been questioned, his reputation does not fall into the same league as those of Amin and Qaddafi.

15. **(b)** The AREA of a figure is 225 square units. With no additional given information, one must assume that the figure is a square. One side of the figure is 15 units long because the square root of 225 is 15. The analogy asks for the volume of the cube based upon the figure related to its area. $15 \times 15 \times 15 = 3375$ cubic units.

16. **(d)** QUEUE and CUE are homophones, different in meaning but pronounced the same; BROOM and BROUGHAM are also pronounced the same.

17. **(a)** A COLONEL leads a REGIMENT; a MAJOR leads a BATTALION.

18. **(d)** A characteristic of a HOYDEN is her CAREFREE attitude; a characteristic of DILETTANTE, a dabbler, is a tendency to be SUPERFICIAL.

19. **(b)** This is a part-to-part analogy. A RECEIVER and a DIAL are parts of a telephone; a KEYBOARD and a CHIP are parts of a computer.

20. **(a)** The relationship is one of action to object. To improve a poor or unfortunate condition one may RECTIFY a MISTAKE, and one may REGAIN a LOSS.

21. **(b)** In this sequence analogy, the INDEX comes at the end of a book, the FRONTISPIECE comes at the beginning; MATURITY comes in the latter part of life, INFANCY comes in the beginning.

22. **(b)** TAUTOLOGICAL is a synonym for REDUNDANT; INCHOATE, which means at an early state of development, is a synonym for INCIPIENT.

23. **(d)** QUADRUPLET refers to a group of four; a COUPLET consists of two successive rhyming lines of verse. Since a SQUARE has four sides, a term involving a pair must be chosen to complete the analogy. A DUET, a composition for two performers, is the only possible choice.

24. **(a)** In this place analogy, MAY, FEAR, and COD are all names of capes. To complete the analogy, another cape must be selected, and Cape HORN is the correct choice.

25. **(c)** In the alphabet, W is the fourth letter after S; L is the fourth letter after H.

26. **(d)** CHOLERIC, which means bad-tempered, and PHLEGMATIC, meaning easy-going, are opposites; TEMERARIOUS, which means rash and reckless, and CIRCUMSPECT, meaning careful, are opposites.

27. **(d)** In this product-to-source analogy; OIL in its rough state is called CRUDE oil; IRON in its rough state is called PIG iron.

28. **(b)** A STAR takes the leading role in a PLAY; a SOLOIST takes the leading role in a CONCERT.

29. **(a)** A SALUTE, TROOP, and EAGLE are all things associated with the Boy Scouts. To complete the analogy, another element of scouting should be selected, and MOTTO is the correct choice. Reveille and mess are associated with Boy Scout camping, but it is not necessary to extend to camping to complete this analogy.

30. **(d)** In this worker-to-job analogy, a QUARTERMASTER's job is to secure PROVISIONS for an army; a SCRIVENER's job is to copy a MANUSCRIPT.

31. **(b)** ATLANTIS, SHANGRI-LA, and EL DORADO are related because each is an undocumented place. XANADU, the only undocumented place among the answer choices, correctly completes this analogy.

32. **(c)** In this cause-and-effect analogy, one effect of excessive WIND is soil EROSION; an effect of an excessive DEFICIT is BORROWING to make up for expenditures. Excessive spending is a cause of a deficit, not an effect.

33. **(a)** The correspondence is one of part to whole. A VALVE is part of a TRUMPET; a SLOT is part of a HARMONICA.

34. **(d)** To FLAUNT is to act BOASTFULLY; to BETRAY is to act DECEPTIVELY.

35. **(c)** In *Gulliver's Travels* by Jonathan Swift, a HOUYHNHNM symbolizes intelligence and REASON, whereas a YAHOO symbolizes the opposite, stupidity or IGNORANCE.

36. **(c)** In this nonsemantic rhyming analogy, DEFIED rhymes with ASTRIDE; EARTH rhymes with BIRTH.

37. **(b)** ISTANBUL was formerly called CONSTANTINOPLE; LENINGRAD was formerly called ST. PETERSBURG.

38. **(c)** In this sequence analogy, the difference between 1901 and 1910 is nine years; the difference between 1950 and 1959 is nine years. The mathematics of this problem is simple, but the use of dates is deceptive. When dates appear to be meaningless, you must look for a relationship along another dimension, just as when words appear unrelated you must seek a grammatical or nonsemantic relationship.

39. **(d)** AMELIORATE, meaning to improve or to make better, is the opposite of IMPAIR, meaning to make worse. The opposite of ADVOCATE, meaning to support or to plead in favor of, is IMPUGN, meaning to deny or to attack as false.

40. **(a)** The connection among HENRY MOORE, DONATELLO, and BERNINI is that they are all sculptors. To complete the analogy, another sculptor must be chosen, and RODIN is the correct choice.

41. **(b)** HO CHI MINH and GANDHI were both leaders of independence movements in countries colonized by European nations. Ho Chi Minh, a leftist revolutionary, fought to expel FRANCE from Indochina. Gandhi, an advocate of nonviolence and passive resistance, led the movement to expel GREAT BRITAIN from India.

42. **(c)** A HEDGER trims SHRUBBERY; a WHITTLER trims a STICK.

43. **(c)** The relationship is a numerical ratio of one to two. A WHEELBARROW has one wheel; a BICYCLE has two. Similarly, a MAN has two legs, and an ELEPHANT has four. Approach this analogy by looking first at the two adjacent capitalized words. You will instantly recognize that a wheelbarrow has one wheel and a bicycle has two. Man uses both a wheelbarrow and a bicycle, and none of the choices logically uses either, so you should begin to suspect a numerical analogy. A centipede with its 100 legs is a distractor which also serves as a clue. Since the wheel ratio is one to two, you must be careful not to choose the bird, which has the same number of legs as the man.

44. **(b)** VISCOSITY is the resistance of a FLUID to flow just as FRICTION is the resistance to relative motion between two SOLIDs.

45. **(c)** A CANTON is a territorial division in SWITZERLAND; a COUNTY is a territorial division in IRELAND.

46. **(b)** In this measurement analogy, a PECK is equal to 8 quarts. A PINT is half of a quart; therefore, 1 peck is equal to 16 pints.

47. **(d)** The relationship among TWEEZERS, BLEACH, and a PICK-POCKET is that they all remove something. Among the choices, an ERASER also removes something, a written mistake.

48. **(a)** In this purpose analogy, a purpose of FILIBUSTERING is to OB-STRUCT passage of legislation. The purpose of JAWBONING is to PER-SUADE or coax another party to accept your position.

49. **(a)** SHERRY has no carbonation; BEER has carbonation; PORT has no carbonation; CHAMPAGNE has carbonation.

50. **(d)** The proper way to refer to people in certain positions or ranks is to say his HONOR, the GOVERNOR, and his GRACE, the DUKE.

51. **(a)** An ANDIRON holds a LOG; a PEDESTAL holds a STATUE.

52. **(d)** In this association analogy, STARS symbolize the rank of GENERAL; an EAGLE symbolizes the rank of COLONEL.

53. **(c)** The relationship is one of degree. LAZY, meaning sluggish, is a lesser degree of immobility than INERT; to DEMUR, meaning to hesitate, delay or object, is a lesser degree of protestation than to REFUSE.

54. **(d)** It is often said that the ways of the HEART are the opposite to the ways of the HEAD; the opposite of VENERY, the gratification of desires, is RESTRAINT.

55. **(a)** A CALORIE is a measure of the heat-producing or ENERGY-producing value of food. A CENTURY is a measure of TIME.

56. **(a)** In this place analogy, SAUDI ARABIA and IRAN are both countries bordering on the Persian Gulf; FLORIDA and LOUISIANA are states which border on the Gulf of Mexico. And, just as Saudi Arabia and Iran do not border on each other, so also Florida and Louisiana do not have a common border.

57. **(c)** *KING LEAR* and *MACBETH* are both Shakespearean tragedies. *DIE FLEDERMAUS* and *RUDDIGORE* are both comic operas. The writer of the two comedies is irrelevant since no other choice is a comedy.

58. **(d)** A BOARDWALK is a kind of walkway along a STRAND or beach; an ESCALATOR is a kind of walkway in a department STORE.

59. **(d)** The SENATE and the House of LORDS are the upper houses of the U.S. Congress and the British Parliament, respectively; the HOUSE of Representatives and House of COMMONS are the lower houses.

60. **(b)** The dates mark the beginnings of two highly significant revolutions. 1776 was the beginning of the revolution in what was to become the UNITED STATES; 1789 was the beginning year of the revolution in FRANCE.

61. **(a)** This is a part-to-part relationship. MALLARD and CANVASBACK both belong to the group "ducks." CANADA and SNOW both belong to the group "geese."

62. **(c)** The relationship is that of cause to effect. An IMPECUNIOUS person, one with little or no money, is likely to be HUNGRY; a WEALTHY person is likely to be WELL-FED.

63. **(b)** In Greek mythology, ICARUS is the son of DAEDALUS; in Shakespeare's play *Hamlet,* LAERTES is the son of POLONIUS.

64. **(d)** SYRACUSE, GOSHEN, CARTHAGE, and ALEXANDRIA are all names of ancient historical communities.

65. **(b)** PALL and CLOY are synonyms; INNUENDO and INSINUATION are also synonyms.

66. **(d)** In this whole-to-part analogy, an ORGANISM is made up of CELLs; LIGHT consists physically of WAVEs.

67. **(a)** The German name for COLOGNE is KOLN; the German name for VIENNA is WIEN.

68. **(b)** If you are required to perform mathematical calculations with large Roman numerals, you may be pretty certain that the calculations will be very simple ones. Begin by translating into Arabic numerals. DCX = 610. MDCCCXXX = 1830. By inspection you can see that $610 \times 3 = 1830$. Now translate the third Roman numeral. CXIII = 113. The fourth term must be one-third of 123 or 41, which is XLI.

69. **(b)** The relationship is one of association. A ROBIN is associated with the coming of SPRING; an OWL is associated with great WISDOM.

70. **(b)** An early stage in the development of the BUTTERFLY is the CHRYSALIS; an early stage in the development of the SILKWORM is the COCOON. *Chrysalis* and *cocoon* are synonyms. *Butterfly* and *silkworm* are not synonyms, but they do bear the same sequential relationship to the enveloped stage of development.

71. **(c)** NORWAY is a monarchy headed by a KING; ICELAND is a republic headed by a PRESIDENT.

72. **(d)** DENMARK, ITALY, and FRANCE are all members of the European Economic Community, also known as the Common Market. Of the choices, only BELGIUM is also a member of the Common Market. Algeria is not located in Europe. Rumania and Hungary are Communist countries and as such are not included in free Europe's trade agreements.

73. **(b)** A CYLINDER is part of a MOTOR; a LOCK is part of a a CANAL. This is a difficult analogy because a cylinder is also part of a lock. However, if you begin and stick with this relationship, you can then choose only that a shaft is part of a motor, which is a reverse relationship and creates an incorrect analogy.

74. **(a)** BUTTER is yellow and SKY is blue; since a BANANA is yellow, the task is to find the choice that is blue: a SAPPHIRE.

75. **(d)** In this action-to-object analogy, you may GNASH your TEETH or WRING your HANDS in anger or dismay. All of the other choices are also activities that can be done with your hands, but they are not characteristically a sign of anger or dismay.

76. **(a)** An OPOSSUM and a KANGAROO are both classified as marsupials, pouched mammals: a CHICKEN and a COCKROACH are both related as oviparous or egg-bearing.

77. **(b)** APHRODITE is the Greek goddess of love and beauty; VENUS is her Roman counterpart. ARES is the Greek god of war; MARS is his Roman counterpart.

78. **(c)** The four terms of this analogy are all related in that they, EPISTEMOLOGY, ETHICS, METAPHYSICS, and LOGIC, constitute four of the five branches of philosophy. The fifth is aesthetics.

79. **(c)** A CLARINET is a WIND instrument; a PIANO is a PERCUSSION instrument.

80. **(b)** An ELEVATOR is used to ascend and descend once inside a SKYSCRAPER; a COMPANIONWAY, a ship's staircase, is used for the same purpose in a SHIP.

81. **(c)** In this degree analogy, a PROPENSITY is a lesser degree of opinion than is a BIAS; a CLUB is a less ominous weapon than a MACE, which is a spiked club.

82. **(c)** STRATFORD is the birthplace of SHAKESPEARE; SALZBURG is the birthplace of MOZART.

83. **(d)** FLAMMABLE and INFLAMMABLE are synonyms; PERTINENT and RELEVANT are also synonyms.

84. **(c)** In this cause-and-effect analogy, FRICTION causes something to RESIST moving; TORQUE causes something to ROTATE. The effects are opposite, but the cause-to-effect relationship is the same.

85. **(a)** In this product-source analogy, a SPECTRUM is created by a PRISM; WANT is produced by a FAMINE, which is a scarcity.

86. **(b)** The LOOP and the HUB are nicknames for the downtown business districts of Chicago and Boston, respectively; Chicago is known for its BEEF, and Boston is known for its BEANS.

87. **(c)** We have a number of firsts here: JANUARY is the first month; SUNDAY is the first day of the week; MERCURY is the first planet in distance from the sun; and WASHINGTON was the first U.S. president.

88. **(d)** LIFT is the British word for an ELEVATOR; PETROL is the British word for GASOLINE.

89. **(c)** In this numerical analogy, 1/4 of 3/4 is 3/16; 1/4 of 2/5 is 1/10.

90. **(b)** A TORT is a wrong that entails LITIGATION; a CONTRACT is an agreement that entails OBLIGATION.

91. **(c)** The BULL (Taurus), FISH (Pisces), CRAB (Cancer), and LION (Leo) are all signs of the zodiac.

92. **(c)** EQUINOX refers to either of the two times each year when the sun crosses the equator and day and night are everywhere of equal length, occurring about March 21 and SEPTEMBER 23. SOLSTICE refers to one of the two points at which the sun's apparent position on the celestial sphere reaches its greatest distance above or below the celestial equator, occurring about JUNE 22 and December 22.

93. **(b)** In this action-to-object analogy, one may KNIT a BROW and one may TAKE DICTATION.

94. **(c)** The correspondence is one of cause and effect. GARROTING (strangling) commonly causes DEATH; CANVASSING (soliciting for support) commonly results in VOTES.

95. **(d)** Miller Analogies tend to get into some esoteric vocabulary, but not much. If the words seem excessively long or obscure, look for another relationship before trying to define and determine meaningful relationships. In this analogy based upon grammar, PUSILLANIMOUS, INVIDIOUS, and SANCTIMONIOUS are all adjectives. The only choice which is an adjective is PERFUNCTORY. Paronomasia you should know by its ending to be a noun; slather is a verb or a noun; melodramatically is an adverb.

96. **(b)** In this symbol analogy, the SICKLE (in conjunction with the hammer) is a symbol of RUSSIA; the CRESCENT is a symbol of TURKEY.

97. **(d)** CICERO and DEMOSTHENES are related as orators; ROOSEVELT and CHURCHILL are related as statesmen.

98. **(b)** The opposite of TURPITUDE, which means baseness, is PROBITY, meaning uprightness. An antonym for TYRO, a beginner, is MASTER.

99. **(b)** In this product-source analogy, COKE is obtained by heating COAL; PLANKS are formed by cutting TIMBER.

100. **(d)** A SAW and a GEAR both have teeth; a SHOE and a BELL both have a tongue.

ANSWER SHEET
MILLER ANALOGIES SAMPLE TEST VI

1 Ⓐ Ⓑ Ⓒ Ⓓ	21 Ⓐ Ⓑ Ⓒ Ⓓ	41 Ⓐ Ⓑ Ⓒ Ⓓ	61 Ⓐ Ⓑ Ⓒ Ⓓ	81 Ⓐ Ⓑ Ⓒ Ⓓ
2 Ⓐ Ⓑ Ⓒ Ⓓ	22 Ⓐ Ⓑ Ⓒ Ⓓ	42 Ⓐ Ⓑ Ⓒ Ⓓ	62 Ⓐ Ⓑ Ⓒ Ⓓ	82 Ⓐ Ⓑ Ⓒ Ⓓ
3 Ⓐ Ⓑ Ⓒ Ⓓ	23 Ⓐ Ⓑ Ⓒ Ⓓ	43 Ⓐ Ⓑ Ⓒ Ⓓ	63 Ⓐ Ⓑ Ⓒ Ⓓ	83 Ⓐ Ⓑ Ⓒ Ⓓ
4 Ⓐ Ⓑ Ⓒ Ⓓ	24 Ⓐ Ⓑ Ⓒ Ⓓ	44 Ⓐ Ⓑ Ⓒ Ⓓ	64 Ⓐ Ⓑ Ⓒ Ⓓ	84 Ⓐ Ⓑ Ⓒ Ⓓ
5 Ⓐ Ⓑ Ⓒ Ⓓ	25 Ⓐ Ⓑ Ⓒ Ⓓ	45 Ⓐ Ⓑ Ⓒ Ⓓ	65 Ⓐ Ⓑ Ⓒ Ⓓ	85 Ⓐ Ⓑ Ⓒ Ⓓ
6 Ⓐ Ⓑ Ⓒ Ⓓ	26 Ⓐ Ⓑ Ⓒ Ⓓ	46 Ⓐ Ⓑ Ⓒ Ⓓ	66 Ⓐ Ⓑ Ⓒ Ⓓ	86 Ⓐ Ⓑ Ⓒ Ⓓ
7 Ⓐ Ⓑ Ⓒ Ⓓ	27 Ⓐ Ⓑ Ⓒ Ⓓ	47 Ⓐ Ⓑ Ⓒ Ⓓ	67 Ⓐ Ⓑ Ⓒ Ⓓ	87 Ⓐ Ⓑ Ⓒ Ⓓ
8 Ⓐ Ⓑ Ⓒ Ⓓ	28 Ⓐ Ⓑ Ⓒ Ⓓ	48 Ⓐ Ⓑ Ⓒ Ⓓ	68 Ⓐ Ⓑ Ⓒ Ⓓ	88 Ⓐ Ⓑ Ⓒ Ⓓ
9 Ⓐ Ⓑ Ⓒ Ⓓ	29 Ⓐ Ⓑ Ⓒ Ⓓ	49 Ⓐ Ⓑ Ⓒ Ⓓ	69 Ⓐ Ⓑ Ⓒ Ⓓ	89 Ⓐ Ⓑ Ⓒ Ⓓ
10 Ⓐ Ⓑ Ⓒ Ⓓ	30 Ⓐ Ⓑ Ⓒ Ⓓ	50 Ⓐ Ⓑ Ⓒ Ⓓ	70 Ⓐ Ⓑ Ⓒ Ⓓ	90 Ⓐ Ⓑ Ⓒ Ⓓ
11 Ⓐ Ⓑ Ⓒ Ⓓ	31 Ⓐ Ⓑ Ⓒ Ⓓ	51 Ⓐ Ⓑ Ⓒ Ⓓ	71 Ⓐ Ⓑ Ⓒ Ⓓ	91 Ⓐ Ⓑ Ⓒ Ⓓ
12 Ⓐ Ⓑ Ⓒ Ⓓ	32 Ⓐ Ⓑ Ⓒ Ⓓ	52 Ⓐ Ⓑ Ⓒ Ⓓ	72 Ⓐ Ⓑ Ⓒ Ⓓ	92 Ⓐ Ⓑ Ⓒ Ⓓ
13 Ⓐ Ⓑ Ⓒ Ⓓ	33 Ⓐ Ⓑ Ⓒ Ⓓ	53 Ⓐ Ⓑ Ⓒ Ⓓ	73 Ⓐ Ⓑ Ⓒ Ⓓ	93 Ⓐ Ⓑ Ⓒ Ⓓ
14 Ⓐ Ⓑ Ⓒ Ⓓ	34 Ⓐ Ⓑ Ⓒ Ⓓ	54 Ⓐ Ⓑ Ⓒ Ⓓ	74 Ⓐ Ⓑ Ⓒ Ⓓ	94 Ⓐ Ⓑ Ⓒ Ⓓ
15 Ⓐ Ⓑ Ⓒ Ⓓ	35 Ⓐ Ⓑ Ⓒ Ⓓ	55 Ⓐ Ⓑ Ⓒ Ⓓ	75 Ⓐ Ⓑ Ⓒ Ⓓ	95 Ⓐ Ⓑ Ⓒ Ⓓ
16 Ⓐ Ⓑ Ⓒ Ⓓ	36 Ⓐ Ⓑ Ⓒ Ⓓ	56 Ⓐ Ⓑ Ⓒ Ⓓ	76 Ⓐ Ⓑ Ⓒ Ⓓ	96 Ⓐ Ⓑ Ⓒ Ⓓ
17 Ⓐ Ⓑ Ⓒ Ⓓ	37 Ⓐ Ⓑ Ⓒ Ⓓ	57 Ⓐ Ⓑ Ⓒ Ⓓ	77 Ⓐ Ⓑ Ⓒ Ⓓ	97 Ⓐ Ⓑ Ⓒ Ⓓ
18 Ⓐ Ⓑ Ⓒ Ⓓ	38 Ⓐ Ⓑ Ⓒ Ⓓ	58 Ⓐ Ⓑ Ⓒ Ⓓ	78 Ⓐ Ⓑ Ⓒ Ⓓ	98 Ⓐ Ⓑ Ⓒ Ⓓ
19 Ⓐ Ⓑ Ⓒ Ⓓ	39 Ⓐ Ⓑ Ⓒ Ⓓ	59 Ⓐ Ⓑ Ⓒ Ⓓ	79 Ⓐ Ⓑ Ⓒ Ⓓ	99 Ⓐ Ⓑ Ⓒ Ⓓ
20 Ⓐ Ⓑ Ⓒ Ⓓ	40 Ⓐ Ⓑ Ⓒ Ⓓ	60 Ⓐ Ⓑ Ⓒ Ⓓ	80 Ⓐ Ⓑ Ⓒ Ⓓ	100 Ⓐ Ⓑ Ⓒ Ⓓ

Tear Here

MILLER ANALOGIES
SAMPLE TEST VI

Time: 50 Minutes. 100 Questions.

Directions: Each of these test questions consists of three CAPITALIZED words and four lettered words enclosed in parentheses. Two of the capitalized words are related in some way. Find the two related words and establish the nature of the relationship. Then study the four words lettered a, b, c, and d. Select the one lettered word which is related to the remaining capitalized word in the same way that the first two capitalized words are related. Mark the answer sheet for the letter of the word you select.

1. SHINGLE : (a. siding, b. hair, c. thatch, d. roof) :: TILE : SLATE

2. SCRUB : SHINE :: (a. turn, b. top, c. spiral, d. dance) : SPIN

3. (a. larva, b. embryo, c. caduceus, d. tadpole) : FROG :: CATERPILLAR : BUTTERFLY

4. LEAP : STRIDE :: JUMP : (a. fall, b. step, c. skip, d. bound)

5. CAT : MOUSE :: (a. polar bear, b. lion, c. orca, d. rat) : ELAND

6. MERCURY : MICA :: QUICKSILVER : (a. formica, b. saltpeter, c. isinglass, d. hydroxide)

7. ROMEO : JULIET :: (a. Pyramus, b. Hercules, c. Endymion, d. Philemon) : THISBE

8. QUEENSLAND : (a. Kingscote, b. Brisbane, c. Victoria, d. Canberra) :: ALBERTA : ONTARIO

9. BOUILLABAISSE : L'ORANGE :: (a. paella, b. a la mode, c. stew, d. chowder) : PEKING

10. (a. Annapolis, b. Mary, c. Baltimore, d. McHenry) : MARYLAND :: PENN : PENNSYLVANIA

11. 1/2 : .5 :: 5/20 : (a. 1./5, b. 02, c. 1/4, d. .25)

12. HYDE PARK : ROOSEVELT :: OYSTER BAY : (a. Kennedy, b. Tyler, c. Coolidge, d. Roosevelt)

13. PEPSIN : PTYALIN :: PROTEIN : (a. meat, b. starch, c. saliva, d. vitamins)

14. KOCH : *MAYOR* :: (a. Cuomo, b. Truman, c. Meir, d. Dior) : *MY LIFE.*

15. GOBI : (a. Mojave, b. Swahili, c. Masai, d. Azalea) :: TIGRIS : EUPHRATES

16. CAPON : (a. rooster, b. turkey, c. chicken, d. steer) :: MULE : TANGELO

17. 12 : 3 :: 44 : (a. 33, b. 3, c. 11, d. 22)

18. GO : WENT :: READ : (a. write, b. learned, c. listen, d. read)

19. (a. "Lycidas," b. "Thanatopsis," c. "Adonais," d. "Astrophel") : "ELEGY" :: BRYANT : GRAY

20. *MAINE* : (a. Spanish-American War, b. Pearl Harbor, c. War of 1812, d. Civil War) :: ALAMO : TEXAS WAR OF INDEPENDENCE

21. PLUTO : URANUS :: (a. Ursa, b. Mercury, c. Haley, d. Sirius) :: POLARIS

22. TRUMAN : (a. Reconstruction, b. policy, c. Containment, d. Re-armament) :: CHAMBERLAIN : APPEASEMENT

23. ARI : URIS :: (a. Michael, b. Gaetano, c. Richard, d. Mario) : PUZO

24. SAMISEN : (a. junk, b. sampan, c. tea pot, d. banjo) :: AMOEBA : PARAMECIUM

25. BIENNIAL : BIANNUAL :: TWO : (a. one, b. one half, c. two, d. eight)

26. *PYGMALION : MY FAIR LADY* :: (a. *A Doll's House,* b. *The Pawnbroker,* c. *The Matchmaker,* d. *A House Is Not a Home*) : *HELLO DOLLY*

27. JACKSON : VAN BUREN :: WILSON : (a. Buchanan, b. Tyler, c. Taft, d. Ford)

28. (a. Algeria, b. Zimbabwe, c. Zambia, d. Liberia) : SIERRA LEONE :: ANGOLA : MOZAMBIQUE

29. FISSION : ENERGY :: (a. fusion, b. inertia, c. mass, d. entropy) : ENERGY

30. CHRISTIE : (a. Queen, b. Holmes, c. Seaman, d. Gardner) :: POIROT : MASON

31. BACH : DA VINCI :: MONET : (a. Bronte, b. Kant, c. Jefferson, d. Sibelius)

32. 9 : 27 :: 81 : (a. 9, b. 99, c. 18, d. 3)

33. (a. C.S.A., b. O.S.S., c. A.C.W., d. O.P.A.) : C.I.A. :: I.W.W. : C.I.O.

34. SUNNITE : SHI'ITE :: (a. Presbyterian, b. Jew, c. Catholic, d. Protestant) : EPISCOPALIAN

35. *ANIMAL FARM* : (a. Eric Blair, b. William Blake, c. William Porter, d. Thomas Wolfe) :: *PUDD'NHEAD WILSON* : SAMUEL CLEMENS

36. STRIKE : LOCKOUT :: GAINSAY : (a. appeal, b. repeat, c. agree, d. annul)

37. COLLIER : MINER :: (a. phobia, b. remission, c. bracelet, d. talisman) : AMULET

38. LOBSTER : SPIDER :: (a. arthropod, b. crayfish, c. clam, d. crustacean) : ARACHNID

39. HOMER : (a. Pindar, b. Ovid, c. Heraclitus, d. Aeneas) :: HERODOTUS : THUCYDIDES

40. HAIL : HALE :: (a. pale, b. pair, c. pear, d. whale) : PARE

41. MANET : "PROUST" :: GAINSBOROUGH : (a. Goya, b. "La Maja," c. "Blue Boy," d. Addison)

42. INFLAMMABLE : FLAMMABLE :: INVALUABLE : (a. priceless, b. worthless, c. untrue, d. deteriorating)

43. 3280.8 ft. : (a. mile, b. kilometer, c. fathom, d. league) :: 946 ml. : QUART

44. OIL : (a. sun, b. gasoline, c. fuel, d. olive) :: COAL : WIND

45. (a. Brahms, b. Beethoven, c. Debussy, d. Haydn) : TCHAIKOVSKY :: "PASTORALE" : "PATHETIQUE"

46. ESTONIA : RUSSIA :: (a. Georgia, b. China, c. Cuba, d. Monaco) : CZECHOSLOVAKIA

47. FLAMINGO : (a. horned owl, b. flicker, c. catbird, d. demoiselle) :: CHICKEN : TURKEY

48. 1^2 : 1 :: 5^2 : (a. 3, b. 25, c. 1, d. 10)

49. RUSSIA : USSR :: HOLLAND : (a. The Netherlands, b. Flanders, c. Europe, d. Belgium)

50. (a. griffin, b. giraffe, c. zebra, d. dinosaur) : DODO :: UNICORN : MASTODON

51. ANOPHELES : MALARIA :: AEDES : (a. cholera, b. dengue, c. bubonic plague, d. typhus)

52. OVOLO : CAVETTO :: (a. fertile, b. sheepish, c. convex, d. poetic) : CONCAVE

53. ADANO : (a. Hersey, b. Hemingway, c. Greene, d. Forster) :: CASTERBRIDGE : HARDY

54. (a. laugh, b. weep, c. cringe, d. geese) : QUAIL :: GAGGLE : COVEY

55. MANY : RAINDROPS :: MUCH : (a. flood, b. snowflakes, c. puddle, d. water)

56. HEART : STOMACH :: (a. veins, b. arteries, c. intestines, d. capillaries) : DUODENUM

57. SETA : (a. razor, b. toothbrush, c. monkey, d. flower) :: FEATHERS : DUSTER

58. CHEETAH : LEOPARD :: WOLF : (a. feline, b. canine, c. dog, d. lupus)

59. QUOITS : (a. boots, b. clangs, c. citations, d. horseshoes) :: OVAL : TRACK

60. (a. state house, b. battlement, c. church, d. fortress) : CHURCH :: CITADEL : CATHEDRAL

61. $5 : \sqrt{36} :: 8 : $ (a. 9, b. $\sqrt{81}$, c. $\sqrt{9}$, d. $\sqrt{64}$)

62. (a. crime, b. punishment, c. jury, d. verdict) : SENTENCE :: ANTEPENULT : PENULT

63. PANDA : (a. condor, b. bear, c. goldfish, d. ostrich) :: RACCOON : CROW

64. *LUSITANIA* : BRITAIN :: 007 : (a. Japan, b. Korea, c. Russia, d. James Bond)

65. NYBBLE : BYTE :: (a. eclipse, b. new, c. half, d. moon) : FULL

66. LANGSTON HUGHES : DOUGHTRY LONG :: (a. Marianne Moore, b. Gwendolyn Brooks, c. Gertrude Stein, d. Emily Dickinson) : NAOMI LONG MADGETT

67. SAT : (a. PEP, b. ACT, c. TAT, d. NTE) :: GRE : MAT

68. TULIP : ASTER :: SPRING : (a. chicken, b. jump, c. fall, d. well)

69. BOLL WEEVIL : GYPSY MOTH :: (a. assassin fly, b. termite, c. cockroach, d. louse) : PRAYING MANTIS

70. GHENT : (a. American Revolution, b. World War I, c. War of 1812, d. Hundred Years' War) :: PANMUNJOM : KOREAN WAR

71. (a. Nymph, b. Syrinx, c. Naiad, d. Chaos) : PAN :: ECHO : NARCISSUS

72. (a. terrapin, b. terrestrial, c. teuton, d. termagent) : SYCOPHANT :: VIRAGO : TOADY

73. KNESSET : ISRAEL :: DIET : (Kashrut, b. Luther, c. Japan, d. Congress)

74. *LES MISÉRABLES* : VICTOR HUGO :: (a. *Le Rouge et le Noir,* b. *Nôtre Dame de Paris,* c. *Les Trois Mousquetaires,* d. *Madame Bovary)* : ALEXANDRE DUMAS

75. ITS : IT'S :: (a. their, b. their's, c. there, d. there's) : THEY'RE

76. NICTATE : WINK :: (a. oscillate, b. osculate, c. ossify, d. oscultate) : KISS

77. DOWN'S SYNDROME : MENTAL RETARDATION :: HODGKIN'S DISEASE : (a. schizophrenia, b. kidney disease, c. leprosy, d. cancer)

78. 28 : 82 :: 56 : (a. 54, b. 30, c. 65, d. 136)

79. MAMA LUCIA : (a. *Lucia de Lamermoor,* b. *Cavalleria Rusticana,* c. *Marriage of Figaro,* d. *Tosca)* :: FIGARO : BARBER OF SEVILLE

80. MINNEAPOLIS : NEW ORLEANS :: ALBANY : (a. Boston, b. Cleveland, c. New York, d. Louisiana)

81. FRANCIS : BILLY : FRANCES : (a. William, b. Hinny, c. Kid, d. Nanny)

82. ROGET : (a. bridge, b. synonyms, c. thesaurus, d. quiz shows) :: MILLER : ANALOGIES

83. OCULIST : OPHTHALMOLOGIST :: CHIROPODIST : (a. chiropractor, b. pediatrician, c. osteopath, d. podiatrist)

84. GNU : GNAT :: (a. koala, b. knight, c. kestrell, d. kangaroo) : KNAVE

85. ALLAH : (a. Islam, b. Mohammed, c. Christianity, d. God) :: HORUS : NEPTUNE

86. 15 : 5 :: 23 : (a. 1, b. 2, c. 5, d. 6)

87. CYRILLIC : RUSSIAN :: ROMAN : (a. Gypsy, b. English, c. numerals, d. Arabic)

88. PASTERN : (a. flank, b. rural, c. horse, d. duck) :: PISTIL : STAMEN

89. @ : & :: 2 : (a. #, b. 5, c. 7, d. ½)

90. *IZVESTIA* : TASS :: (a. Reuters, b. *The New York Times,* c. CBS, d. State Department) : AP

91. (a. Alice, b. Medusa, c. King Arthur, d. Minerva) : ADONIS :: QUASIMODO : SNOW WHITE

92. ANTHROPOLOGY : MARGARET MEAD :: (a. archeology, b. history, c. philosophy, d. psychology) : HOWARD CARTER

93. AMBITION : MACBETH :: JEALOUSY : (a. Caesar, b. Brutus, c. Othello, d. Shylock)

94. *FAUST* : (a. Mephistopheles, b. Goethe, c. folklore, d. underworld) :: *FAUST* : GOUNOD

95. (a. ibid, b. etc., c. asst., d. dz.) : ET AL. :: OP. CIT. : CF.

96. YALTA : ROOSEVELT :: (a. Munich, b. Potsdam, c. Bastogne, d. Corregidor) : TRUMAN

97. *THE MAGIC FLUTE* : (a. *Iolanthe,* b. *Turandot,* c. *Il Trovatore,* d. *Don Giovanni*) :: *AIDA* : *DON CARLOS*

98. OXYGEN : (a. air, b. water, c. carbon dioxide, d. carbon monoxide) :: FAUNA : FLORA

99. (a. Sleeping Beauty, b. Cinderella, c. Rapunzel, d. Goldilocks) : PRINCE CHARMING :: FROG : PRINCESS

100. 9 : 104 :: BEETHOVEN : (a. Mozart, b. Sibelius, c. Haydn, d. Casals)

ANSWER KEY FOR
MILLER ANALOGIES SAMPLE TEST VI

1. c	21. d	41. c	61. b	81. d
2. a	22. c	42. a	62. d	82. b
3. d	23. a	43. b	63. a	83. d
4. b	24. d	44. a	64. b	84. b
5. b	25. b	45. b	65. c	85. d
6. c	26. c	46. a	66. b	86. d
7. a	27. b	47. d	67. b	87. b
8. c	28. b	48. b	68. c	88. a
9. d	29. a	49. a	69. a	89. c
10. c	30. d	50. a	70. c	90. b
11. d	31. c	51. b	71. b	91. b
12. d	32. b	52. c	72. d	92. a
13. b	33. b	53. a	73. c	93. c
14. c	34. c	54. d	74. c	94. b
15. a	35. a	55. d	75. a	95. a
16. d	36. c	56. b	76. b	96. b
17. c	37. d	57. b	77. d	97. d
18. d	38. d	58. c	78. c	98. c
19. b	39. a	59. d	79. b	99. a
20. a	40. b	60. d	80. c	100. c

EXPLANATORY ANSWERS FOR
MILLER ANALOGIES SAMPLE TEST VI

1. **(c)** The analogy is one of part to part. TILE and SLATE are both roofing materials; SHINGLE and THATCH are roofing materials as well.

2. **(a)** In this cause-and-effect analogy, to SCRUB something causes it to SHINE and to TURN something causes it to SPIN.

3. **(d)** This is a sequential analogy; the TADPOLE stage precedes the FROG, and a CATERPILLAR precedes a BUTTERFLY.

4. **(b)** The relationship is one of degree. A LEAP is a very large JUMP; a STRIDE is a very large STEP.

5. **(b)** The relationship of CAT to MOUSE is that of predator to prey. An ELAND is an African antelope preyed upon by LIONs.

6. **(c)** The relationship is that of synonyms. MERCURY is popularly known as QUICKSILVER; MICA is popularly called ISINGLASS.

7. **(a)** ROMEO and JULIET were tragic lovers whose parents forbade their marriage. This story closely parallels that of the mythological PYRAMUS and THISBE, whose love was also thwarted by their parents.

8. **(c)** The relationship is that of part to part. ALBERTA and ONTARIO are both Canadian provinces; QUEENSLAND and VICTORIA are both Australian provinces.

9. **(d)** L'ORANGE and PEKING are ways of preparing duck; BOUILLA-BAISSE and CHOWDER are different kinds of fish stews.

10. **(c)** William PENN established the colony which later became the state of PENNSYLVANIA; Lord BALTIMORE established the colony which became the state of MARYLAND.

11. **(d)** The relationship is that of a fraction to its decimal equivalent. 1/2 = .5; 5/20 = .25.

12. **(d)** HYDE PARK was the family home of Franklin D. ROOSEVELT; OYSTER BAY was the family home of Theodore ROOSEVELT.

13. **(b)** PEPSIN is an enzyme which breaks down PROTEIN into amino acids; PTYALIN is the enzyme which decomposes STARCH. The analogy is one of function.

14. **(c)** Edward KOCH is the author of the autobiography entitled *MAYOR;* Golda MEIR is the author of the autobiography entitled *MY LIFE*.

15. **(a)** GOBI and MOJAVE are both deserts; TIGRIS and EUPHRATES are both rivers.

16. **(d)** The analogy is one of shared characteristic. MULE and TANGELO share the characteristic that both are man-made hybrids. CAPON and STEER also share a characteristic: both are castrated males of their species which are raised specially for their meat.

17. **(c)** The analogy stems from the divisibility of the first number by the second and the answer yielded by the division. 12 ÷ 3 = 4; 44 ÷ 11 = 4. The sign "::" does not necessarily mean "equals."

18. **(d)** This is a grammatical analogy. WENT is the past tense of GO; READ is the past tense of READ.

19. **(b)** Thomas GRAY wrote *Elegy Written in a Country Churchyard,* commonly known as GRAY's "ELEGY"; William Cullen BRYANT wrote "THANATOPSIS."

20. **(a)** The battle of the ALAMO, a fort in Texas at which all defenders were killed, was the turning point of the TEXAS WAR OF INDEPENDENCE. The rallying cry of the Texans was "Remember the Alamo." The sinking

of the battleship *MAINE* in Havana Harbor brought the United States into the SPANISH-AMERICAN WAR. The American call to battle was "Remember the *Maine*."

21. **(d)** PLUTO and URANUS are both planets; SIRIUS (the dog star) and POLARIS (the north star) are both stars.

22. **(c)** In this analogy of association, just as British Prime Minister Neville CHAMBERLAIN is associated with the policy of APPEASEMENT, so President Harry TRUMAN is associated with the policy of Soviet CONTAINMENT.

23. **(a.)** The relationship is between the hero of a novel and the author of that novel. ARI is the hero of Leon URIS' novel *Exodus*; MICHAEL is the hero of Mario PUZO's *The Godfather*.

24. **(d)** AMOEBA and PARAMECIUM are both simple water organisms; SAMISEN and BANJO are both simple stringed instruments.

25. **(b)** A BIENNIAL event happens once every TWO years; a BIANNUAL event occurs twice a year or every ONE-HALF year.

26. **(c)** *PYGMALION* is the George Bernard Shaw play upon which the musical *MY FAIR LADY* was based; *THE MATCHMAKER* is the Thornton Wilder play upon which the musical *HELLO DOLLY* was based.

27. **(b)** JACKSON and VAN BUREN both entered the White House as widowers and remained single throughout their tenure; both WILSON and TYLER married second wives while in the White House.

28. **(b)** ANGOLA and MOZAMBIQUE before they achieved their independence were colonies of Portugal; SIERRA LEONE and ZIMBABWE were British colonies. Algeria was French; Zambia was Belgian; Liberia was always independent.

29. **(a)** This is a cause-and-effect analogy. Both nuclear FISSION and nuclear FUSION create ENERGY. None of the other choices creates energy.

30. **(d)** In this analogy, there is a relationship between the mystery writer and the character created by the author. Agatha CHRISTIE is the creator of Hercule POIROT; Erle Stanley GARDNER is the creator of Perry MASON.

31. **(c)** The relationship is between specialist and generalist. BACH was a famous Baroque composer. He is well known only for his musical compositions. DA VINCI is equally well known as an artist, sculptor, architect, engineer, inventor, and student of anatomy. MONET is famous only as an impressionist painter, while JEFFERSON is famous as President, statesman, landscape architect, composer, and musician.

32. **(b)** The relationship is based upon simple addition. 27 is 18 more than 9. On the other side of the proportion, 18 must be added to 81 to yield 99. Avoid the temptation to say "2 plus 7 = 9. therefore since 8 plus 1 = 9 (a) is the answer." Such reasoning reverses the direction and does not complete the analogy

33. **(b)** This is a sequence analogy. The O.S.S. (Office of Strategic Services) was an intelligence-gathering unit during World War II and was a forerunner of the C.I.A. (Central Intelligence Agency); the I.W.W. (Industrial Workers of the World) was an early labor union and was a forerunner of the C.I.O. (Congress of Industrial Organizations).

34. **(c)** This analogy is one of degree. The SUNNITEs are the original body of Moslems; the SHI'ITE sect broke away from the SUNNITEs and practices a less orthodox version of Islam. The CATHOLICs were the original body of Christians; the EPISCOPALIANs broke away from the CATHOLICs and formed a less orthodox group.

35. **(a)** *PUDD'NHEAD WILSON* is a book written by SAMUEL CLEMENS whose pen name was Mark Twain; *ANIMAL FARM* is a book written by ERIC BLAIR whose pen name was George Orwell.

36. **(c)** This analogy is based upon antonyms. In a STRIKE, management welcomes the workers but the workers refuse to work, while in a LOCKOUT the workers are willing but management does not allow them to work. To GAINSAY is to contradict, which is the antonym of to AGREE.

37. **(d)** This analogy is based upon synonyms. A COLLIER is a coal MINER; a TALISMAN is a good luck charm, as is an AMULET.

38. **(d)** A SPIDER is an ARACHNID, a member of the class Arachnida of the phylum Arthropoda; a LOBSTER is a CRUSTACEAN, a member of the class Crustacea of the phylum Arthropoda.

39. **(a)** HERODOTUS and THUCYDIDES were both Greek historians; HOMER and PINDAR were both Greek poets. Ovid was a Roman poet.

40. **(b)** This is a nonsemantic relationship. The words of the first pair HAIL and HALE are homonyms. Both (b) and (c) create a pair of homonyms with PARE, however, (b) is the best answer because its spelling is analogous to that of the first member of the initial word pair.

41. **(c)** The artist MANET painted a portrait of his friend the novelist Marcel PROUST; the artist GAINSBOROUGH painted a famous portrait of a young man in blue called "BLUE BOY."

42. **(a)** INFLAMMABLE and FLAMMABLE are synonyms; INVALUABLE and PRICELESS are synonyms. Often the prefix *in* means *not,* but in both these instances the initial *in* does not mean that the word is negative.

43. **(b)** 946 ml. is equal to one QUART; 3280.8 ft. is equal to one KILO-METER.

44. **(a)** COAL is a fossil fuel; WIND is a nonfossil power source. OIL is a fossil fuel while SUN is a nonfossil power source.

45. **(b)** TCHAIKOVSKY's sixth symphony is named the "PATHE-TIQUE;" BEETHOVEN's sixth symphony is named the "PASTOR-ALE."

46. **(a)** ESTONIA and RUSSIA are both constituent republics of the USSR (Union of Soviet Socialist Republics). GEORGIA and CZECHOSLO-VAKIA are also member states of the USSR.

47. **(d)** CHICKEN and TURKEY are both barnyard fowl. FLAMINGO and DEMOISELLE (a small crane) are both wading birds.

48. **(b)** This analogy is simply that of the square of a number to the number.

49. **(a)** This is a part-to-whole analogy. RUSSIA is a part of the USSR, which is commonly considered to be the whole of the country. HOLLAND is a province of THE NETHERLANDS, which is often incorrectly thought to be the whole of the country.

50. **(a)** A UNICORN is a mythological animal; a MASTODON is an extinct animal. A GRIFFIN is a mythological animal; a DODO is an extinct animal.

51. **(b)** The ANOPHELES mosquito transmits MALARIA; the AEDES mosquito transmits DENGUE and yellow fever.

52. **(c)** OVOLO and CAVETTO are moldings. OVOLO is a CONVEX molding; CAVETTO is a CONCAVE molding.

53. **(a)** ADANO is the town in the John HERSEY novel *A Bell for Adano;* CASTERBRIDGE is the city in the Thomas HARDY novel *The Mayor of Casterbridge*.

54. **(d)** A COVEY is a flock of QUAIL; a GAGGLE is a flock of GEESE.

55. **(d)** This is a grammatical analogy. The adjective MANY is used to describe a quantity of an object that can be counted; the adjective MUCH is used to describe a volume that cannot be counted.

56. **(b)** The contents of the STOMACH empty directly into the DUO-DENUM (the top part of the small intestine); blood from the HEART goes directly into ARTERIES for distribution.

57. **(b)** FEATHERS are part of a feather DUSTER: SETA (bristles) are part of a TOOTHBRUSH. This is a part-to-whole analogy.

58. **(c)** This is a part-to-part analogy. CHEETAH and LEOPARD are both members of the feline family; WOLF and DOG are both members of the canine family.

59. **(d)** This is an analogy of synonyms or near synonyms. A race TRACK is often called an OVAL; QUOITS are flattened circles or semicircles of metal sometimes used in place of HORSESHOES. The game of QUOITS is played in the same way as the game of HORSESHOES and the terms are interchangeable.

60. **(d)** A CATHEDRAL is a CHURCH; a CITADEL is a FORTRESS.

61. **(b)** The relationship is between a number and the expression of a square root. 5 is one less than the square root of 36; 8 is one less than the square root of 81. Therefore the analogy should read $5 : \sqrt{36} :: 8 : \sqrt{81}$. Choice (a) makes a correct statement but not a perfect analogy. If choice (b) were not offered, (a) would suffice. However, you must always choose the answer which creates the most perfect analogy.

62. **(d)** This is a sequential analogy. The ANTEPENULT is the third syllable from the end of a word; the PENULT is the next-to-the-last syllable of a word. In the sequence of events from crime to punishment, VERDICT comes immediately before SENTENCE.

63. **(a)** RACCOON and CROW are both plentiful, common creatures; PANDA and CONDOR are both members of endangered species.

64. **(b)** The *LUSITANIA* was a BRITISH ship which was sunk by the Germans; flight 007 was a KOREAN airplane which was shot down and sunk by the Russians in the sea of Japan. The salient relationship is that between the vessel and the country to which it belonged.

65. **(c)** In computer parlance, a NYBBLE is half a BYTE. In speaking of the moon, a HALF moon is half of a FULL moon.

66. **(b)** LANGSTON HUGHES and DOUGHTRY LONG are both black male poets; GWENDOLYN BROOK and NAOMI LONG MADGETT are both black female poets.

67. **(b)** GRE (Graduate Record Exam) and MAT (Miller Analogies Test) are both qualifying examinations for graduate school; SAT (Scholastic Aptitude Test) and ACT (American College Testing Program) are both qualifying examinations for college admission.

68. **(c)** The nature of the relationship is association. TULIP is a flower associated with SPRING; ASTER is a flower associated with FALL.

69. **(a)** BOLL WEEVIL and GYPSY MOTH are both harmful insects. ASSASSIN FLY and PRAYING MANTIS are both beneficial insects which prey upon harmful insects.

70. **(c)** PANMUNJOM was the site of the signing of the Peace Treaty of the KOREAN WAR; GHENT (in Belgium) was the site of the signing of the Peace Treaty of the WAR OF 1812.

71. **(b)** ECHO was a nymph loved by NARCISSUS; SYRINX was a nymph loved by PAN.

72. **(d)** On each side of the proportion the words are synonyms. A VIRAGO is a quarrelsome woman, a shrew or a TERMAGENT; a TOADY is a fawning person, a flatterer or a SYCOPHANT.

73. **(c)** The KNESSET is the lawmaking body of the government of ISRAEL; the DIET serves as the congressional arm of the government of JAPAN.

74. **(c)** *LES MISÉRABLES* is a novel written by VICTOR HUGO; *LES TROIS MOUSQUETAIRES* is a novel written by ALEXANDRE DUMAS.

75. **(a)** This is a grammatical analogy. Simply stated, the relationship on both sides of the proportion is possessive : contraction. ITS is the possessive of *it*, while IT'S is the contraction for *it is;* THEIR is the possessive of *they,* while THEY'RE is the contraction for *they are.*

76. **(b)** The analogy is based upon synonyms. To NICTATE is to WINK; to OSCULATE is to KISS.

77. **(d)** DOWN'S SYNDROME is one form of MENTAL RETARDATION; HODGKIN'S DISEASE is a form of CANCER.

78. **(c)** The relationship of the numbers is a nonmathematical one. The second number is merely a mirror image of the first.

79. **(b)** FIGARO is a character in the opera BARBER OF SEVILLE; MAMA LUCIA is a character in the opera CAVALLERIA RUSTICANA.

80. **(c)** The source of the Mississippi River is in Minnesota very close to the city of MINNEAPOLIS while the mouth of the Mississippi River is at NEW ORLEANS; the source of the Hudson River is very close to the city of ALBANY while the mouth of the Hudson River is at NEW YORK City.

81. **(d)** This analogy is based upon gender, that is, the relationship of male to female. FRANCIS is male; FRANCES is female. BILLY is the commonly used term referring to a male goat; NANNY is the counterpart for a female goat.

82. **(b)** The subject of the examination devised by W.S. MILLER is ANALOGIES; the subject of the book compiled by ROGET is SYNONYMS.

83. **(d)** The analogy is based upon similarity of function. Both OCULIST and OPHTHALMOLOGIST are eye doctors; both CHIROPODIST and PODIATRIST are foot doctors.

84. **(b)** This is a nonsemantic analogy. Both GNU and GNAT are creatures whose names begin with a silent letter *g*; both KNIGHT and KNAVE are persons whose names begin with a silent letter *k*.

85. **(d)** HORUS and NEPTUNE are both gods in polytheistic religions; both ALLAH and GOD are the deities of monotheistic religions.

86. **(d)** This is a different style of relationship, found by multiplying the two numbers in each double digit number (15 and 23). $1 \times 5 = 5$; $2 \times 3 = 6$.

87. **(b)** The RUSSIAN language is written in the CYRILLIC alphabet; the ENGLISH language is written in the ROMAN alphabet.

88. **(a)** PISTIL and STAMEN are both parts of a flower; PASTERN and FLANK are both parts of a horse. The relationship is that of part to part.

89. **(c)** This analogy is based upon the location of certain symbols on the typewriter keyboard. @ is on the same key as 2; & shares a key with 7.

90. **(b)** *IZVESTIA* is a Russian newspaper, TASS a Russian wire service; *THE NEW YORK TIMES* is an American newspaper, AP (Associated Press) an American wire service.

91. **(b)** The analogy is between hideous ugliness and great beauty. QUASIMODO was the hunchback in Victor Hugo's *Hunchback of Notre Dame* while SNOW WHITE was a beautiful fairy tale heroine. MEDUSA, in Greek mythology, was a Gorgon and very ugly, while ADONIS, also from Greek mythology, was the epitome of male beauty.

92. **(a)** MARGARET MEAD was a famous ANTHROPOLOGIST; HOWARD CARTER was an English ARCHEOLOGIST.

93. **(c)** AMBITION was the force which drove MACBETH; JEALOUSY was the force which drove OTHELLO.

94. **(b)** The analogy is one of product to its creator. The dramatic poem *FAUST* was written by GOETHE; the opera *FAUST* was written by GOUNOD.

95. **(a)** The analogy is based upon the location at which the abbreviation is likely to be found. OP.CIT. (in the work cited) and CF. (compare) are both abbreviations from the Latin commonly used in footnotes. IBID. (in the same place) and ET AL. (and others) are also footnote abbreviations.

96. **(b)** YALTA was the site of a conference of the three major allies of World War II at which President ROOSEVELT represented the United States; POTSDAM was the site of a later conference at which President TRUMAN represented the United States.

97. **(d)** *AIDA* and *DON CARLOS* are both operas written by Verdi; *THE MAGIC FLUTE* and *DON GIOVANNI* are operas written by Mozart.

98. **(c)** The relationship of FAUNA (animal life) to OXYGEN is that animals breathe in oxygen. The relationship of FLORA (plant life) to CARBON DIOXIDE is that plants breathe in carbon dioxide.

99. **(a)** The FROG was under a wicked spell which was broken by the kiss of the PRINCESS; SLEEPING BEAUTY was under a wicked spell which was broken by the kiss of PRINCE CHARMING.

100. **(c)** BEETHOVEN wrote 9 symphonies; HAYDN was very prolific and wrote 104.

ANSWER SHEET
MILLER ANALOGIES SAMPLE TEST VII

1 Ⓐ Ⓑ Ⓒ Ⓓ   21 Ⓐ Ⓑ Ⓒ Ⓓ   41 Ⓐ Ⓑ Ⓒ Ⓓ   61 Ⓐ Ⓑ Ⓒ Ⓓ   81 Ⓐ Ⓑ Ⓒ Ⓓ
2 Ⓐ Ⓑ Ⓒ Ⓓ   22 Ⓐ Ⓑ Ⓒ Ⓓ   42 Ⓐ Ⓑ Ⓒ Ⓓ   62 Ⓐ Ⓑ Ⓒ Ⓓ   82 Ⓐ Ⓑ Ⓒ Ⓓ
3 Ⓐ Ⓑ Ⓒ Ⓓ   23 Ⓐ Ⓑ Ⓒ Ⓓ   43 Ⓐ Ⓑ Ⓒ Ⓓ   63 Ⓐ Ⓑ Ⓒ Ⓓ   83 Ⓐ Ⓑ Ⓒ Ⓓ
4 Ⓐ Ⓑ Ⓒ Ⓓ   24 Ⓐ Ⓑ Ⓒ Ⓓ   44 Ⓐ Ⓑ Ⓒ Ⓓ   64 Ⓐ Ⓑ Ⓒ Ⓓ   84 Ⓐ Ⓑ Ⓒ Ⓓ
5 Ⓐ Ⓑ Ⓒ Ⓓ   25 Ⓐ Ⓑ Ⓒ Ⓓ   45 Ⓐ Ⓑ Ⓒ Ⓓ   65 Ⓐ Ⓑ Ⓒ Ⓓ   85 Ⓐ Ⓑ Ⓒ Ⓓ
6 Ⓐ Ⓑ Ⓒ Ⓓ   26 Ⓐ Ⓑ Ⓒ Ⓓ   46 Ⓐ Ⓑ Ⓒ Ⓓ   66 Ⓐ Ⓑ Ⓒ Ⓓ   86 Ⓐ Ⓑ Ⓒ Ⓓ
7 Ⓐ Ⓑ Ⓒ Ⓓ   27 Ⓐ Ⓑ Ⓒ Ⓓ   47 Ⓐ Ⓑ Ⓒ Ⓓ   67 Ⓐ Ⓑ Ⓒ Ⓓ   87 Ⓐ Ⓑ Ⓒ Ⓓ
8 Ⓐ Ⓑ Ⓒ Ⓓ   28 Ⓐ Ⓑ Ⓒ Ⓓ   48 Ⓐ Ⓑ Ⓒ Ⓓ   68 Ⓐ Ⓑ Ⓒ Ⓓ   88 Ⓐ Ⓑ Ⓒ Ⓓ
9 Ⓐ Ⓑ Ⓒ Ⓓ   29 Ⓐ Ⓑ Ⓒ Ⓓ   49 Ⓐ Ⓑ Ⓒ Ⓓ   69 Ⓐ Ⓑ Ⓒ Ⓓ   89 Ⓐ Ⓑ Ⓒ Ⓓ
10 Ⓐ Ⓑ Ⓒ Ⓓ   30 Ⓐ Ⓑ Ⓒ Ⓓ   50 Ⓐ Ⓑ Ⓒ Ⓓ   70 Ⓐ Ⓑ Ⓒ Ⓓ   90 Ⓐ Ⓑ Ⓒ Ⓓ
11 Ⓐ Ⓑ Ⓒ Ⓓ   31 Ⓐ Ⓑ Ⓒ Ⓓ   51 Ⓐ Ⓑ Ⓒ Ⓓ   71 Ⓐ Ⓑ Ⓒ Ⓓ   91 Ⓐ Ⓑ Ⓒ Ⓓ
12 Ⓐ Ⓑ Ⓒ Ⓓ   32 Ⓐ Ⓑ Ⓒ Ⓓ   52 Ⓐ Ⓑ Ⓒ Ⓓ   72 Ⓐ Ⓑ Ⓒ Ⓓ   92 Ⓐ Ⓑ Ⓒ Ⓓ
13 Ⓐ Ⓑ Ⓒ Ⓓ   33 Ⓐ Ⓑ Ⓒ Ⓓ   53 Ⓐ Ⓑ Ⓒ Ⓓ   73 Ⓐ Ⓑ Ⓒ Ⓓ   93 Ⓐ Ⓑ Ⓒ Ⓓ
14 Ⓐ Ⓑ Ⓒ Ⓓ   34 Ⓐ Ⓑ Ⓒ Ⓓ   54 Ⓐ Ⓑ Ⓒ Ⓓ   74 Ⓐ Ⓑ Ⓒ Ⓓ   94 Ⓐ Ⓑ Ⓒ Ⓓ
15 Ⓐ Ⓑ Ⓒ Ⓓ   35 Ⓐ Ⓑ Ⓒ Ⓓ   55 Ⓐ Ⓑ Ⓒ Ⓓ   75 Ⓐ Ⓑ Ⓒ Ⓓ   95 Ⓐ Ⓑ Ⓒ Ⓓ
16 Ⓐ Ⓑ Ⓒ Ⓓ   36 Ⓐ Ⓑ Ⓒ Ⓓ   56 Ⓐ Ⓑ Ⓒ Ⓓ   76 Ⓐ Ⓑ Ⓒ Ⓓ   96 Ⓐ Ⓑ Ⓒ Ⓓ
17 Ⓐ Ⓑ Ⓒ Ⓓ   37 Ⓐ Ⓑ Ⓒ Ⓓ   57 Ⓐ Ⓑ Ⓒ Ⓓ   77 Ⓐ Ⓑ Ⓒ Ⓓ   97 Ⓐ Ⓑ Ⓒ Ⓓ
18 Ⓐ Ⓑ Ⓒ Ⓓ   38 Ⓐ Ⓑ Ⓒ Ⓓ   58 Ⓐ Ⓑ Ⓒ Ⓓ   78 Ⓐ Ⓑ Ⓒ Ⓓ   98 Ⓐ Ⓑ Ⓒ Ⓓ
19 Ⓐ Ⓑ Ⓒ Ⓓ   39 Ⓐ Ⓑ Ⓒ Ⓓ   59 Ⓐ Ⓑ Ⓒ Ⓓ   79 Ⓐ Ⓑ Ⓒ Ⓓ   99 Ⓐ Ⓑ Ⓒ Ⓓ
20 Ⓐ Ⓑ Ⓒ Ⓓ   40 Ⓐ Ⓑ Ⓒ Ⓓ   60 Ⓐ Ⓑ Ⓒ Ⓓ   80 Ⓐ Ⓑ Ⓒ Ⓓ   100 Ⓐ Ⓑ Ⓒ Ⓓ

Tear Here

MILLER ANALOGIES
SAMPLE TEST VII

Time: 50 Minutes. 100 Questions.

Directions: Each of these test questions consists of three CAPITALIZED words and four lettered words enclosed in parentheses. Two of the capitalized words are related in some way. Find the two related words and establish the nature of the relationship. Then study the four words lettered a, b, c, and d. Select the one lettered word which is related to the remaining capitalized word in the same way that the first two capitalized words are related. Mark the answer sheet for the letter of the word you select.

1. TINY : (a. dwarf, b. small, c. infinitesimal, d. huge) :: BIG : ENORMOUS

2. LAMP : LIGHT :: CHAIR : (a. stool, b. table, c. back, d. seat)

3. (a. bud, b. spring, c. flower, d. blossom) : BLOOM :: FADE : FALL

4. BLUE : (a. gold, b. gray, c. red, d. green) :: NORTH : SOUTH

5. DOCKET : COURT :: (a. agenda, b. itinerary, c. calendar, d. route) : TRIP

6. NEITHER : WEIRD :: (a. friend, b. yield, c. receipt, d. height) : LEISURE

7. BERING STRAIT : SEWARD PENINSULA :: STRAIT OF MAGELLAN : (a. Trazos-Montes, b. Tierra del Fuego, c. Matan, d. Malay Peninsula)

8. *LORD OF THE FLIES* : *LORD OF THE RING* :: GOLDING : (a. Swift, b. King Arthur, c. Tolkien, d. Burnett)

9. ATROPHY : (a. eyes, b. muscles, c. teeth, d. veins) :: THICKENING : JOINTS

10. ERNEST : RUDYARD :: HEMINGWAY : (a. Proust, b. Loftus, c. Kipling, d. Brecht)

11. 4/8 : 8/4 :: 5/15 : (a. 1/3, b. 2/3, c. 15/5, d. 3/1)

12. MAY DAY : (a. Labor Day, b. Christmas, c. Bastille Day, d. Tet) :: RAMADAN : LENT

13. INGENUOUS : (a. frank, b. aloof, c. clever, d. pretty) :: INIQUITOUS : WICKED

14. PROTRACTOR : ANGLES :: COMPASS : (a. tones, b. area, c. directions, d. curves)

15. TENNESSEE WILLIAMS : *THE GLASS MENAGERIE* :: (a. Thornton Wilder, b. Luigi Pirandello, c. Maxwell Anderson, d. Noel Coward) : *SIX CHARACTERS IN SEARCH OF AN AUTHOR*

16. INJURY : PARAPLEGIA :: STROKE : (a. aphasia, b. quadriplegia, c. fantasia, d. hemiplegia)

17. LIKES : EVERYONE :: (a. hate, b. wish, c. loves, d. care) : NOBODY

18. OCTOBER : (a. July, b. January, c. Thursday, d. planting) :: HARVEST MOON : THUNDER MOON

19. ERATO : THALIA :: (a. movies, b. sleep, c. poetry, d. death) : COMEDY

20. (a. agar, b. alga, c. alum, d. agnus) : BUROWS SOLUTION :: ALOE : COLD CREAM

21. 6 : −6 :: 31 : (a. −2, b. 3, c. −13, d. 19)

22. RIVE GAUCHE : PARIS :: (a. New Jersey, b. Statue of Liberty, c. Riker's Island, d. Brooklyn) : NEW YORK

23. SURINAM : (a. Guyana, b. British Honduras, c. Belize, d. Dutch Guiana) :: ZIMBABWE : RHODESIA

24. BAROQUE : BACH :: (a. Classical, b. Romantic, c. Rococo, d. Impressionist) : SCHUMANN

25. OBSEQUIOUS : OBSTINATE :: DIFFIDENT : (a. indifferent, b. shy, c. distinct, d. defiant)

26. SHIITE : (a. Arab, b. Muslim, c. Sunni, d. Iran) :: ROMAN CATHOLIC : PROTESTANT

27. HONOR : CITATION :: SPEEDING : (a. citation, b. hurry, c. race, d. stop)

28. *HEDDA GABLER* : (a. *The Cherry Orchard,* b. *Riders to the Sea,* c. *An Enemy of the People,* d. *Blood Wedding*) :: *ANNA CHRISTIE : MOON FOR THE MISBEGOTTEN*

29. YELLOW : (a. jonquil, b. cornflower, c. rose, d. jacket) :: RED : SALVIA

30. ANODE : CATHODE :: OXIDATION : (a. erosion, b. reduction, c. carbonization, d. hydrogenation)

31. VIOLA DA GAMBA : VIOLIN :: (a. clarinet, b. French horn, c. accordion, d. rebec) : ENGLISH HORN

32. JOAN OF ARC : (a. Pope, b. stake, c. king, d. saint) :: GALILEO : SUN

33. (a. Yeats, b. Shakespeare, c. Chaucer, d. Tennyson) : SONNETS :: NASH : LIMERICKS

34. SQUASH : PLATFORM TENNIS :: HOCKEY : (a. badminton, b. rugby, c. volleyball, d. curling)

35. LENINGRAD : HERMITAGE :: (a. Spain, b. Majorca, c. Madrid, d. Seville) : PRADO

36. ABSCISSA : (a. ordinate, b. mantissa, c. coordinate, d. precision) :: X : Y

37. SKINNER : BEHAVIORISM :: (a. Adler, b. Terman, c. Kant, d. Wertheimer) : GESTALT

38. HESTER : FIDELITY :: (a. Goneril, b. Cordelia, c. Ophelia, d. Cassandra) : DEVOTION

39. CAPILLARIES : CIRCULATION :: VILLI : (a. respiration, b. digestion, c. recreation, d. procreation)

40. SAN MARINO : ITALY :: (a. Ethiopia, b. Capetown, c. Lesotho, d. Swaziland) : SOUTH AFRICA

41. (a. Florida, b. New Mexico, c. Puerto Rico, d. Texas) : ALASKA :: SPAIN : RUSSIA

42. KEYNES : ECONOMICS :: DEWEY : (a. politics, b. electronics, c. medicine, d. education)

43. NEIL ARMSTRONG : URI GAGARIN :: CHARLES LINDBERGH : (a. George Washington, b. Albert Einstein, c. Orville Wright, d. Guglielmo Marconi)

44. *PILGRIM'S PROGRESS* : (a. *Inferno,* b. *Paradise Lost,* c. *De Monarchia,* d. *Divine Comedy)* :: BUNYAN : DANTE

45. GHENGIS KAHN : MONGOLS :: ATILLA : (a. Roman Empire, b. Germany, c. Huns, d. Tartars)

46. HARE : (a. rabbit, b. tortoise, c. terrapin, d. hart) :: FOX : GRAPES

47. 4 : 6 :: (a. 10, b. 6, c. 9, d. 16) : 36

48. THOMAS MANN : *BUDDENBROOKS* :: THOMAS WOLFE : (a. *Death in Venice,* b. *Look Homeward Angel,* c. *The Magic Mountain,* d. *Joseph and His Brothers*)

49. (a. Earth, b. moon, c. Russia, d. Stalin) : SPUTNIK :: JUPITER : IO

50. FREYA : ASGARD :: (a. Hera, b. Venus, c. Minerva, d. Aphrodite) : OLYMPUS

51. (a. isosceles, b. scalene, c. right, d. obtuse) : EQUILATERAL :: DUPLE : TRIPLE

52. ORR : PELE :: (a. hockey, b. baseball, c. football, d. horseracing) : SOCCER

53. OBVERSE : (a. coin, b. sweater, c. reverse, d. crochet) :: KNIT : PURL

54. PASTEL : MUTED :: LIGHT : (a. sound, b. voice, c. trumpet, d. wheel)

55. (a. one, b. two, c. three, d. nine) : BETWEEN :: SIX : AMONG

56. XENOPHOBIA : PREJUDICE :: PECCATOPHOBIA : (a. tantrums, b. bad habits, c. clumsiness, d. virtue)

57. HARPSICHORD : VIRGINAL :: (a. piccolo, b. saxophone, c. sousaphone, d. oboe) : CLARINET

58. ROMANY : LAPP :: NOMADIC : (a. stationary, b. migratory, c. aquatic, d. ascetic)

59. ATOM : MOLECULE :: GENE : (a. heredity, b. genetics, c. DNA, d. chromosome)

60. FIRE : SMOKE :: (a. pipe, b. hose, c. leak, d. break) : STAIN

61. BUTTER : MARGARINE :: LEATHER : (a. fur, b. linoleum, c. naugahyde, d. canvas)

62. TOM SAWYER : (a. Mark Twain, b. Samuel Clemens, c. Becky Thatcher, d. David Copperfield) :: HAZEL : FIVER

63. (a. white, b. blue, c. blanch, d. yellow) : BLEACH :: HENNA : ANIL

64. CHECKERS : RICHARD NIXON :: TRAVELLER : (a. Robert E. Lee, b. Franklin Roosevelt, c. Dwight Eisenhower, d. Aristotle Onassis)

65. BRUTE : SQUIRE :: TUBER : (a. leaves, b. yams, c. quires, d. stems)

66. 1/8 : 12.5% :: (a. 1/6, b. 3/11, c. 2/7, d. 3/8) : 37.5%

67. CRETACEOUS : DINOSAURS :: TERTIARY : (a. vampires, b. fish, c. reptiles, d. mammals)

68. MAPLE : (a. syrup, b. oak, c. cyanide, d. leaf) :: PRIVET : HEMLOCK

69. (a. Washington, b. Jefferson, c. Franklin, d. Lincoln) : MADISON :: DECLARATION OF INDEPENDENCE : CONSTITUTION

70. ALZHEIMER'S DISEASE : HANSEN'S DISEASE :: (a. cerebral palsy, b. copper deficiency, c. senility, d. lymphatic cancer) : LEPROSY

71. GEORGES BRAQUE : FERNAND LEGER :: (a. e.e. cummings, b. William Wordsworth, c. Jack London, d. Leo Tolstoy) : DON MARQUIS

72. INDEPENDENCE : COOPERATION :: PHOTOSYNTHESIS : (a. parasitism, b. parthenogenesis, c. symbiosis, d. carbohydrates)

73. (a. stars, b. restaurants, c. tires, d. highways) : MICHELIN :: GASOLINE : MOBIL

74. SWIFT : (a. Barrie, b. Kipling, c. Dorothy, d. Baum) :: LILLIPUT : OZ

75. FOUR : BASEBALL :: (a. ten, b. eleven, c. fifty, d. one hundred twenty) : FOOTBALL

76. (a. remuneration, b. stipend, c. pay, d. overtime) : SALARY :: COMMISSION : ROYALTY

77. LAWYER : BARRISTER :: ATTORNEY : (a. judge, b. juror, c. advocate, d. appellant)

78. KOALA : (a. eucalyptus, b. wallaby, c. bamboo, d. mulberry) :: WHALE : PLANKTON

79. DEER : (a. deer, b. moose, c. dear, d. swan) :: GOOSE : GEESE

80. 27 : (a. 3, b. 9, c. 5.19, d. 729) :: 125 : 5

81. EGG : CHICKEN :: CHICKEN : (a. rooster, b. capon, c. egg, d. hen)

82. PARIS : FRANCE :: (a. Amsterdam, b. Holland, c. Rotterdam, d. the Hague) : NETHERLANDS

83. CCC : TVA :: FDIC : (a. OPA, b. WMC, c. OSS, d. FHA)

84. ELABORATE : (a. streamlined, b. boring, c. oblique, d. obligatory) :: SERIF : SANS SERIF

85. BULL RUN : MANASSAS :: STREAM : (a. battle, b. town, c. war, d. tribe)

86. GREENWICH VILLAGE : (a. London, b. Kensington, c. New York, d. Picadilly Circus) :: MONTMARTRE : PARIS

87. TALIPES : HARELIP :: HYDROCEPHALUS : (a. hydrophobia, b. spina bifida, c. hemiplegia, d. poliomyelitis)

88. ZOLA : *NANA* :: (a. Humbert Humbert, b. Don Juan, c. Don Quixote, d. Nabokov) : *LOLITA*

89. KANT : CATEGORICAL IMPERATIVE :: (a. Descartes, b. Neitzche, c. Sartre, d. Mill) : UTILITY

90. NOON : EVE :: (a. pop, b. dine, c. moon, d. morn) : SUP

91. MENTICIDE : BRAINWASHING :: OPPROBRIUM : (a. commendation, b. reproach, c. indoctrination, d. repression)

92. CALPURNIA : (a. Oedipus, b. Caesar, c. King Lear, d. Cicero) :: CRESSIDA : TROILUS

93. BLIND : DEAF :: (a. Milton, b. Scott, c. Mozart, d. Justice) : BEETHOVEN

94. REMUS : (a. Brer Rabbit, b. Aquarius, c. Quisling, d. Romulus) :: CASTOR : POLLUX

95. DOG : FLEA :: HORSE : (a. rider, b. fly, c. mane, d. shoe)

96. 10 : (a. decimal, b. common, c. unnatural, d. metric) :: e : NATURAL

97. BROUGHAM : CARRIAGE :: HOME : (a. house, b. town, c. marriage, d. family)

98. EZEKIEL : (a. Hosea, b. Isaiah, c. Peter, d. Ecclesiastes) :: CHRONICLES : ACTS

99. (a. Shangri-La, b. Lilliput, c. Atlantis, d. Ilium) : BRIGADOON :: FOUNTAIN OF YOUTH : NEVER-NEVER LAND

100. PANTHEON : PARTHENON :: (a. Al Aksa, b. Cathedral of Saint John the Divine, c. Shrine of Our Lady of Guadaloupe, d. Teopancali) : ST. PETER'S BASILICA

ANSWER KEY FOR
MILLER ANALOGIES SAMPLE TEST VII

1. c	21. d	41. a	61. c	81. c
2. d	22. d	42. d	62. c	82. d
3. a	23. d	43. c	63. b	83. d
4. b	24. b	44. d	64. a	84. a
5. b	25. d	45. c	65. c	85. b
6. d	26. c	46. b	66. d	86. c
7. b	27. a	47. d	67. d	87. b
8. c	28. c	48. b	68. b	88. d
9. b	29. a	49. a	69. b	89. d
10. c	30. b	50. d	70. c	90. b
11. c	31. a	51. a	71. a	91. b
12. a	32. c	52. a	72. c	92. b
13. a	33. b	53. c	73. c	93. a
14. d	34. d	54. a	74. d	94. d
15. b	35. c	55. b	75. a	95. b
16. d	36. a	56. d	76. b	96. b
17. c	37. d	57. d	77. c	97. c
18. a	38. a	58. b	78. a	98. c
19. c	39. b	59. d	79. a	99. a
20. c	40. c	60. c	80. a	100. d

EXPLANATORY ANSWERS FOR
MILLER ANALOGIES SAMPLE TEST VII

1. **(c)** This is an analogy of degree. ENORMOUS is an intense degree of BIG, INFINITESIMAL is an intense degree of TINY.

2. **(d)** This is an analogy not of true synonyms but of synonyms as used in common parlance. Thus, "Turn on a LIGHT" is used interchangeably with "Turn on a LAMP," and "Have a SEAT" is used interchangeably with "Have a CHAIR."

3. **(a)** This analogy is based upon sequence. A flower must FADE before it FALLS. The same flower must BUD before it can BLOOM. The sequence is BUD, BLOOM, FADE, FALL.

4. **(b)** During the Civil War, the uniforms of the NORTH were BLUE and the uniforms of the SOUTH were GRAY. This is an analogy of association.

5. **(b)** The COURT DOCKET is the official register of cases to be tried; the TRIP ITINERARY is the step-by-step schedule for a trip including route to be traveled, sights to be seen, and stops to be made.

6. **(d)** This is a grammatical analogy. It is based upon the fact that the related words are all exceptions to the "*i* before *e* except after *c*" spelling rule. NEITHER and WEIRD are both exceptions to this rule; so are HEIGHT and LEISURE.

7. **(b)** The BERING STRAIT separates the SEWARD PENINSULA from Russia; the STRAIT OF MAGELLAN separates TIERRA DEL FUEGO from mainland South America.

8. **(c)** GOLDING is the author of *LORD OF THE FLIES*; TOLKIEN is the author of *LORD OF THE RING*.

9. **(b)** The analogy is based upon what happens to a body part with disuse. When JOINTS are not used for a long period of time, they THICKEN; when MUSCLES are not used for a long period of time they ATROPHY or waste away.

10. **(c)** In this literary analogy, the relationship is based upon association of first and last names. ERNEST HEMINGWAY was an author as was RUD-YARD KIPLING.

11. **(c)** This is a simple relationship. The second term is the reciprocal of the first. 8/4 is the reciprocal of 4/8; 15/5 is the reciprocal of 5/15.

12. **(a)** RAMADAN and LENT are both prolonged periods of fasting and prayer, RAMADAN for the Moslems and LENT for Christians. MAY DAY and LABOR DAY are both secular holidays in celebration of labor.

13. **(a)** This is an analogy of synonyms. INIQUITOUS means WICKED; IN-GENUOUS means FRANK or open.

14. **(d)** This analogy is based upon function. The function of a PROTRAC-TOR is to measure ANGLES; the function of a COMPASS is to measure CURVES.

15. **(b)** TENNESSEE WILLIAMS is the author of the play, *THE GLASS MENAGERIE;* LUIGI PIRANDELLO is the author of the play, *SIX CHARACTERS IN SEARCH OF AN AUTHOR.*

16. **(d)** An INJURY to the spinal column may cause paralysis of the lower half of the body—PARAPLEGIA; a STROKE may cause paralysis of either the right or left half of the body—HEMIPLEGIA.

17. **(c)** This analogy is a grammatical one. EVERYONE is a singular pronoun which takes the singular form of the verb, LIKES; NOBODY is a singular pronoun which takes the singular form of the verb, LOVES.

18. **(a)** The HARVEST MOON, the full moon following the autumnal equi-nox, falls in OCTOBER; the THUNDER MOON, the full moon following the summer solstice, falls in JULY.

19. **(c)** ERATO and THALIA are both muses. ERATO is the muse of PO-ETRY; THALIA is the muse of COMEDY.

20. **(c)** ALOE is a succulent plant whose spears secrete a skin lubricant when they are rubbed; COLD CREAM is also a skin lubricant. ALUM is a chemical compound used as an astringent; BUROWS SOLUTION is also an astringent.

21. **(d)** The only feasible mathematical relationship is that of subtraction. $6 - 12 = -6$; $31 - 12 = 19$. The analogy is correct because on both sides of the proportion, 12 was subtracted from the first number to yield the second number.

22. **(d)** The RIVE GAUCHE is a part of PARIS located across the river from the main business part of the city; BROOKLYN is a part of the city of NEW YORK located across the river from the main business section.

23. **(d)** ZIMBABWE is the current name for that African country which used to be called RHODESIA; SURINAM is the name taken when that South American country gained its independence and ceased being DUTCH GUIANA.

24. **(b)** The music composed by BACH was of the BAROQUE style; SCHU-MANN was strictly a ROMANTIC composer.

25. **(d)** This is an analogy of antonyms. The OBSEQUIOUS person is spine-less and overly agreeable whereas the OBSTINATE person is stubborn and stands his or her ground. The DIFFIDENT person is shy and lacking is self-confidence while the DEFIANT person is confident and bold.

26. **(c)** ROMAN CATHOLIC and PROTESTANT are terms for two leading branches of Christianity. SHIITE and SUNNI are terms for two leading branches of Islam.

27. **(a)** The relationship in the analogy is one of cause and effect. When you are to be HONORED, you receive a CITATION, which is a formal document describing your achievements. When you are stopped for SPEEDING, you receive a CITATION, which is an official summons to appear in court. Citation is a word with two very different meanings.

28. **(c)** *ANNA CHRISTIE* and *MOON FOR THE MISBEGOTTEN* are both plays written by Eugene O'Neill; *HEDDA GABLER* and *AN ENEMY OF THE PEOPLE* are both plays written by Henrik Ibsen.

29. **(a)** This analogy is one of characteristic. The characteristic color of SALVIA is flaming RED; the characteristic color of a JONQUIL is YELLOW. A cornflower is blue.

30. **(b)** The ANODE is the site of OXIDATION in an electrical cell; the CATHODE is the site of REDUCTION in that same electrical cell.

31. **(a)** VIOLA DA GAMBA and VIOLIN are both stringed instruments; CLARINET and ENGLISH HORN are both woodwinds with sounds produced by reeds. A rebec is an ancient stringed instrument.

32. **(c)** GALILEO fell out of favor with the Church because of his insistence that the SUN was the center of the universe; JOAN OF ARC fell out of favor with the Church because of her defense of the KING as the ruler on earth.

33. **(b)** Ogden NASH is well known as a writer of LIMERICKS; SHAKE-SPEARE is well known for his SONNETS as well as his plays.

34. **(d)** SQUASH and PLATFORM TENNIS are both racquet sports played within an enclosed court; HOCKEY and CURLING are both played on ice.

35. **(c)** The HERMITAGE is a famous art gallery in the city of LENIN-GRAD; the PRADO is a famous art gallery in the city of MADRID.

36. **(a)** In coordinate geometry, an ABSCISSA is the horizontal coordinate of a point in a plane obtained by measuring parallel to the X-axis; an ORDINATE is obtained by measuring parallel to the Y-axis.

37. **(d)** B.F. SKINNER is a psychologist closely associated with the school of psychology called BEHAVIORISM; Max WERTHEIMER was the founder of the GESTALT school of psychology.

38. **(a)** This analogy is based upon lacking characteristics. HESTER Prynne in Hawthorne's *Scarlet Letter* was an adultress; FIDELITY was not one of her characteristics. GONERIL in Shakespeare's *King Lear* was one of the rejecting daughters; DEVOTION was not one of her characteristics.

39. **(b)** CAPILLARIES, the smallest blood vessels, are part of the CIR-CULATORY system; VILLI, fingerlike projections in the small intestine which help absorb nutrients, are part of the DIGESTIVE system.

40. **(c)** SAN MARINO is a tiny independent country which exists entirely within the boundaries of ITALY; LESOTHO is a small independent country entirely encapsulated by SOUTH AFRICA.

41. **(a)** ALASKA was purchased from RUSSIA; FLORIDA was purchased from SPAIN.

42. **(d)** John Maynard KEYNES formulated and published controversial and influential theories in ECONOMICS; John DEWEY was equally influential for his novel theories in EDUCATION.

43. **(c)** The four analogous people were all pioneers in flight. NEIL ARM-STRONG was the first person to fly to the moon and then walk upon it;

URI GAGARIN, a Russian, was the first person to go into outer space; CHARLES LINDBERGH was the first aviator to cross the Atlantic alone; ORVILLE WRIGHT was the first person to fly in an airplane.

44. **(d)** *PILGRIM'S PROGRESS* is a religious allegory written by John BUNYON; *THE DIVINE COMEDY* is an allegorical autobiography heavily religious in content, written by DANTE.

45. **(c)** GHENGIS KAHN was leader of the MONGOLS, conquerors of the 13th century; ATTILA was leader of the HUNS who conquered most of the Roman Empire in the middle of the 5th century.

46. **(b)** The analogy is based upon the association of significant elements in two of *Aesop's Fables*. The FOX attempts to reach the GRAPEs; the HARE attempts to win a race with the TORTOISE.

47. **(d)** This is an A : C :: B : D correspondence. 6 squared is 36; 4 squared is 16. On one side of the proportion are the square roots; on the other side, in the same order, the squares.

48. **(b)** THOMAS MANN is the author of *BUDDENBROOKS;* THOMAS WOLFE is the author of *LOOK HOMEWARD ANGEL*.

49. **(a)** IO is the first moon of the planet JUPITER. A moon is a satellite. SPUTNIK was the first man-made satellite of the planet EARTH.

50. **(d)** The Norse gods live at ASGARD; the Norse goddess of love and beauty is FREYA. The Greed gods live at OLYMPUS; the Greek goddess of love and beauty is APHRODITE.

51. **(a)** In music, DUPLE time is time that is divisible by two; TRIPLE time is time that is divisible by three (into equal segments). An ISOSCELES triangle is one in which two sides are equal; all three sides of an EQUILATERAL triangle are of equal length.

52. **(a)** This analogy is based upon the association between the athlete and the sport in which he excels. Bobby ORR is a famous HOCKEY player and PELE a well-known SOCCER player.

53. **(c)** KNIT and PURL are basically opposite stitches though the entire activity is called "knitting." OBVERSE and REVERSE are the opposite sides of a coin.

54. **(a)** Color is created by LIGHT waves. A PASTEL color is one which has been softened. Thus PASTEL color is softened LIGHT waves. When a SOUND has been softened, we say that it has been MUTED.

55. **(b)** This is a grammatical analogy. The preposition AMONG is used for comparison of more than two persons or things; the preposition BETWEEN is used for comparisons between only TWO persons or things.

56. **(d)** This is a cause-and-effect relationship. XENOPHOBIA (fear of strangers) leads to PREJUDICE; PECCATOPHOBIA (fear of sinning) leads to VIRTUE.

57. **(d)** A HARPSICHORD is a manual double-keyboard instrument, while a VIRGINAL is a single-keyboard instrument closely related to the harpsichord; the OBOE is a double-reed wind instrument while the CLARINET is a single-reed woodwind.

58. **(b)** ROMANY gypsies are NOMADIC. They have no established residence and roam at will from one location to another. LAPPs are MIGRATORY. They have both summer and winter homes which are dictated by the migrations of their food sources.

59. **(d)** This analogy is based upon a part-to-whole relationship. An ATOM is a constituent part of a MOLECULE; a GENE is a constituent part of a CHROMOSOME.

60. **(c)** SMOKE is presumptive evidence of FIRE; a STAIN is presumptive evidence of a LEAK.

61. **(c)** MARGARINE is a synthetic shortening used in place of BUTTER and closely resembling butter in taste and color; NAUGAHYDE is a synthetic substance which closely resembles LEATHER in look, texture, and durability and is often used as a leather substitute.

62. **(c)** The analogy is based upon the friendship of two characters in the same novel. HAZEL and FIVER are two main characters in Richard Adams' novel *Watership Down;* TOM SAWYER and BECKY THATCHER are two main characters in Mark Twain's novel *The Adventures of Tom Sawyer.*

63. **(b)** HENNA and ANIL are both plants which yield dyeing agents. BLUEing and BLEACH are both agents which serve to whiten or remove dye.

64. **(c)** This analogy is based upon animals and the famous persons with whom their names are closely associated. CHECKERS was RICHARD NIXON's dog. TRAVELLER was ROBERT E. LEE's horse.

65. **(c)** This nonsemantic analogy is based upon anagrams. TUBER is an anagram of BRUTE; QUIRES is an anagram of SQUIRE. The fact that there is absolutely no meaningful relationship between any two of the capitalized words should immediately alert you to a nonsemantic analogy. All the words are nouns, though *brute* could be an adjective and *squire* a verb, so no grammatical analogy is feasible. The *qu* in *squire* leads you directly to the correct answer.

66. **(d)** The relationship here is between the fraction and its percent equivalent. 1/8 is equivalent to 12.5%; 3/8 is equivalent to 37.5%.

67. **(d)** This analogy refers to geologic periods. During the CRETACEOUS period, DINOSAURS were the predominant animal form; during the TERTIARY period, MAMMALS were predominant.

68. **(b)** The analogy is based upon function. PRIVET and HEMLOCK serve as hedges on or between properties; MAPLE and OAK serve as shade trees.

69. **(b)** The relationship in this analogy is between the author and the document. Although both documents were the products of many men's thinking, the acknowledged author of the CONSTITUTION was MADISON, and the authorship of the DECLARATION OF INDEPENDENCE is attributed to JEFFERSON.

70. **(c)** This analogy is based upon alternative names for the same disease. HANSEN'S DISEASE is LEPROSY; ALZHEIMER'S DISEASE is a form of SENILITY.

71. **(a)** GEORGES BRAQUE and FERNAND LEGER are both famous Cubist painters; E.E. CUMMINGS and DON MARQUIS are both writers who are famous for writing only in lower case.

72. **(c)** PHOTOSYNTHESIS is the INDEPENDENT creation of food (carbohydrates) by chloryphyll-bearing plants; SYMBIOSIS is the COOPERATIVE arrangement by which two plants, two animals, or an animal and a plant live together and mutually supply each other's needs.

73. **(c)** GASOLINE is the chief product of MOBIL; TIRES are the chief product of MICHELIN.

74. **(d)** In this analogy, fictional countries are paired with their creators. Jonathan SWIFT was the creator of LILLIPUT in his social novel *Gulliver's Travels;* Frank BAUM created the land of OZ in *The Wizard of Oz.*

75. **(a)** FOUR balls in BASEBALL entitle the batter to walk to first base; the game then continues without the team's changing sides. TEN yards in FOOTBALL constitutes a first down; the game continues with the same team in possession of the ball.

76. **(b)** COMMISSION and ROYALTY are both forms of payment which are based upon a percentage of the money brought in; SALARY and STIPEND are both fixed rates of payment.

77. **(c)** All four words are synonyms or near synonyms. LAWYER and ATTORNEY are terms most often used in the United States while BARRISTER and ADVOCATE are more often used in England.

78. **(a)** The chief food of the WHALE is PLANKTON; the sole food of the KOALA is leaves of the EUCALYPTUS tree.

79. **(a)** This is a grammatical analogy. On both sides of the proportion are words which form their plurals in an irregular manner. The plural of GOOSE is GEESE; the plural of DEER is DEER.

80. **(a)** 125 is the cube of 5; 27 is the cube of 3. Conversely, 5 is the cube root of 125; 3 is the cube root of 27.

81. **(c)** The relationship in this analogy is not only sequential, it is circular. There is a conundrum, "Which came first, the chicken or the egg?" The answer is that the CHICKEN comes from an EGG and an EGG comes from a CHICKEN. The sequence is analogous on both sides of the proportion.

82. **(d)** The relationship is that of the capital city to the country of which it is the capital. PARIS is the capital of FRANCE; THE HAGUE is the capital of the NETHERLANDS.

83. **(d)** All four related terms are agencies which were set up early in the Franklin D. Roosevelt administration to help the nation to recover from the Depression. CCC is the Civilian Conservation Corps; TVA, the Tennessee Valley Authority; FDIC, the Federal Deposit Insurance Corporation; and FHA, the Federal Housing Administration. OPA (Office of Price Administration) and OSS (Office of Security Services) were Second World War agencies. WMC is the Women's Marine Corps.

84. **(a)** SERIF and SANS SERIF refer to typefaces. SERIF type has ELABORATE little cross strokes at the tops and bottoms of capital letters. SANS SERIF type has no such embellishments, hence it is STREAMLINED.

85. **(b)** In Civil War histories the labels First BATTLE OF BULL RUN and BATTLE OF MANASSAS are used interchangeably to refer to the same battle. Northerners named battles for STREAMs; Southerners called the battles by the names of the TOWNs they were in or near.

86. **(c)** MONTMARTRE is the artists' district of PARIS; GREENWICH VILLAGE is the artists' district of NEW YORK City.

87. **(b)** All four terms in this analogy are birth defects. TALIPES (clubfoot) is a birth defect as is HARELIP (cleft palate); HYDROCEPHALUS (water on the brain) leads to retardation while SPINA BIFIDA (failure of the spinal column to fully enclose the spinal cord) is a severe crippler.

88. **(d)** Emile ZOLA is the author of the novel *NANA*: Vladimir NABOKOV is the author of the novel *LOLITA*.

89. **(d)** KANT's test of the morality of an action was the CATEGORICAL IMPERATIVE, the test of whether or not the action would be pleasing to another person in a particular situation; MILL's test of the morality

of an action was its UTILITY, that is, whether it would be pleasing to the greatest number of people.

90. **(b)** This is a sequential relationship, NOON comes before EVE; DINE comes before SUP. Or you may see the relationship as being one of characteristic. At NOON one DINEs; in the EVE one SUPs. The first two terms may mislead you to look first for more palindromes (words that read the same forwards and backwards), but the absence of palindromes on the right should encourage you to shift gears quickly and to look for a meaningful relationship.

91. **(b)** This is an analogy based on synonyms. MENTICIDE is BRAIN-WASHING; OPPROBRIUM is REPROACH.

92. **(b)** On both sides of this analogy we find women who warned their men of impending danger. In Shakespeare's *Troilus and Cressida,* CRESSIDA warns her brother of the perils of fighting the Greeks. In Shakespeare's *Julius Caesar,* CALPURNIA warns her husband CAESAR of the dangers of going to the Senate.

93. **(a)** This is an analogy of characteristic. The composer BEETHOVEN was DEAF; the poet MILTON was BLIND.

94. **(d)** CASTOR and POLLUX are mythological twins and are the astronomical constellations which make up the zodiac sign Gemini; REMUS and ROMULUS were mythological twins who founded the city of Rome. The analogy is based upon the fact that both pairs are twins.

95. **(b)** This analogy is based upon the relationship of object to actor with a very special relationship between the two. The actor acts as irritant to the object. Thus, a FLEA irritates a DOG; a FLY irritates a HORSE. The *rider* may at times irritate the *horse* though not as consistently as the *fly.*

96. **(b)** A logarithm to the base e is a NATURAL logarithm; a logarithm to the base 10 is a COMMON logarithm.

97. **(c)** This analogy is based upon rhyme. BROUGHAM rhymes with HOME; CARRIAGE rhymes with MARRIAGE. *House* is a tempting wrong answer, but while a brougham is a kind of carriage, a home is not a kind of house.

98. **(c)** This analogy is based upon the relationship of an Old Testament book to a New Testament book. CHRONICLES is a book of the Old Testament while ACTS is a book of the New Testament. EZEKIEL is a prophet after whom a book of the Old Testament is named, while PETER is a disciple whose letters appear in the New Testament in books bearing his name.

99. **(a)** The four related terms are all places in which time stands still and people never age.

100. **(d)** In this analogy, a place of worship devoted to many gods is paired with a place of worship devoted to one god. The PANTHEON in Rome was devoted to the worship of all the Roman gods; the PARTHENON in Greece was devoted to the worship of ATHENA. TEOPANCALI in Mitla, Oaxaca, Mexico, was devoted to the worship of all the Mixtecan gods; ST. PETER'S BASILICA in Rome is devoted to the worship of one God. Once you have determined that the relationship of Pantheon to Parthenon is "many to one," Teopancali is your only possible choice even if you have never heard of it.

Part III

Verbal Analogies for Other Graduate-Level Examinations

ANALOGY PAIRS

The analogy question is acknowledged to be one of the most sensitive measures of general intelligence and of reasoning ability. As such, it is used on many standardized examinations for graduate level study and for higher level employment.

The examinations that large corporations and foundations have designed for their own use for making employment and grant recipient decisions often combine a measure of specific knowledge with the measure of reasoning ability. Among standardized exams, the best known such exam is the Minnesota Engineering Analogies Test (MEAT). The subject matter of the MEAT is strictly confined to science and mathematics. The examination presupposes more than a superficial background in these areas. The questions become increasingly technical. The format of the MEAT is similar to that of the MAT: three given terms and a choice of one of four to complete the analogy. In the MEAT, the fourth term is always the missing term, and the choices are numbered rather than lettered. Thus, a MEAT item reads: A : B :: C : 1, 2, 3, or 4.

Of the nationally distributed graduate-level exams that utilize the analogy question, the best-known and most widely used is the Graduate Record Examination (GRE). Questions on the GRE are intended to measure only reasoning ability and vocabulary. The GRE does not test knowledge in specific fields such as literature, philosophy or chemistry. In measuring the breadth of vocabulary, however, the GRE analogy questions do reach into the vocabulary of the various fields.

The GRE and some other exams present the analogy question in a format somewhat different from that of the MAT. Instead of supplying only one missing term as on the MAT, you must select a pair of words whose relationship to each other most closely parallels the relationship expressed by the first word pair.

Sample Analogy Pair

SNAPSHOT : SCRAPBOOK ::
(A) memo : file
(B) photograph : book jacket
(C) camera : case
(D) film : frame
(E) career : portfolio

Answer: **(A)** A SNAPSHOT is stored for future reference in a SCRAPBOOK in the same way that a MEMO is stored in a FILE.

Although the format of these analogy problems differs from the format of MAT problems, the same strategies apply. First you must determine the nature of the relationship between the terms of the given word pair, and then you must select the one pair from the choices offered in which the terms are related in exactly the same way.

Let us "walk together" through a typical analogy problem of the missing pair format.

SPANIEL : DOG ::
(A) kitten : cat
(B) lion : tiger
(C) spider : fly
(D) robin : bird
(E) fish : trout

The words are familiar ones, so you can slip right through the definition of terms phase. Now look at the initial pair. A SPANIEL is a specific kind of DOG. Look at the answer choices. You are seeking a choice in which the first word is a specific kind of the second word. Begin by eliminating the answers which are obviously incorrect. (B) and (C) may both be eliminated because a LION is not a specific type of TIGER, and a SPIDER is not a specific type of FLY. Now return to choice (A). A KITTEN is a young CAT. If there were no better answer offered, you might consider marking (A), but you must not be satisfied with a dubiously correct answer without carefully searching for a truly correct one. A KITTEN really is not a specific type of CAT. At first glance, both (D) and (E) might appear to be correct. A ROBIN is a specific type of BIRD; a TROUT is a specific type of FISH. However, (E) reverses the sequence of the original relationship. In (E), FISH is the larger group of which TROUT is a specific kind, whereas in the original pair, the specific kind is named before the larger group. Thus (D), which maintains the relationship in the same sequence, is the correct completion of this analogy.

The A : C :: B : D relationship occurs much less frequently among analogies in which you choose pairs rather than single words. However, this relationship is not precluded by the pair format, and you must not rule out the possibility when you cannot find a relationship between A and B.

You'll get plenty of practice with the paired analogy problem in the pages that follow. The practice questions are divided into short tests in order to allow you to complete a set even when you have only a few minutes to spare. At the end of the chapter you will find both correct and explanatory answers for all questions. Be sure to study ALL the explanations. Each has something to teach in terms of vocabulary, relationships, or reasoning processes.

If you will be taking the GRE, these exercises are a must for you. If not, try to do them justice and gain whatever benefits you can.

ANSWER SHEET FOR ANALOGY PAIRS

Analogy Pairs Test I

1 Ⓐ Ⓑ Ⓒ Ⓓ Ⓔ   5 Ⓐ Ⓑ Ⓒ Ⓓ Ⓔ   9 Ⓐ Ⓑ Ⓒ Ⓓ Ⓔ   13 Ⓐ Ⓑ Ⓒ Ⓓ Ⓔ   17 Ⓐ Ⓑ Ⓒ Ⓓ Ⓔ
2 Ⓐ Ⓑ Ⓒ Ⓓ Ⓔ   6 Ⓐ Ⓑ Ⓒ Ⓓ Ⓔ   10 Ⓐ Ⓑ Ⓒ Ⓓ Ⓔ   14 Ⓐ Ⓑ Ⓒ Ⓓ Ⓔ   18 Ⓐ Ⓑ Ⓒ Ⓓ Ⓔ
3 Ⓐ Ⓑ Ⓒ Ⓓ Ⓔ   7 Ⓐ Ⓑ Ⓒ Ⓓ Ⓔ   11 Ⓐ Ⓑ Ⓒ Ⓓ Ⓔ   15 Ⓐ Ⓑ Ⓒ Ⓓ Ⓔ   19 Ⓐ Ⓑ Ⓒ Ⓓ Ⓔ
4 Ⓐ Ⓑ Ⓒ Ⓓ Ⓔ   8 Ⓐ Ⓑ Ⓒ Ⓓ Ⓔ   12 Ⓐ Ⓑ Ⓒ Ⓓ Ⓔ   16 Ⓐ Ⓑ Ⓒ Ⓓ Ⓔ   20 Ⓐ Ⓑ Ⓒ Ⓓ Ⓔ

Analogy Pairs Test II

1 Ⓐ Ⓑ Ⓒ Ⓓ Ⓔ   5 Ⓐ Ⓑ Ⓒ Ⓓ Ⓔ   9 Ⓐ Ⓑ Ⓒ Ⓓ Ⓔ   13 Ⓐ Ⓑ Ⓒ Ⓓ Ⓔ   17 Ⓐ Ⓑ Ⓒ Ⓓ Ⓔ
2 Ⓐ Ⓑ Ⓒ Ⓓ Ⓔ   6 Ⓐ Ⓑ Ⓒ Ⓓ Ⓔ   10 Ⓐ Ⓑ Ⓒ Ⓓ Ⓔ   14 Ⓐ Ⓑ Ⓒ Ⓓ Ⓔ   18 Ⓐ Ⓑ Ⓒ Ⓓ Ⓔ
3 Ⓐ Ⓑ Ⓒ Ⓓ Ⓔ   7 Ⓐ Ⓑ Ⓒ Ⓓ Ⓔ   11 Ⓐ Ⓑ Ⓒ Ⓓ Ⓔ   15 Ⓐ Ⓑ Ⓒ Ⓓ Ⓔ   19 Ⓐ Ⓑ Ⓒ Ⓓ Ⓔ
4 Ⓐ Ⓑ Ⓒ Ⓓ Ⓔ   8 Ⓐ Ⓑ Ⓒ Ⓓ Ⓔ   12 Ⓐ Ⓑ Ⓒ Ⓓ Ⓔ   16 Ⓐ Ⓑ Ⓒ Ⓓ Ⓔ   20 Ⓐ Ⓑ Ⓒ Ⓓ Ⓔ

Analogy Pairs Test III

1 Ⓐ Ⓑ Ⓒ Ⓓ Ⓔ   5 Ⓐ Ⓑ Ⓒ Ⓓ Ⓔ   9 Ⓐ Ⓑ Ⓒ Ⓓ Ⓔ   13 Ⓐ Ⓑ Ⓒ Ⓓ Ⓔ   17 Ⓐ Ⓑ Ⓒ Ⓓ Ⓔ
2 Ⓐ Ⓑ Ⓒ Ⓓ Ⓔ   6 Ⓐ Ⓑ Ⓒ Ⓔ Ⓔ   10 Ⓐ Ⓑ Ⓒ Ⓓ Ⓔ   14 Ⓐ Ⓑ Ⓒ Ⓓ Ⓔ   18 Ⓐ Ⓑ Ⓒ Ⓓ Ⓔ
3 Ⓐ Ⓑ Ⓒ Ⓓ Ⓔ   7 Ⓐ Ⓑ Ⓒ Ⓓ Ⓔ   11 Ⓐ Ⓑ Ⓒ Ⓓ Ⓔ   15 Ⓐ Ⓑ Ⓒ Ⓓ Ⓔ   19 Ⓐ Ⓑ Ⓒ Ⓓ Ⓔ
4 Ⓐ Ⓑ Ⓒ Ⓓ Ⓔ   8 Ⓐ Ⓑ Ⓒ Ⓓ Ⓔ   12 Ⓐ Ⓑ Ⓒ Ⓓ Ⓔ   16 Ⓐ Ⓑ Ⓒ Ⓓ Ⓔ   20 Ⓐ Ⓑ Ⓒ Ⓓ Ⓔ

Analogy Pairs Test IV

1 Ⓐ Ⓑ Ⓒ Ⓓ Ⓔ   5 Ⓐ Ⓑ Ⓒ Ⓓ Ⓔ   9 Ⓐ Ⓑ Ⓒ Ⓓ Ⓔ   13 Ⓐ Ⓑ Ⓒ Ⓓ Ⓔ   17 Ⓐ Ⓑ Ⓒ Ⓓ Ⓔ
2 Ⓐ Ⓑ Ⓒ Ⓓ Ⓔ   6 Ⓐ Ⓑ Ⓒ Ⓓ Ⓔ   10 Ⓐ Ⓑ Ⓒ Ⓓ Ⓔ   14 Ⓐ Ⓑ Ⓒ Ⓓ Ⓔ   18 Ⓐ Ⓑ Ⓒ Ⓓ Ⓔ
3 Ⓐ Ⓑ Ⓒ Ⓓ Ⓔ   7 Ⓐ Ⓑ Ⓒ Ⓓ Ⓔ   11 Ⓐ Ⓑ Ⓒ Ⓓ Ⓔ   15 Ⓐ Ⓑ Ⓒ Ⓓ Ⓔ   19 Ⓐ Ⓑ Ⓒ Ⓓ Ⓔ
4 Ⓐ Ⓑ Ⓒ Ⓓ Ⓔ   8 Ⓐ Ⓑ Ⓒ Ⓓ Ⓔ   12 Ⓐ Ⓑ Ⓒ Ⓓ Ⓔ   16 Ⓐ Ⓑ Ⓒ Ⓓ Ⓔ   20 Ⓐ Ⓑ Ⓒ Ⓓ Ⓔ

Tear Here

Analogy Pairs Test V

1 Ⓐ Ⓑ Ⓒ Ⓓ Ⓔ   5 Ⓐ Ⓑ Ⓒ Ⓓ Ⓔ   9 Ⓐ Ⓑ Ⓒ Ⓓ Ⓔ   13 Ⓐ Ⓑ Ⓒ Ⓓ Ⓔ   17 Ⓐ Ⓑ Ⓒ Ⓓ Ⓔ
2 Ⓐ Ⓑ Ⓒ Ⓓ Ⓔ   6 Ⓐ Ⓑ Ⓒ Ⓓ Ⓔ   10 Ⓐ Ⓑ Ⓒ Ⓓ Ⓔ   14 Ⓐ Ⓑ Ⓒ Ⓓ Ⓔ   18 Ⓐ Ⓑ Ⓒ Ⓓ Ⓔ
3 Ⓐ Ⓑ Ⓒ Ⓓ Ⓔ   7 Ⓐ Ⓑ Ⓒ Ⓓ Ⓔ   11 Ⓐ Ⓑ Ⓒ Ⓓ Ⓔ   15 Ⓐ Ⓑ Ⓒ Ⓓ Ⓔ   19 Ⓐ Ⓑ Ⓒ Ⓓ Ⓔ
4 Ⓐ Ⓑ Ⓒ Ⓓ Ⓔ   8 Ⓐ Ⓑ Ⓒ Ⓓ Ⓔ   12 Ⓐ Ⓑ Ⓒ Ⓓ Ⓔ   16 Ⓐ Ⓑ Ⓒ Ⓓ Ⓔ   20 Ⓐ Ⓑ Ⓒ Ⓓ Ⓔ

Analogy Pairs Test VI

1 Ⓐ Ⓑ Ⓒ Ⓓ Ⓔ   11 Ⓐ Ⓑ Ⓒ Ⓓ Ⓔ   21 Ⓐ Ⓑ Ⓒ Ⓓ Ⓔ   31 Ⓐ Ⓑ Ⓒ Ⓓ Ⓔ   41 Ⓐ Ⓑ Ⓒ Ⓓ Ⓔ
2 Ⓐ Ⓑ Ⓒ Ⓓ Ⓔ   12 Ⓐ Ⓑ Ⓒ Ⓓ Ⓔ   22 Ⓐ Ⓑ Ⓒ Ⓓ Ⓔ   32 Ⓐ Ⓑ Ⓒ Ⓓ Ⓔ   42 Ⓐ Ⓑ Ⓒ Ⓓ Ⓔ
3 Ⓐ Ⓑ Ⓒ Ⓓ Ⓔ   13 Ⓐ Ⓑ Ⓒ Ⓓ Ⓔ   23 Ⓐ Ⓑ Ⓒ Ⓓ Ⓔ   33 Ⓐ Ⓑ Ⓒ Ⓓ Ⓔ   43 Ⓐ Ⓑ Ⓒ Ⓓ Ⓔ
4 Ⓐ Ⓑ Ⓒ Ⓓ Ⓔ   14 Ⓐ Ⓑ Ⓒ Ⓓ Ⓔ   24 Ⓐ Ⓑ Ⓒ Ⓓ Ⓔ   34 Ⓐ Ⓑ Ⓒ Ⓓ Ⓔ   44 Ⓐ Ⓑ Ⓒ Ⓓ Ⓔ
5 Ⓐ Ⓑ Ⓒ Ⓓ Ⓔ   15 Ⓐ Ⓑ Ⓒ Ⓓ Ⓔ   25 Ⓐ Ⓑ Ⓒ Ⓓ Ⓔ   35 Ⓐ Ⓑ Ⓒ Ⓓ Ⓔ   45 Ⓐ Ⓑ Ⓒ Ⓓ Ⓔ
6 Ⓐ Ⓑ Ⓒ Ⓓ Ⓔ   16 Ⓐ Ⓑ Ⓒ Ⓓ Ⓔ   26 Ⓐ Ⓑ Ⓒ Ⓓ Ⓔ   36 Ⓐ Ⓑ Ⓒ Ⓓ Ⓔ   46 Ⓐ Ⓑ Ⓒ Ⓓ Ⓔ
7 Ⓐ Ⓑ Ⓒ Ⓓ Ⓔ   17 Ⓐ Ⓑ Ⓒ Ⓓ Ⓔ   27 Ⓐ Ⓑ Ⓒ Ⓓ Ⓔ   37 Ⓐ Ⓑ Ⓒ Ⓓ Ⓔ   47 Ⓐ Ⓑ Ⓒ Ⓓ Ⓔ
8 Ⓐ Ⓑ Ⓒ Ⓓ Ⓔ   18 Ⓐ Ⓑ Ⓒ Ⓓ Ⓔ   28 Ⓐ Ⓑ Ⓒ Ⓓ Ⓔ   38 Ⓐ Ⓑ Ⓒ Ⓓ Ⓔ   48 Ⓐ Ⓑ Ⓒ Ⓓ Ⓔ
9 Ⓐ Ⓑ Ⓒ Ⓓ Ⓔ   19 Ⓐ Ⓑ Ⓒ Ⓓ Ⓔ   29 Ⓐ Ⓑ Ⓒ Ⓓ Ⓔ   39 Ⓐ Ⓑ Ⓒ Ⓓ Ⓔ   49 Ⓐ Ⓑ Ⓒ Ⓓ Ⓔ
10 Ⓐ Ⓑ Ⓒ Ⓓ Ⓔ   20 Ⓐ Ⓑ Ⓒ Ⓓ Ⓔ   30 Ⓐ Ⓑ Ⓒ Ⓓ Ⓔ   40 Ⓐ Ⓑ Ⓒ Ⓓ Ⓔ   50 Ⓐ Ⓑ Ⓒ Ⓓ Ⓔ

Tear Here

TEST I. ANALOGY PAIRS

Time. 10 Minutes. 20 Questions.

Directions: Each of these test questions begins with two CAPITAL-IZED words which are related to each other in some way. Find out how they are related. Then study the five pairs of words that follow. They are lettered (A) (B) (C) (D) (E). Select the two words which are related to each other in the same way that the two capitalized words are related.

1. LINEAR : CURVILINEAR ::
   (A) throw : reach
   (B) sunrise : sunset
   (C) absolute : relative
   (D) arrow : bow
   (E) bow : arrow

2. LETTUCE : LEAF ::
   (A) potato : eye
   (B) rose : thorn
   (C) onion : bulb
   (D) grass : stem
   (E) grape : vine

3. INTERRUPT : HECKLE ::
   (A) disrupt : intrude
   (B) tease : hector
   (C) maintain : uphold
   (D) condemn : implore
   (E) speech : performance

4. DAM : WATER ::
   (A) over : under
   (B) embargo : trade
   (C) curse : H₂O
   (D) beaver : fish
   (E) river : stream

5. ALLAY : PAIN ::
   (A) damp : noise
   (B) create : noise
   (C) regain : consciousness
   (D) fray : edge
   (E) nerves : soothe

6. LATENT : LATE ::
   (A) crude : callous
   (B) potential : tardy
   (C) natty : nettled
   (D) obvious : concealed
   (E) decorous : deceased

7. CALIBER : RIFLE ::
   (A) reputation : blast
   (B) compass : bore
   (C) army : navy
   (D) gauge : rails
   (E) cavalry : infantry

8. CHOP : MINCE ::
   (A) fry : bake
   (B) meat : cake
   (C) axe : mallet
   (D) Washington : Lincoln
   (E) stir : beat

9. PECCADILLO : CRIME ::
   (A) district attorney : criminal
   (B) hesitate : procrastinate
   (C) armadillo : bone
   (D) bushel : peck
   (E) sheriff : jail

10. WOOD : PAPER ::
    (A) iron : steel
    (B) chair : wall
    (C) cut : clip
    (D) fireplace : lighter
    (E) forest : fire

11. FRENETIC : SANGUINE ::
    (A) cool : hot
    (B) ardent : involved
    (C) frantic : unruffled
    (D) unharried : unsullied
    (E) uncouth : rude

12. COMPETITION :
    COMPENSATION ::
    (A) absurdity : serenity
    (B) commendation : condensation
    (C) contending : amends
    (D) striving : contriving
    (E) geniality : cordiality

13. CANDID : DEVIOUS ::
    (A) unnerved : unhinged
    (B) unruffled : unnerved
    (C) unhinged : unspoken
    (D) unsullied : unruffled
    (E) upright : underhanded

14. PUBLICATION : LIBEL ::
    (A) newspaper : editorial
    (B) radio : television
    (C) information : liability
    (D) journalism : attack
    (E) speech : slander

15. CANAL : PANAMA ::
    (A) sea : land
    (B) ships : commerce
    (C) chord : circle
    (D) locks : waterway
    (E) country : continent

16. ALLEVIATE : AGGRAVATE ::
    (A) joke : worry
    (B) elevate : agree
    (C) level : grade
    (D) plastic : rigid
    (E) alluvial : gravelly

17. BEHAVIOR : IMPROPRIETY ::
    (A) honesty : morality
    (B) freedom : servitude
    (C) response : stimulus
    (D) word : malapropism
    (E) grammar : usage

18. ELM : TREE ::
    (A) dollar : dime
    (B) currency : dime
    (C) map : leaves
    (D) oak : maple
    (E) dollar : money

19. DOCTOR : DISEASE ::
    (A) miser : money
    (B) illness : prescription
    (C) sheriff : crime
    (D) theft : punishment
    (E) intern : hospital

20. EXAMINATION : CHEAT ::
    (A) lawyer : defendant
    (B) compromise : principles
    (C) army : gripe
    (D) swindle : business
    (E) politics : graft

TEST II. ANALOGY PAIRS

Time: 10 Minutes. 20 Questions.

Directions: Each of these test questions begins with two CAPITAL-IZED words which are related to each other in some way. Find out how they are related. Then study the five pairs of words that follow. They are lettered (A) (B) (C) (D) (E). Select the two words which are related to each other in the same way that the two capitalized words are related.

1. ADVERSITY : HAPPINESS ::
   (A) fear : misfortune
   (B) solace : adversity
   (C) vehemence : serenity
   (D) troublesome : petulance
   (E) graduation : felicitation

2. LUTE : STRING ::
   (A) flute : treble
   (B) xylophone : percussion
   (C) drum : rhythm
   (D) violin : concert
   (E) piano : octave

3. FEATHERS : PLUCK ::
   (A) goose : duck
   (B) garment : weave
   (C) car : drive
   (D) wool : shear
   (E) duck : down

4. MODESTY : ARROGANCE ::
   (A) debility : strength
   (B) cause : purpose
   (C) passion : emotion
   (D) finance : Wall Street
   (E) practice : perfection

5. BLOW : HORN ::
   (A) switch : tracks
   (B) tune : lights
   (C) go over : map
   (D) accelerate : engine
   (E) turn on : radio

6. BAY : SEA ::
   (A) mountain : valley
   (B) plain : forest
   (C) peninsula : land
   (D) cape : reef
   (E) island : sound

7. DECEMBER : WINTER ::
   (A) April : showers
   (B) September : summer
   (C) June : fall
   (D) March : spring
   (E) February : autumn

8. GIGATON : MEGATON ::
   (A) megacycle : kilocycle
   (B) deciliter : liter
   (C) milligram : centigram
   (D) microsecond : millisecond
   (E) decivolt : dekavolt

9. AERIALIST : MINER ::
   (A) subterranean : aetherial
   (B) flier : youth
   (C) terrestrial : celestial
   (D) trapeze : pick
   (E) arboreal : sartorial

10. INTERRUPT : SPEAK ::
    (A) shout : yell
    (B) intrude : enter
    (C) assist : interfere
    (D) telephone : telegraph
    (E) concede : defend

11. ENCOURAGE : RESTRICT ::
    (A) gain : succeed
    (B) deprive : supply
    (C) see : believe
    (D) detain : deny
    (E) finish : complete

12. BEFOUL : TIDY ::
    (A) animate : inanimate
    (B) extricate : intricate
    (C) introvert : extrovert
    (D) cloth : clergy
    (E) indict : acquit

13. ITALY : MILAN ::
    (A) Paris : Moscow
    (B) Moscow : Russia
    (C) Spain : Madrid
    (D) Manhattan : New York
    (E) Norway : Sweden

14. MIST : RAIN ::
    (A) wind : hurricane
    (B) hail : thunder
    (C) snow : freeze
    (D) clouds : sky
    (E) sun : warm

15. GUN : HOLSTER ::
    (A) shoe : soldier
    (B) sword : warrior
    (C) ink : pen
    (D) books : school bag
    (E) cannon : plunder

16. MACE : MAJESTY ::
    (A) king : crown
    (B) sword : soldier
    (C) diploma : knowledge
    (D) book : knowledge
    (E) house : security

17. VIXEN : SCOLD ::
    (A) wound : scar
    (B) hero : winner
    (C) bee : sting
    (D) pimple : irritate
    (E) duck : walk

18. DEBATE : SOLILOQUY ::
    (A) crowd : mob
    (B) Hamlet : Macbeth
    (C) Lincoln : Douglas
    (D) group : hermit
    (E) fight : defend

19. THREAT : INSECURITY ::
    (A) challenge : fight
    (B) reason : anger
    (C) thunder : lightning
    (D) speed : acceleration
    (E) discipline : learning

20. LARGE : ENORMOUS ::
    (A) cat : tiger
    (B) warmth : frost
    (C) plump : fat
    (D) royal : regal
    (E) happy : solemn

TEST III. ANALOGY PAIRS

Time: 10 Minutes. 20 Questions.

Directions: Each of these test questions begins with two CAPITAL-IZED words which are related to each other in some way. Find out how they are related. Then study the five pairs of words that follow. They are lettered (A) (B) (C) (D) (E). Select the two words which are related to each other in the same way that the two capitalized words are related.

1. FIN : FISH ::
   (A) engine : auto
   (B) propeller : airplane
   (C) five : ten
   (D) teeth : stomach
   (E) leg : chair

2. RESTRAIN : REPRESS ::
   (A) advance : capitulate
   (B) surround : surrender
   (C) march : refrain
   (D) retire : battle
   (E) urge : spur

3. CONCERT : MUSIC ::
   (A) performance : artist
   (B) exhibition : art
   (C) play : actor
   (D) operetta : singer
   (E) flute : soloist

4. KEY : DOOR ::
   (A) combination : safe
   (B) keyhole : porthole
   (C) lock : key
   (D) opening : closing
   (E) bolt : safety

5. THROW : BOUNCE ::
   (A) carry : lift
   (B) drop : break
   (C) catch : hop
   (D) hold : miss
   (E) run : hide

6. AFTERNOON : DUSK ::
   (A) breakfast : dinner
   (B) yesterday : tomorrow
   (C) Sunday : Saturday
   (D) night : dawn
   (E) age : youth

7. STUDYING : LEARNING ::
   (A) running : jumping
   (B) investigating : discovering
   (C) reading : writing
   (D) dancing : singing
   (E) feeling : thinking

8. PULP : PAPER ::
   (A) rope : hemp
   (B) box : package
   (C) fabric : yarn
   (D) paper : package
   (E) cellulose : rayon

9. DYNAST : SERF ::
   (A) lord : master
   (B) regal : lowly
   (C) king : courtly
   (D) royalty : gentry
   (E) vassal : fief

10. OBSTRUCTION : BUOY ::
    (A) construction : building
    (B) boy : girl
    (C) danger : red light
    (D) iceberg : titanic
    (E) barricade : wall

11. EXPEDITE : HASTEN ::
(A) illuminate : disturb
(B) refine : refute
(C) inflate : distend
(D) scour : squeeze
(E) augment : lessen

12. VIBRATION : SOUND ::
(A) gravity : pull
(B) watercolor : paint
(C) accident : death
(D) worm : reptile
(E) drought : plague

13. WRITE : LETTER ::
(A) pen : paper
(B) drink : glass
(C) act : part
(D) rhyme : poem
(E) memorize : book

14. DEPRESSION : MASOCHISM ::
(A) man : animal
(B) one : many
(C) psychiatry : cure
(D) revenge : sadism
(E) greed : avarice

15. SKIN : MAN ::
(A) scaled : fur
(B) hide : hair
(C) walls : room
(D) window : house
(E) clothes : lady

16. ELIXIR : PILL ::
(A) life : health
(B) water : ice
(C) bottle : box
(D) mystery : medicine
(E) nurse : doctor

17. FRUGAL : ECONOMICAL ::
(A) fragile : solid
(B) prosperous : wealthy
(C) fruitful : sunny
(D) regal : comical
(E) spendthrift : miser

18. MUNDANE : TEMPORAL ::
(A) earthly : heavenly
(B) celestial : starry
(C) spiritual : everlasting
(D) angelic : religious
(E) ephemeral : eternal

19. CLARINET : MUSIC ::
(A) symbol : sign
(B) chalk : writing
(C) daughter : father
(D) pencil : pen
(E) bread : flour

20. FURIOUS : ANGRY ::
(A) cold : frozen
(B) love : like
(C) embrace : hug
(D) slap : hit
(E) wish : fulfillment

TEST IV. ANALOGY PAIRS

Time: 10 Minutes. 20 Questions.

Directions: Each of these test questions begins with two CAPITAL-IZED words which are related to each other in some way. Find out how they are related. Then study the five pairs of words that follow. They are lettered (A) (B) (C) (D) (E). Select the two words which are related to each other in the same way that the two capitalized words are related.

1. RAIN : DROPS ::
   (A) ice : winter
   (B) cloud : sky
   (C) flake : snow
   (D) ocean : stream
   (E) mankind : men

2. PUPIL : LEARN ::
   (A) book : read
   (B) wheel : tire
   (C) knife : bread
   (D) press : print
   (E) teacher : learn

3. HORSE : CENTAUR ::
   (A) stable : barn
   (B) decade : century
   (C) pig : sty
   (D) fish : mermaid
   (E) hydra : chimera

4. MODEST : QUIET ::
   (A) cynical : determined
   (B) conceited : loquacious
   (C) capable : stubborn
   (D) egocentric : reserved
   (E) demure : brash

5. IMPORTANT : CRUCIAL ::
   (A) orange : lemon
   (B) sorrow : death
   (C) misdemeanor : felony
   (D) poverty : uncleanliness
   (E) axiom : hypothesis

6. WATER : SWIMMING ::
   (A) egg : breaking
   (B) fire : flaming
   (C) chair : sitting
   (D) learning : knowledge
   (E) deed : owning

7. TOWER : CASTLE ::
   (A) car : motor
   (B) grass : prairie
   (C) house : chimney
   (D) rider : horse
   (E) dungeon : sepulcher

8. WANTON : SAINT ::
   (A) prolific : bounteous
   (B) kindly : stingy
   (C) atheistic : priest
   (D) stolid : stoic
   (E) capitalistic : anapest

9. PEOPLE : ELECT ::
   (A) statesmen : govern
   (B) debate : lawyers
   (C) teach : teachers
   (D) diplomats : judge
   (E) journalists : news

10. JUSTICE : SCALES ::
    (A) ruler : education
    (B) weathervane : cock
    (C) tree : farm
    (D) court : crime
    (E) pearl : wisdom

11. UXORIOUS : MISOGYNOUS ::
    (A) philanthropic : charitable
    (B) useless : mystic
    (C) satanic : angelic
    (D) tender : gracious
    (E) domestic : national

12. RULE : KINGDOM ::
    (A) starvation : famine
    (B) oppression : serfdom
    (C) proof : reason
    (D) reign : ruler
    (E) discipline : children

13. UNFRIENDLY : HOSTILE ::
    (A) weak : ill
    (B) weak : strong
    (C) blaze : flame
    (D) useful : necessary
    (E) violence : danger

14. PAMPHLET : BOOK ::
    (A) dress : sweater
    (B) discomfort : pain
    (C) height : weight
    (D) swimming : wading
    (E) epilogue : summary

15. CONSTELLATION : STARS ::
    (A) state : country
    (B) library : book
    (C) archipelago : islands
    (D) continent : peninsula
    (E) dollar : penny

16. CALIBRATOR : MEASURE ::
    (A) plumber : wrench
    (B) clamp : hold
    (C) ruler : line
    (D) measure : tolerance
    (E) thermometer : temperature

17. PAPER : REAM ::
    (A) eggs : dozen
    (B) newspaper : stand
    (C) apartment : room
    (D) candy : wrapper
    (E) gaggle : geese

18. SAIL : SALE ::
    (A) cat : rat
    (B) blue : blew
    (C) tar : car
    (D) flew : flaw
    (E) hug : huge

19. GOURMAND : GOURMET ::
    (A) wisdom : epicureanism
    (B) spaghetti : chopped liver
    (C) atrophy : empathy
    (D) good : plenty
    (E) undiscriminating : selective

20. GOOD FRIDAY : CHRISTMAS ::
    (A) opening : closing
    (B) holiday : school
    (C) end : beginning
    (D) New Year : Christmas
    (E) crucifixion : resurrection

TEST V. ANALOGY PAIRS

Time: 10 Minutes. 20 Questions.

Directions: Each of these test questions begins with two CAPITAL-IZED words which are related to each other in some way. Find out how they are related. Then study the five pairs of words that follow. They are lettered (A) (B) (C) (D) (E). Select the two words which are related to each other in the same way that the two capitalized words are related.

1. SEWER : SEWER ::
    (A) pickle : tank
    (B) lance : philosophy
    (C) seed : spore
    (D) service : plaintiff
    (E) drain : needle

2. AUTHOR : NOVEL ::
    (A) teacher : student
    (B) reader : interest
    (C) hero : conquest
    (D) carpenter : cabinet
    (E) doctor : cure

3. SELL : PURCHASE ::
    (A) pay : charge
    (B) eager : anxious
    (C) gift : earned
    (D) sale : sold
    (E) give : receive

4. AMENITIES : GENTLEMEN ::
    (A) regulations : player
    (B) society : lady
    (C) profanity : hobo
    (D) requirements : professor
    (E) media : journalist

5. MEDICINE : SCIENCE ::
    (A) daughter : father
    (B) tomato : fruit
    (C) penicillin : aspirin
    (D) school : college
    (E) mammal : reptile

6. AIMLESSNESS :
    DELINQUENCY ::
    (A) aggression : appeasement
    (B) belligerence : mischief
    (C) slum : dirt
    (D) boredom : mischief
    (E) crime : vandalism

7. SADIST : INJURY ::
    (A) dentist : teeth
    (B) thief : robbery
    (C) priest : church
    (D) pupil : desk
    (E) opportunist : generosity

8. RUBBER : FLEXIBILITY ::
    (A) iron : pliability
    (B) wood : plastic
    (C) steel : rigidity
    (D) iron : elasticity
    (E) synthetics : natural

9. MEDIAN : MEAN ::
    (A) mean : unkind
    (B) fashion : mode
    (C) middle : average
    (D) mode : mean
    (E) divide : multiply

10. RECKLESSNESS : VALOR ::
    (A) courage : cowardice
    (B) reliance : dependability
    (C) restitution : confirmation
    (D) usury : interest
    (E) conservation : ecology

11. WICKED : SCORN ::
    (A) commendable : emulate
    (B) devilish : revere
    (C) celebrated : exculpate
    (D) weak : oust
    (E) honor : award

12. BELL : RING ::
    (A) clock : build
    (B) alarm : activate
    (C) light : switch
    (D) scissors : handle
    (E) bicycle : ride

13. BOY : MAN ::
    (A) wall : floor
    (B) calf : cow
    (C) seat : chair
    (D) knob : door
    (E) history : legend

14. PINK : RED ::
    (A) chartreuse : green
    (B) blue : torquoise
    (C) blue : pink
    (D) yellow : white
    (E) gray : beige

15. ABSENCE : PRESENCE ::
    (A) steady : secure
    (B) poor : influential
    (C) fresh : salted
    (D) safe : influential
    (E) stable : changeable

16. JUDICIAL : LEGISLATIVE ::
    (A) administer : veto
    (B) enforce : pass
    (C) elected : appointed
    (D) bench : bicameral
    (E) federal : state

17. RABBIT'S FOOT : FOUR-LEAF CLOVER ::
    (A) wishing well : pennies
    (B) devil : Satan
    (C) 13 : black cat
    (D) horseshoe : horse
    (E) 7 : white cat

18. SYMPATHY : ADVERSITY ::
    (A) acceptance : pathos
    (B) happiness : sadness
    (C) suppression : emotion
    (D) condolences : grief
    (E) innocence : guilt

19. FLUID : LIGHTER ::
    (A) wood : pencil
    (B) gas : automobile
    (C) chair : table
    (D) dust : chalk
    (E) oil : lubrication

20. POSSIBLE : PROBABLE ::
    (A) likely : unlikely
    (B) best : better
    (C) willing : eager
    (D) quick : fast
    (E) frighten : worry

TEST VI. ANALOGY PAIRS

Time: 25 Minutes. 50 Questions.

Directions: Each of these test questions begins with two CAPITAL-IZED words which are related to each other in some way. Find out how they are related. Then study the five pairs of words that follow. They are lettered (A) (B) (C) (D) (E). Select the two words which are related to each other in the same way that the two capitalized words are related.

1. HAIR : BALD ::
   (A) wig : head
   (B) egg : eggshell
   (C) rain : drought
   (D) skin : scar
   (E) healthy : sick

2. BOAT : SHIP ::
   (A) book : volume
   (B) canoe : paddle
   (C) oar : water
   (D) aft : stern
   (E) land : sea

3. SCYTHE : DEATH ::
   (A) fall : winter
   (B) knife : murder
   (C) sickle : grain
   (D) harvest : crops
   (E) arrow : love

4. CARNIVORE : ANIMALS ::
   (A) omnivore : omelets
   (B) vegetarian : vegetables
   (C) trace : minerals
   (D) herbivore : healthy
   (E) pollination : plants

5. MAUVE : COLOR ::
   (A) basil : spice
   (B) colorless : colored
   (C) light : dark
   (D) tan : brown
   (E) blue : rainbow

6. MUFFLE : SILENCE ::
   (A) cover : bell
   (B) sound : hearing
   (C) cry : loud
   (D) stymie : defeat
   (E) glimpse : look

7. DEARTH : PAUCITY ::
   (A) few : many
   (B) scarcity : shortage
   (C) shortage : plethora
   (D) empty : container
   (E) commodity : expectation

8. WATERMARK : BIRTHMARK ::
   (A) buoy : stamp
   (B) paper : person
   (C) tide : character
   (D) line : signal
   (E) meaning : significance

9. BRIGHT : BRILLIANT ::
   (A) color : red
   (B) yellow : red
   (C) window : light
   (D) light : fire
   (E) happy : ecstatic

10. POWERFUL : MIGHTY ::
    (A) muscle : boxer
    (B) same : alike
    (C) strength : exercise
    (D) weak : small
    (E) great : bigger

11. NEWS REPORT : DESCRIPTIVE ::
    (A) weather report : unpredictable
    (B) editorial : objective
    (C) feature story : newsworthy
    (D) commercial : prescriptive
    (E) joke : funny

12. AGREEMENT : CONSENSUS ::
    (A) count : census
    (B) pleasure : enjoy
    (C) peace : tranquility
    (D) argument : solution
    (E) action : incite

13. WATER : HYDRAULIC ::
    (A) energy : atomic
    (B) power : electric
    (C) gasoline : combustion
    (D) pressure : compress
    (E) air : pneumatic

14. STABLE : HORSE ::
    (A) cow : barn
    (B) sty : pig
    (C) fold : ram
    (D) coop : hen
    (E) zoo : lioness

15. ROLE : ACTOR ::
    (A) aria : soprano
    (B) private : soldier
    (C) melody : singer
    (D) position : ballplayer
    (E) character : part

16. PROW : SHIP ::
    (A) snout : hog
    (B) nose : airplane
    (C) bird : beak
    (D) wheel : car
    (E) point : shaft

17. MAXIMUM : MINIMUM ::
    (A) pessimist : optimist
    (B) minimum : optimum
    (C) best : good
    (D) most : least
    (E) wane : wax

18. SENSATION : ANESTHETIC ::
    (A) breath : lung
    (B) drug : reaction
    (C) satisfaction : disappointment
    (D) poison : antidote
    (E) observation : sight

19. DISEMBARK : SHIP ::
    (A) board : train
    (B) dismount : horse
    (C) intern : jail
    (D) discharge : navy
    (E) dismantle : clock

20. PROTEIN : MEAT ::
    (A) calories : cream
    (B) energy : sugar
    (C) cyclamates : diet
    (D) starch : potatoes
    (E) fat : cholesterol

21. NECK : NAPE ::
    (A) foot : heel
    (B) head : forehead
    (C) arm : wrist
    (D) stomach : back
    (E) eye : lid

22. GRIPPING : PLIERS ::
    (A) chisel : gouging
    (B) breaking : hammer
    (C) elevating : jack
    (D) killing : knife
    (E) fastening : screwdriver

23. RADIUS : CIRCLE ::
    (A) rubber : tire
    (B) bisect : angle
    (C) equator : earth
    (D) cord : circumference
    (E) spoke : wheel

24. HAIR : HORSE ::
    (A) feather : bird
    (B) wool : sheep
    (C) down : pillow
    (D) peach : fuzz
    (E) fur : animal

25. GOBBLE : TURKEY ::
(A) poison : cobra
(B) bark : tree
(C) trunk : elephant
(D) twitter : bird
(E) king : lion

26. ASTUTE : STUPID ::
(A) scholar : idiotic
(B) agile : clumsy
(C) lonely : clown
(D) dance : ignorant
(E) intelligent : smart

27. WHALE : FISH ::
(A) collie : dog
(B) fly : insect
(C) bat : bird
(D) clue : detective
(E) mako : shark

28. GOLD : PROSPECTOR ::
(A) medicine : doctor
(B) prayer : preacher
(C) wood : carpenter
(D) clue : detective
(E) iron : machinist

29. COUPLET : POEM ::
(A) page : letter
(B) sentence : paragraph
(C) number : address
(D) epic : poetry
(E) biography : novel

30. OIL : WELL ::
(A) water : faucet
(B) iron : ore
(C) silver : mine
(D) gas : tank
(E) lumber : yard

31. TILLER : SHIP ::
(A) wheel : car
(B) motor : truck
(C) row : boat
(D) kite : string
(E) wing : plane

32. STALLION : ROOSTER ::
(A) buck : doe
(B) filly : colt
(C) horse : chicken
(D) foal : calf
(E) mare : hen

33. READ : BOOK ::
(A) taste : salty
(B) attend : movie
(C) smell : odor
(D) listen : record
(E) touch : paper

34. PARROT : SPARROW ::
(A) dog : poodle
(B) elephant : ant
(C) goldfish : guppy
(D) lion : cat
(E) eagle : butterfly

35. BONES : LIGAMENT ::
(A) break : stretch
(B) muscles : tendon
(C) fat : cell
(D) knuckle : finger
(E) knee : joint

36. SPICY : INSIPID ::
(A) pepper : salt
(B) hot : creamy
(C) exciting : dull
(D) cucumber : pickle
(E) bland : sharp

37. BURL : TREE ::
(A) silver : ore
(B) bronze : copper
(C) plank : wood
(D) glass : sand
(E) pearl : oyster

38. YEAST : LEAVEN ::
(A) soda : bubble
(B) iodine : antiseptic
(C) aspirin : medicine
(D) flour : dough
(E) penicillin : plant

39. SOLECISM : GRAMMAR ::
(A) separation : marriage
(B) foul : game
(C) incest : family
(D) race : stumble
(E) apostasy : dogma

40. EXPURGATE : PASSAGES ::
(A) defoliate : leaves
(B) cancel : checks
(C) incorporate : privacy
(D) invade : privacy
(E) till : fields

41. PHARMACIST : DRUGS ::
(A) psychiatrist : ideas
(B) mentor : drills
(C) mechanic : troubles
(D) chef : foods
(E) nurse : diseases

42. CONQUER : SUBJUGATE ::
(A) esteem : respect
(B) slander : vilify
(C) discern : observe
(D) ponder : deliberate
(E) freedom : slavery

43. ENGRAVING : CHISEL ::
(A) printing : paper
(B) photography : camera
(C) lithography : stone
(D) printing : ink
(E) etching : acid

44. DECIBEL : SOUND ::
(A) calorie : weight
(B) volt : electricity
(C) temperature : weather
(D) color : light
(E) area : distance

45. HOMONYM : SOUND ::
(A) synonym : same
(B) antonym : meaning
(C) acronym : ideas
(D) pseudonym : fake
(E) synopsis : summary

46. CHAIR : FURNITURE ::
(A) tire : rubber
(B) tree : plant
(C) food : meat
(D) boat : float
(E) transport : car

47. VALUELESS : INVALUABLE ::
(A) miserly : philanthropic
(B) frugality : wealth
(C) thriftiness : cheap
(D) costly : cut-rate
(E) cheap : unstable

48. TRIANGLE : PRISM ::
(A) sphere : earth
(B) square : rhomboid
(C) rectangle : building
(D) circle : cylinder
(E) polygon : diamond

49. YOKE : OX ::
(A) saddle : stallion
(B) tether : cow
(C) herd : sheep
(D) brand : steer
(E) harness : horse

50. COW : BUTTER ::
(A) chicken : omelets
(B) tree : fruit
(C) steer : mutton
(D) water : ice
(E) grape : raisin

CORRECT ANSWERS

Test I. Analogy Pairs

1. D	5. A	9. B	13. E	17. D
2. C	6. B	10. A	14. E	18. E
3. B	7. D	11. C	15. C	19. C
4. B	8. E	12. C	16. D	20. E

Test II. Analogy Pairs

1. C	5. E	9. D	13. C	17. C
2. B	6. C	10. B	14. A	18. D
3. D	7. D	11. B	15. D	19. A
4. A	8. A	12. E	16. C	20. C

Test III. Analogy Pairs

1. B	5. B	9. B	13. C	17. B
2. E	6. D	10. C	14. D	18. C
3. B	7. B	11. C	15. C	19. B
4. A	8. E	12. A	16. B	20. B

Test IV. Analogy Pairs

1. E	5. C	9. A	13. D	17. A
2. D	6. C	10. B	14. B	18. B
3. D	7. D	11. C	15. C	19. E
4. B	8. C	12. E	16. B	20. C

Test V. Analogy Pairs

1. E	5. B	9. C	13. B	17. C
2. D	6. D	10. D	14. A	18. D
3. E	7. B	11. A	15. E	19. B
4. A	8. C	12. B	16. B	20. C

Test VI. Analogy Pairs

1. C	11. D	21. A	31. A	41. D
2. A	12. C	22. C	32. E	42. B
3. E	13. E	23. E	33. D	43. E
4. B	14. B	24. B	34. C	44. B
5. A	15. D	25. D	35. B	45. B
6. D	16. B	26. B	36. C	46. B
7. B	17. D	27. C	37. E	47. A
8. B	18. D	28. D	38. B	48. D
9. E	19. B	29. B	39. B	49. E
10. B	20. D	30. C	40. A	50. A

EXPLANATORY ANSWERS

Test I. Analogy Pairs

1. **(D)** LINEAR and CURVILINEAR refer to equations which, when graphed, describe straight and curved lines, respectively. The only answer choice that suggests first a straight and then a curved line is ARROW : BOW. Choice (E) is incorrect because the order of the shapes is reversed.

2. **(C)** Humans consider both the LEAF of the LETTUCE and the BULB of the ONION to be edible.

3. **(B)** HECKLING is forceful and unpleasant INTERRUPTING. HECTORING is forceful and unpleasant TEASING.

4. **(B)** A DAM obstructs the flow of WATER; an EMBARGO obstructs the flow of TRADE.

5. **(A)** One ALLAYs (reduces) PAIN: one DAMPs (reduces) NOISE.

6. **(B)** LATENT means POTENTIAL; LATE means TARDY.

7. **(D)** CALIBER is a standard of measurement for a RIFLE: GAUGE is a standard of measurement for RAILS.

8. **(E)** To MINCE is more extreme than to CHOP; to BEAT is more extreme than to STIR.

9. **(B)** A PECCADILLO is a small offense; a CRIME is a large one. To HESITATE is brief; to PROCRASTINATE is extended.

10. **(A)** WOOD is used to make PAPER; IRON is used to make STEEL.

11. **(C)** FRENETIC and SANGUINE are opposites meaning the same as FRANTIC and UNRUFFLED, respectively. Choice (A) is incorrect because the opposites are in reverse order.

12. **(C)** Since there appears to be no functional relationship between COMPETITION and COMPENSATION, look for an answer which provides a synonym for each word. Only (C) CONTENDING : AMENDS, provides synonyms for both key words.

13. **(E)** CANDID and DEVIOUS are antonyms. Both (B) and (E) provide antonym pairs; however, (E) is the better match for the key pair because UPRIGHT means the same as candid and UNDERHANDED means the same as devious.

14. **(E)** LIBEL is written defamation; it appears in a PUBLICATION. SLANDER is oral defamation; it appears in SPEECH.

15. **(C)** A CANAL cuts right through the country of PANAMA; a CHORD cuts right through a CIRCLE.

16. **(D)** ALLEVIATE and AGGRAVATE are antonyms; so are PLASTIC and RIGID.

17. **(D)** An unacceptable form of BEHAVIOR is an IMPROPRIETY; an incorrect use of a WORD is a MALAPROPISM.

18. **(E)** An ELM is a type of TREE; a DOLLAR is a type of MONEY.

19. **(C)** A DOCTOR seeks to eliminate DISEASE; a SHERIFF seeks to eliminate CRIME.

20. **(E)** To CHEAT on an EXAMINATION is against regulations; to accept GRAFT in POLITICS is against the law.

Test II. Analogy Pairs

1. **(C)** ADVERSITY causes unhappiness, the opposite of HAPPINESS; VEHEMENCE causes conflict, the opposite of SERENITY.

2. **(B)** The LUTE is a STRING instrument, just as the XYLOPHONE is a PERCUSSION instrument.

3. **(D)** One PLUCKs FEATHERS and SHEARs WOOL. The relationship is one of product to action involved in taking that product from an animal.

4. (A) MODESTY is the opposite of ARROGANCE; DEBILITY is the opposite of STRENGTH.

5. (E) When we BLOW on a HORN we produce a sound, just as when we TURN ON a RADIO.

6. (C) A BAY is smaller than a SEA and an extension of it, just as a PENINSULA is smaller than the LAND mass from which it protrudes. The relationship is one of part to whole.

7. (D) DECEMBER is the first month of WINTER; MARCH is the first month of SPRING.

8. (A) A GIGATON, which is a billion tons, is a thousand times larger than a MEGATON, a million tons. A MEGACYCLE, a million cycles, is a thousand times larger than a KILOCYCLE, which is a thousand cycles.

9. (D) The AERIALIST uses a TRAPEZE in the performance of his work just as the MINER uses a PICK.

10. (B) When one SPEAKS at the wrong time, one might INTERRUPT; when one ENTERS at the wrong time, one might INTRUDE.

11. (B) ENCOURAGE is the opposite of RESTRICT. DEPRIVE is the opposite of SUPPLY.

12. (E) The key words are opposites as are answer choices (A), (C), and (E). BEFOUL is strongly negative in feeling, while TIDY is decidedly positive. Only INDICT : ACQUIT conveys the same negative-positive relationship.

13. (C) ITALY is the country in which MILAN is located. Similarly, SPAIN is the country in which MADRID is located.

14. (A) MIST is a minor kind of RAIN, just as WIND is a lesser kind of HURRICANE. The relationship is one of degree.

15. (D) A HOLSTER is used to carry a GUN; a SCHOOL BAG is used to carry BOOKS.

16. (C) A MACE is an ornamental staff borne as a symbol of authority or MAJESTY; a DIPLOMA is a symbol of educational achievement or the acquisition of KNOWLEDGE.

17. (C) A VIXEN attacks by SCOLDing; a BEE attacks by STINGing.

18. (D) A DEBATE is engaged in by two or more people; one person conducts a SOLILOQUY. A GROUP consists of several people; a HERMIT lives alone. The relationship is one of plural to singular.

19. **(A)** A THREAT often results in INSECURITY; a CHALLENGE often results in a FIGHT. The relationship is one of cause and effect.

20. **(C)** ENORMOUS means very LARGE; FAT means very PLUMP. The relationship is one of degree.

Test III. Analogy Pairs

1. **(B)** A FIN propels a FISH; a PROPELLER propels an AIRPLANE.

2. **(E)** RESTRAIN and REPRESS are synonyms, as are URGE and SPUR.

3. **(B)** You hear MUSIC at a CONCERT; you see ART at an EXHIBITION.

4. **(A)** The right KEY opens the DOOR; the right COMBINATION opens the SAFE.

5. **(B)** If you THROW a certain type of object (like a rubber ball) at a solid surface, it may BOUNCE. If you DROP a certain type of object (like an egg) on a solid surface, it may BREAK. If you think of *throw* and *bounce* as comparable activities, you will have trouble with this one. As soon as you recognize the cause-and-effect relationship, the solution is obvious.

6. **(D)** In this sequence relationship, AFTERNOON precedes DUSK as NIGHT precedes DAWN.

7. **(B)** STUDYING is required for LEARNING; INVESTIGATING is required for DISCOVERING.

8. **(E)** PULP is used in making PAPER; CELLULOSE is used in making RAYON.

9. **(B)** A DYNAST is a ruler; a SERF is a peasant. Only REGAL and LOWLY repeat this contrast.

10. **(C)** A BUOY warns of an OBSTRUCTION; a RED LIGHT warns of DANGER.

11. **(C)** EXPEDITE and HASTEN are synonyms, as are INFLATE and DISTEND.

12. **(A)** SOUND is caused by VIBRATION; PULL is caused by GRAVITY. The relationship is one of cause and effect.

13. **(C)** One WRITES a LETTER and ACTS a PART in this action-to-object relationship.

14. **(D)** DEPRESSION and MASOCHISM refer to pain or injury to oneself; REVENGE and SADISM refer to pain or injury to another.

15. **(C)** SKIN encloses a MAN; WALLS enclose a ROOM.

16. **(B)** An ELIXIR is a liquid medicine; a PILL is a solid medicine. WATER is liquid, ICE is solid.

17. **(B)** FRUGAL and ECONOMICAL are synonyms, as are PROSPEROUS and WEALTHY.

18. **(C)** What is MUNDANE is usually considered TEMPORAL; what is SPIRITUAL is usually considered EVERLASTING.

19. **(B)** A CLARINET is used to produce MUSIC; CHALK is used for WRITING.

20. **(B)** Being FURIOUS is a more intense emotion than being ANGRY; LOVE is a more intense emotion than LIKE. The relationship is one of degree.

Test IV. Analogy Pairs

1. **(E)** RAIN is made up of DROPS; MANKIND is made up of MEN. The relationship is that of whole to part.

2. **(D)** The role of a PUPIL is to LEARN; the purpose of a PRESS is to PRINT.

3. **(D)** A CENTAUR has as its upper part a man and as its lower part a HORSE; a MERMAID is part woman and part FISH. Both a centaur and a mermaid are legendary. The relationship is that of a component part to the whole legendary creature.

4. **(B)** A MODEST person is usually QUIET; a CONCEITED person is usually LOQUACIOUS. The relationship is one of characteristic.

5. **(C)** In this analogy of degree, something that is CRUCIAL is very IMPORTANT; a FELONY is a more serious offense than a MISDEMEANOR.

6. **(C)** WATER might be used for SWIMMING. A CHAIR is usually used for SITTING. Note that water and chair are both concrete nouns. The relationship is one of medium or implement to its associated use.

7. **(D)** A TOWER is atop a CASTLE; a RIDER is atop a HORSE. Choice (C) reverses the relationship.

8. **(C)** The relationship between the key words—"If you are A you are not B"—exists only in choices (B) and (C). However, only choice (C) is in the relationship of adjective : noun as established by the key word pair.

9. **(A)** PEOPLE are known to ELECT and STATESMEN are known to GOVERN. The relationship is that of a particular group to its associated activity.

10. **(B)** We associate JUSTICE with SCALES. We associate a WEATHER-VANE with a COCK; in fact a weathervane is often called a weathercock. We also associate pearls with wisdom, but here the order of the relationship is reversed.

11. **(C)** UXORIOUS and MISOGYNOUS are opposites, as are SATANIC and ANGELIC.

12. **(E)** We speak of the RULE (control) of a KINGDOM and the DISCIPLINE (control) of CHILDREN. The relationship is one of action to object.

13. **(D)** In this analogy of degree, HOSTILE is more intensive than UN-FRIENDLY, and NECESSARY is more intense than USEFUL. The degree relationship in (C) is reversed.

14. **(B)** A PAMPHLET is a short printed work; a BOOK is longer. DISCOM-FORT is a milder form of PAIN. The relationship is one of degree.

15. **(C)** A group of STARS make up a CONSTELLATION; a group of IS-LANDS make up an ARCHIPELAGO. The relationship is that of whole to part.

16. **(B)** A CALIBRATOR is used to MEASURE; a CLAMP is used to HOLD. The relationship is one of tool to function.

17. **(A)** PAPER is counted by the REAM; EGGS are counted by the DOZEN. The relationship is one of item to unit of measure.

18. **(B)** SAIL-SALE and BLUE-BLEW are homophone pairs, or homonyms. A homophone is a word identical with another in pronunciation but differing in spelling and meaning.

19. **(E)** A GOURMAND is UNDISCRIMINATING in his love of food. A GOURMET is SELECTIVE in his choice of food.

20. **(C)** GOOD FRIDAY commemorates the death of Christ; CHRISTMAS commemorates the birth of Christ. The answer hinges on the relationship of END to BEGINNING.

Test V. Analogy Pairs

1. **(E)** A SEWER uses a DRAIN. A SEWER, one who sews, uses a NEEDLE.

2. **(D)** An AUTHOR writes a NOVEL; a CARPENTER builds a CABINET. The relationship is that of worker to product.

3. **(E)** One SELLs an item to another who thereby PURCHASEs it. One GIVEs an item to another who thereby RECEIVEs it.

4. **(A)** A GENTLEMAN is supposed to observe the social AMENITIES; a PLAYER is supposed to observe the REGULATIONS.

5. **(B)** MEDICINE is one SCIENCE; a TOMATO is one FRUIT. The relationship is that of part to whole.

6. **(D)** AIMLESSNESS often leads to DELINQUENCY; BOREDOM often leads to MISCHIEF. The relationship is one of cause and effect.

7. **(B)** A SADIST commits INJURY to others; a THIEF commits ROBBERY.

8. **(C)** One characteristic of RUBBER is FLEXIBILITY; one characteristic of STEEL is RIGIDITY.

9. **(C)** The MEDIAN is the MIDDLE, having an equal number of items above and below it; the MEAN is the AVERAGE.

10. **(D)** Uncontrolled VALOR may result in RECKLESSNESS, just as uncontrolled INTEREST rates may result in USURY.

11. **(A)** We should SCORN what is WICKED; we should EMULATE what is COMMENDABLE.

12. **(B)** In this action to object analogy, we RING a BELL or ACTIVATE an ALARM to create sound. The creation of sound is an important aspect of this analogy so that one can eliminate choice (C).

13. **(B)** A BOY becomes a MAN and a CALF becomes a COW. It's a matter of sequence.

14. **(A)** PINK is a pale RED; CHARTREUSE is a pale GREEN.

15. **(E)** ABSENCE and PRESENCE are opposites, as are STABLE and CHANGEABLE.

16. **(B)** A JUDICIAL function is to ENFORCE the laws; a LEGISLATIVE function is to PASS the laws.

17. **(C)** The RABBIT'S FOOT and the FOUR-LEAF CLOVER are symbols of good luck. Conversely, the number 13 and the BLACK CAT are symbols of bad luck.

18. **(D)** We give SYMPATHY to a person who experiences ADVERSITY; we give CONDOLENCES to a person who experiences GRIEF.

19. **(B)** We put FLUID into a LIGHTER to make it work; we put GAS into an AUTOMOBILE to make it go.

20. **(C)** Something that is POSSIBLE might be, but it is not necessarily, PROBABLE. Someone who is WILLING might be, but is not necessarily, EAGER. This analogy is based on degree.

Test VI. Analogy Pairs

1. **(C)** To be BALD is to lack HAIR. In a DROUGHT there is a lack of RAIN.

2. **(A)** A SHIP is more than just an ordinary BOAT, and a VOLUME is more than just an ordinary BOOK.

3. **(E)** A SCYTHE is involved in symbolizing DEATH, as an ARROW is in symbolizing LOVE.

4. **(B)** A CARNIVORE eats ANIMALS; a VEGETARIAN eats VEGETABLES.

5. **(A)** MAUVE is a COLOR, and BASIL is a SPICE.

6. **(D)** To MUFFLE something is almost to SILENCE it. To STYMIE something is almost to DEFEAT it.

7. **(B)** PAUCITY is a synonym for DEARTH, and SHORTAGE for SCARCITY.

8. **(B)** PAPER is sometimes identified by a WATERMARK, and a PERSON by a BIRTHMARK.

9. **(E)** A person who is extremely BRIGHT is BRILLIANT. A person who is extremely HAPPY is ECSTATIC.

10. **(B)** Those who are POWERFUL are also MIGHTY. Things that are the SAME are also ALIKE. The two terms of each analogous pair are synonyms of equal intensity which is why (E) is not the correct answer.

11. **(D)** A NEWS REPORT is DESCRIPTIVE of an event, but a COMMERCIAL is PRESCRIPTIVE, recommending rather than describing. (B) is stylistically correct but makes a false statement.

12. **(C)** In a case of CONSENSUS among individuals, there is necessarily AGREEMENT. Where there is TRANQUILITY among individuals, there is necessarily PEACE.

13. **(E)** HYDRAULIC describes something that is operated by means of WATER; PNEUMATIC describes something that is operated by means of AIR.

14. **(B)** A HORSE is usually kept and fed in a STABLE; a PIG is usually kept and fed in a STY. The relationship in (A) is reverse. (C), (D), and (E) do not make a parallel statement because the animals are specified by gender, whereas *horse* includes males and females, as does *pig*.

15. **(D)** The ACTOR plays a ROLE, as a BALLPLAYER plays a POSITION.

16. **(B)** The PROW is the forward part of the SHIP, as the NOSE is the forward part of the AIRPLANE. Ship and airplane are inanimate; hog is an animal, so (A) is not the best choice.

17. **(D)** MAXIMUM and MINIMUM mark extremes in quantity, as do MOST and LEAST. So also do minimum and optimum, but in reverse order.

18. **(D)** One can counteract a SENSATION with an ANESTHETIC and a POISON with an ANTIDOTE.

19. **(B)** One leaves a SHIP by DISEMBARKING and a HORSE by DISMOUNTING.

20. **(D)** MEAT is a food that supplies us with PROTEIN; POTATOES are a food that supplies us with STARCH.

21. **(A)** The NAPE is the back of the NECK, and the HEEL is the back of the FOOT.

22. **(C)** PLIERS are designed for GRIPPING, and a JACK, for ELEVATING. The initial purpose for which the tool was designed governs this answer.

23. **(E)** The RADIUS moves from the center of the CIRCLE to the edge, as the SPOKE moves from the center of the WHEEL to the edge.

24. **(B)** A HORSE is a four-legged animal that is covered with HAIR. A SHEEP is a four-legged animal that is covered with WOOL. When more than one choice seems possible, you must further refine your definition of the related terms. Here you can eliminate choice (A) by specifying the number of legs.

25. **(D)** A GOBBLE is a sound made by a particular kind of bird, a TURKEY. A TWITTER is a sound made by some BIRDS.

26. **(B)** As ASTUTE is in emphatic opposition to STUPID, so is AGILE in opposition to CLUMSY. Both terms go beyond simple denials of the opposing terms.

27. **(C)** A WHALE is a mammal that is mistakenly thought to be a FISH, and a BAT is a mammal that is mistakenly thought to be a BIRD.

28. **(D)** A PROSPECTOR seeks GOLD, and a DETECTIVE seeks a CLUE.

29. **(B)** A COUPLET makes up part of a POEM, and a SENTENCE makes up part of a PARAGRAPH.

30. **(C)** OIL is extracted from the earth by means of a WELL, and SILVER by means of a MINE.

31. **(A)** A TILLER is used in directing a SHIP. A WHEEL is used in directing a CAR.

32. **(E)** A STALLION and a ROOSTER are two different animals of the same sex, as are a MARE and a HEN.

33. **(D)** We assimilate a BOOK through READing, and a RECORD through LISTENing.

34. **(C)** A PARROT and a SPARROW are two very different sorts of birds. A GOLDFISH and a GUPPY are two very different sorts of fish.

35. **(B)** MUSCLES are connected to bones by TENDONS just as BONES are connected to bones by LIGAMENTS.

36. **(C)** Food that is INSIPID is DULL and uninteresting, whereas SPICY food can be said to be EXCITING.

37. **(E)** A BURL is an outgrowth of a TREE, and a PEARL is an outgrowth of an OYSTER.

38. **(B)** YEAST is used as a LEAVEN, and IODINE as an ANTISEPTIC. These functions are more specific than aspirin's function as a medicine.

39. **(B)** A SOLECISM is a violation of the rules of GRAMMAR; a FOUL is a violation of the rules of a GAME.

40. **(A)** One can EXPURGATE (eliminate) PASSAGES as one can DEFOLIATE LEAVES.

41. **(D)** The basic materials of a PHARMACIST are DRUGS; the basic materials of a CHEF are FOODS.

42. **(B)** To CONQUER someone is to SUBJUGATE him. To SLANDER someone is to VILIFY him. In both cases the subject is hostile toward the object.

43. **(E)** A CHISEL can be used to cut out an ENGRAVING. ACID can be used to cut through a surface to create an ETCHING.

44. **(B)** SOUND is measured in DECIBELs, and ELECTRICITY in VOLTs.

45. **(B)** SOUND determines whether two words are HOMONYMs. MEANING determines whether two words are ANTONYMs.

46. **(B)** A CHAIR is a piece of FURNITURE and a TREE is an individual PLANT.

47. **(A)** At one extreme something can be VALUELESS, and at another extreme something can be INVALUABLE. At one extreme an individual can be MISERLY, and at another extreme, PHILANTHROPIC.

48. **(D)** A TRIANGLE has three sides, and a PRISM is a three-sided solid figure. A CIRCLE is circular, and a CYLINDER is a solid figure that is circular.

49. **(E)** An OX is controlled by means of a YOKE. A HORSE is controlled by means of a HARNESS.

50. **(A)** Both a COW and a CHICKEN are animals. Indirectly, BUTTER is a product from the former and OMELETS are products from the latter.

APPENDIX

USEFUL MISCELLANEOUS INFORMATION FOR THE MILLER ANALOGIES TEST-TAKER

MYTHOLOGY

The Greeks had the most highly developed mythology, in terms of geneology, personalities, and lifestyles of the gods. Roman mythology closely parallels Greek mythology; many of the gods and goddesses are counterparts of Greek gods. The other highly developed European mythology is Norse mythology. Norse mythology developed independently of that of the Greeks and Romans, but since mythology existed to explain the same phenomena in each society, there are many similarities.

The Greek gods lived on MT. OLYMPUS. Roman gods had no comparable dwelling place. The home of the Norse gods was at ASGARD where the dining hall of the heroes was VALHALLA and the private dining room of the gods, GIMLI.

KRONOS and RHEA were parents of the six original Greek gods. Their Roman counterparts were SATURN and OPS. The original Greek gods were:

ZEUS—king of the gods, comparable to the Roman JUPITER and the Norse ODIN.

HERA—both sister and wife of Zeus and queen of the gods, comparable to the Roman JUNO, wife of Jupiter, and Norse FRIGG or FRIGGA, wife of Odin.

POSEIDON—ruler of the sea and of earthquakes, comparable to the Roman NEPTUNE and to the Norse NJORD.

HADES—ruler of the dead and god of wealth, comparable to the ROMAN PLUTO.

DEMETER—goddess of agriculture, comparable to Roman CERES.

HESTIA—goddess of the hearth, comparable to Roman VESTA.

Parentage of some of the "younger" gods is consistent from myth to myth. Some of the most important gods of consistently acknowledged parentage are:

ATHENE or ATHENA— who "sprung full-blown from the head of Zeus," goddess of wisdom, cities, heroes in war, and handicrafts. Her Roman counterpart, MINERVA, had the same miraculous birth.

PERSEPHONE—daughter of Zeus and Demeter, goddess of agriculture (like her mother) and queen of the dead; wife of Hades; comparable to the Roman PROSERPINA.

APOLLO and ARTEMIS—twin children of Zeus and Leto. Apollo, god of prophesy, music, and medicine, is a god of purification and giver of oracles. Apollo has no Roman counterpart, but his Norse counterpart is FREYR, twin brother of FREYA. Artemis is goddess of the moon and of the hunt as well as of woods, meadows, wild animals, and fertility. Artemis has a Roman counterpart in DIANA. FREYA, goddess of love and beauty, though Freyr's twin sister, is more comparable to Aphrodite.

HERMES—son of Zeus and Maia, herald of the gods and leader of men, god of trade and eloquence. Hermes' Roman counterpart is MERCURY.

ARES—son of Zeus and Hera, god of war, with a Roman counterpart, MARS.

DIONYSUS—son of Zeus and Semele, god of wine and joy, comparable to Roman BACCHUS.

Some gods and goddesses of disputed or unknown parentage include:

APHRODITE—goddess of sexual love, comparable to Roman VENUS and to Norse FREYA.

HEPHAISTOS—god of fire and thunderbolts, the divine smith and crafts-man, comparable to Roman VULCAN.

ADONIS— god of male beauty, vegetation, and rebirth.

PHOEBUS APOLLO—driver of the sun's chariot in its daily journey across the sky.

EOS—goddess of the dawn, Roman AURORA.

HEBE—god of youth, Roman JUVENTAS.

HYPNOS—god of sleep, Roman SOMNUS.

PAN—god of woods and fields, Roman FAUNUS.

THANATOS—god of death, Roman MORS.

NIKE—goddess of victory, Roman VICTORIA.

Mythology, especially Greek mythology, often makes references to person-ifications in groups. In some groups the individuals have distinctive names. Some of the most common of these are:

MUSES—CLIO, muse of history
    EUTERPE, muse of lyric poetry and flute playing
    THALIA, muse of comedy
    MELPOMENE, muse of music, song, and tragedy
    TERPSICHORE, muse of choral dancing and choral singing
    ERATO, muse of love songs and love poetry
    POLYHYMNIA, muse of serious poetry and hymns, of mime, and
                of geometry
    URANIA, muse of astronomy and astrology
    CALLIOPE, muse of epic poetry
FATES—CLOTHO, spinner of the thread of life—Roman NONA
    LACHESIS, determiner of the length—Roman DECUMA
    ATROPOS, cutter of the thread—Roman MORTA
FURIES—ALECTO, unending
    TISIPHONE, retaliation
    MEGAERA, envious fury
GRACES—AGLAIA, brilliance
    EUPHROSYNE, joy
    THALIA, bloom
WINDS—AEOLUS, keeper of the winds
    BOREAS, the north wind
    EURUS, the east wind
    NOTUS, the south wind
    ZEPHYRUS, the west wind

Half-people, half-animals:

CENTAUR—head and torso of a man, lower half of a horse
HARPY—head of a woman, body of a bird
SATYR—head and torso of a man, lower half of a goat

Minor deities of nature:

DRYADS—tree nymphs
NAIADS—water, stream, and fountain nymphs
NAPAEAE—wood nymphs
NEREIDS—sea nymphs
OCEANIDS—ocean nymphs
OREADS—mountain nymphs

Rivers of the Underworld:

ACHERON—woe
COCYTUS—wailing
PHLEGETHON—fire
LETHE—forgetfulness
STYX—the last river that souls must cross

NATIONS OF THE WORLD

Over the course of history, many nations of the world have changed identities and alliances as well as borders and governments. A brief course in world history and geography is a logical impossibility but this comprehensive list of some of today's nations and their previous identities may prove helpful for the sequential and the language-spoken types of analogy questions.

Current Name	*Previous Name or Names*
Algeria	ancient Numidia
Angola	Portuguese West Africa
Bangladesh	East Pakistan . . . British India
Belize	British Honduras
Benin	Dahomey (French)
Botswana	Bechuanaland (English)
Burkina Faso	Upper Volta (French)
Burundi	Ruanda-Urundi . . . Belgian Congo . . . German East Africa
Cambodia	French Indo-China
Central African Republic	Central African Empire . . . French Equatorial Africa . . . Ubangi-Shari
Chad	French Equatorial Africa
Congo	French Congo
Djibouti	Afars and Issas . . . French Somaliland
Equatorial Guinea	Spanish Guinea
Ethiopia	ancient Abyssinia
France	ancient Gaul
Gabon	French Congo
Ghana	British Gold Coast
Guinea	French West Africa
Guinea-Bissau	Portuguese Guinea
Guyana	British Guiana
Iran	Persia
Iraq	Babylonia and Assyria . . . Mesopotamia
Israel	Palestine . . . Canaan
Jordan	Palestine . . . Edom and Moab
Laos	French Indo-China
Lesotho	Basutoland (English)
Madagascar	Malagasy Republic (French)
Malawi	Nyasaland (English)
Malaysia	Malaya and Sabah (North Borneo) and Sarawak
Mali	French Sudan
Mozambique	Portuguese East Africa
Namibia	South West Africa (English and Afrikaans)
Niger	French West Africa
North Vietnam	French Indo-China

Oman	Muscat and Oman
Pakistan	British India
PDR Yemen (People's Democratic Republic of Yemen)	Aden
Rwanda	Ruanda-Urundi . . . Belgian Congo . . . German East Africa
Senegal	French West Africa
Somalia	Somaliland (English)
South Vietnam	French Indo-China
Sri Lanka	Ceylon (English)
Sudan	Anglo-Egyptian Sudan . . . ancient Nubia
Surinam	Dutch Guiana
Switzerland	ancient Helvetia
Tanzania	Tanganyika and Zanzibar
Thailand	Siam
Togo	Togoland (French)
Tunisia	ancient Carthage
United Arab Emirates	union of the Trucial States which were: Abu Dhabi, Sharja, Ras al Khaima, Dubai, Ajman, Fujaira, and Umm al Qaiman
West Irian	Netherlands New Guinea
Western Sahara	Spanish Sahara
Zaire	Belgian Congo
Zambia	Northern Rhodesia (English)
Zimbabwe	Rhodesia (English)

MATHEMATICS

Some mathematical analogy questions draw upon specific knowledge of algebra, geometry, trigonometry, and calculus. In order to answer these questions, you must have real understanding of the various branches of mathematics. Other mathematical analogies rest upon a more generalized or superficial understanding of the mathematics with, perhaps, more complex reasoning required. The following tables compile in one easy reference source the general mathematical information you are most likely to find useful.

ROMAN NUMERALS

I =	1	D =	500	$\overline{C}$ =	100,000
V =	5	M =	1000	$\overline{D}$ =	500,000
X =	10	$\overline{V}$ =	5000	$\overline{M}$ =	1,000,000
L =	50	$\overline{X}$ =	10,000		
C =	100	$\overline{L}$ =	50,000		

Rules:

1. A letter repeated once or twice repeats its value that many times. (XXX = 30; MM = 2,000)
2. One or more letters placed after another letter of greater value increases the greater value by the amount of the smaller. (XII = 12; DXC = 610)
3. A letter placed before another letter of greater value decreases the greater value by the amount of the smaller. (IX = 9; CD = 400)

General Measures

Time	*Angles and Arcs*	*Counting*
1 minute (min) = 60 seconds (sec)	1 minute (′) = 60 seconds (″)	1 dozen (doz) = 12 units
1 hour (hr) = 60 minutes	1 degree (°) = 60 minutes	1 gross (gr) = 12 dozen
1 day = 24 hours	1 circle = 360 degrees	1 gross = 144 units
1 week = 7 days		
1 year = 52 weeks		
1 calendar year = 365 days		

The Metric System

Length

Unit	Abbreviation	Number of Meters
myriameter	mym	10,000
kilometer	km	1,000
hectometer	hm	100
dekameter	dam	10
meter	m	1
decimeter	dm	0.1
centimeter	cm	0.01
millimeter	mm	0.001

Area

Unit	Abbreviation	Number of Square Meters
square kilometer	sq km *or* km²	1,000,000
hectare	ha	10,000
are	a	100
centare	ca	1
square centimeter	sq cm *or* cm²	0.0001

Volume

Unit	Abbreviation	Number of Cubic Meters
dekastere	das	10
stere	s	1
decistere	ds	0.10
cubic centimeter	cu cm *or* cm³ *or* cc	0.000001

Capacity

Unit	Abbreviation	Number of Liters
kiloliter	kl	1,000
hectoliter	hl	100
dekaliter	dal	10
liter	l	1
deciliter	dl	0.10
centiliter	cl	0.01
milliliter	ml	0.001

Mass and Weight

Unit	Abbreviation	Number of Grams
metric ton	MT *or* t	1,000,000
quintal	q	100,000
kilogram	kg	1,000
hectogram	hg	100
dekagram	dag	10
gram	g *or* gm	1
decigram	dg	0.10
centigram	cg	0.01
milligram	mg	0.001

Temperature

Scale	Abbreviation	
Celsius or Centigrade	°C	Freezing Point 0°C Boiling Point 100°C

American Measures

Length

1 foot (ft or ') = 12 inches (in or ")
1 yard (yd) = 36 inches
1 yard = 3 feet
1 rod (rd) = 16½ feet
1 mile (mi) = 5280 feet
1 mile = 1760 yards
1 mile = 320 rods

Liquid Measure

1 cup (c) = 8 fluid ounces (fl oz)
1 pint (pt) = 2 cups
1 pint = 4 gills (gi)
1 quart (qt) = 2 pints
1 gallon (gal) = 4 quarts
1 barrel (bl) = 31½ gallons

Weight

1 pound (lb) = 16 ounces (oz)
1 hundredweight (cwt) = 100 pounds
1 ton (T) = 2000 pounds

Dry Measure

1 quart (qt) = 2 pints (pt)
1 peck (pk) = 8 quarts
1 bushel (bu) = 4 pecks

Area

1 square foot (ft²) = 144 square inches (in²)
1 square yard (yd²) = 9 square feet

Volume

1 cubic foot (ft³ or cu ft) = 1728 cubic inches
1 cubic yard (yd³ or cu yd) = 27 cubic feet
1 gallon = 231 cubic inches

Temperature

Water freezes at 32°F (Fahrenheit)
Water boils at 212° F

Table of American-Metric Conversions (Approximate)

American to Metric

1 inch = 2.54 centimeters
1 yard = .9 meters
1 mile = 1.6 kilometers
1 ounce = 28 grams
1 pound = 454 grams
1 fluid ounce = 30 milliliters
1 liquid quart = .95 liters
32°F = o°C
212°F = 100°C
°F = 9/5°C + 32

Metric to American

1 centimeter = .39 inches
1 meter = 1.1 yards
1 kilometer = .6 miles
1 kilogram = 2.2 pounds
1 liter = 1.06 liquid quart
0°C = 32°F
100°C = 212°F
°C = 5/9 (°F − 32°)

Table of Metric Conversions*

11 liter = 1000 cubic centimeters (cm³)
1 milliliter = 1 cubic centimeter
1 liter of water weighs 1 kilogram
1 milliliter of water weighs 1 gram

---

*These conversions are exact only under specific conditions. If the conditions are not met, the conversions are approximate.